CARNIVOROUS PLANTS of the WORLD

Carnivorous Plants
of the World

JAMES and PATRICIA PIETROPAOLO

TIMBER PRESS
Portland, Oregon

To
Darcy Ann
and
Robin Louise

Photograph credits:
Cover photographs by Rudolf Schmid,
Department of Integrative Biology, University of California, Berkeley,
clockwise from upper right:
(front) *Dionaea muscipula, Drosera neo-caledonica, Nepenthes vieillardii*;
(back) *Darlingtonia californica, Drosera rotundifolia, D. rotundifolia.*
Text photographs by Patricia Ann Pietropaolo.
Text line drawings by Saundra Dowling.

Paperback edition printed 1996, reprinted 1997, 1999;
reprinted 2001 with updates to appendixes A and B

Printed in Hong Kong

TIMBER PRESS, INC.
The Haseltine Building
133 S.W. Second Avenue, Suite 450
Portland, Oregon 97204, U.S.A.
1-800-327-5680 (U.S.A. and Canada only)

ISBN 0-88192-356-7
Library of Congress catalog card number 87-11932

Contents

Preface

Carnivorous plants are enjoying unprecedented popularity today. Their popularity stems from the realization that they are relatively easy to grow combined with the mystique that surrounds "man-eating plants." Carnivorous plants are immortalized in Saturday morning cartoons, comic books, the late, late shows and monster movies. The fact that carnivorous plants have the ability to lure, capture, and digest organic matter from the animal world has fascinated people for generations. Carnivorous plants rearrange the natural order of nature where plants are usually the meal, not the consumer of animal protein.

Adding to the increasing popularity of growing carnivorous plants is the current availability of species from Europe, Asia, Africa, Central and South America. Enthusiasts as well as novices have a broad range of plants to choose from or specialize in.

We hope that by providing direct, easy-to-follow growing instructions, along with helpful hints and pointing out pitfalls to avoid, this book will tempt the curious individual into growing carnivorous plants and guide the avid enthusiasts in selecting plants, growing methods, and propagation techniques best suited to their situation.

A brief note on the organization and intent of this book and the thinking behind the organization is in order. Our combined backgrounds blend botany, chemistry, and practical experience into a mix that has led us into an inquisitive and investigative approach in caring for and propagating carnivorous plants.

The information gained from our own personal experiences, reading, talking and corresponding with other growers and carnivorous plant enthusiasts is organized within this book.

The first chapters of the book deal with specific information on each group or genus of carnivorous plants, such as the Sundews, Butterworts, and the Venus Fly Trap. Each chapter includes information on the history of the plant, natural environment, trapping mechanism, species that comprise the genus, botanical description, specific cultural requirements and specific propagating techniques as well as information of general interest.

Later chapters are devoted to the general cultural requirements necessary to successfully grow and propagate carnivorous plants as well as information concerning purchasing, growing outdoors, feeding and pest control. The later chapters contain general information pertinent to all carnivorous plants. This information is accumulated in separate chapters for easy reference to avoid repetition. This organization allows the book to be a reference tool as well as a textbook.

Chapters and sections dealing with genera contain lists of species within the genera. The species are organized into groups that have similar cultural requirements. For the species commercially available, more detailed information is included. When species not currently available commercially do become available, cultural information can be gleaned from the group in which it is included.

The intent of this book is to provide cultural data for growing carnivorous plants, including information pertaining to soils, pots, containers, light, water and humidity, dormancy, fertilization, feeding, pest control, germination of seeds, propagation (sexual and asexual), and hybridization.

The contents of this book reflect over 25 years experience in growing, propagating, hybridizing, and selling over 125 species of carnivorous plants. We have also compiled and integrated information gathered by other growers and hobbyists. Thus it provides you with information that will enable you to grow carnivorous plants successfully, and also to experiment on your own. For example, *Sarracenia,* the Pitcher Plants, grow well in several different growing media, even though many people have their favorite media. It could very well be that in a particular environment a specific growing media is most effective. It is doubtful that the growing environment of any two growers is exactly identical. Knowing this, you can select the most readily and/or economically available growing media in your area. The information provided in this book can be the basis for experimentation with other growing media. The same idea can be applied to the other cultural areas such as seed germination, and vegetative reproduction. There is much more that needs to be learned about the cultural requirements of these plants. Therefore, the accumulation of this knowledge will require the efforts of many growers, including you. Once this information is gained it should be shared with others. The best method of disseminating information is through the publications of the various carnivorous plant societies.

Some plants, like people, have their idiosyncrasies, and once these are known, the job of growing them is made much easier. By growing, we mean maintaining plants that are healthy, vigorous, and usually flowering, not just keeping the plants alive for several years with the plant's vigor slowly decreasing each year.

The authors are indebted to innumerable carnivorous plants growers whose continued advice, suggestions, and questions encouraged the writing of this manuscript. We thank our daughters Darcy and Robin for their patience and forebearance during this project.

The fine artwork of Saundra Dowling and the cordial and thoughtful advice of Richard Abel of Timber Press are gratefully acknowledged.

SECTION I

1

Introduction

WHAT IS CARNIVORY?

What is plant carnivory? Or specifically, what characteristics must a plant have to be called carnivorous? Carnivorous means literally "meat eating." When this definition is applied to plants it evokes visions of snarling green jaws snapping at nearby animal life. Although the vision is vivid, it is not in keeping with reality. Most plants are subtle in their means of entrapping animal prey and have evolved sophisticated means of digesting it; *Dionaea* is the proverbial exception.

A good working definition of a carnivorous plant is needed and must account for the following characteristics: attracting prey (lures, odors, and directional guides), trapping of prey, secreting digestive enzymes and absorption of digested materials. A realistic definition of plant carnivory should be based on whether animal nutrients are digested by enzymes produced by the plant. The means of digestion varies in this group of plants. While in some digestion is the result of secreted enzymes and bacterial action, in a few it is totally attributable to bacterial action. At the present time the number of known digestive enzymes secreted by carnivorous plants varies from five in *Nepenthes* to none in *Heliamphora*. In all plants categorized as carnivorous the digestive organs are modified leaves.

One plant which is not carnivorous has seeds that are carnivorous. John T. Barber and colleagues discovered that dead mosquito larvae were attached to single seeds of *Capsella bursa-pastoris*. The larvae were attracted to the seeds by a chemical released by the seed and killed by a toxin produced by the seed. In addition, the seeds secrete an enzyme which digests protein of the larvae and which permits them to subsequently absorb the material. In the plants' natural environment mosquito larvae are not common, so research was continued with organisms such as protozoans, nematodes and motile bacteria which the seeds are more likely to encounter. Preliminary results show that these seeds are able to attract, kill and digest some of these organisms.

There are plants that appear structurally similar to those classified as carnivorous. Although some species of these genera might be carnivorous, this aspect of their nature has not yet been investigated. Some genera containing species in this category are listed below, classified by their type of trapping mechanism.

PLANTS DISPLAYING PASSIVE TRAPPING CHARACTERISTICS

Pitfall—Water Holding Structures
Aquilegia, Asplenium, Azolla, Billergia, Coprinus, Delphinium, Dipsacus, Dischidia, Drynaria, Marcgravia, and liverworts such as *Colura, Lejeunea, Frullania,* and *Physiotum.*

Flypaper—Sticky Hairs
Aeonium, Erica, Geranium, Hydrolea, Linnoea, Lycopersicon, Mirabilis, Nicotiana, Pelargonium, Platylepis, Primula, Proboscidea, Saxifraga, Solanum, and *Sparmannia.*

PLANTS DISPLAYING ACTIVE TRAPPING CHARACTERISTICS

These are plants in which rapid movement of the plant is involved in capturing prey.

Caltha dioneaefolia, which grows in Tierra del Fuego in Argentina, was first described by Dr. Hooke in 1874. He wrote "Delpino, for example, has suggested that a plant, first described by myself from Tierra del Fuego—*Caltha dioneaefolia*—is so analogous in the structure of its leaves to *Dionaea* that it is difficult to resist the conviction that its structure is also adapted for the capture of small insects." Another plant, *Molinia coerulea,* is a grass whose flowers have bracts which act as the jaws of a spring-type trap and can capture insects for a period of time during flowering.

DEVELOPMENT OF CARNIVORY

Plants and animals have evolved to fill all available habitats and ecological niches. Plants inhabit every possible environment including water, air, soil (wet and/or dry), other plants and also animals.

Green plants contain the organic pigment chlorophyll. When provided with light, carbon dioxide, water, and essential minerals they produce carbohydrates through a chemical process called photosynthesis mediated by the pigment chlorophyll. The light energy is converted into the chemical bond energy of a food molecule. The carbohydrate food molecules are utilized by the plant for cellular energy and as the basis for producing other molecules which are essential for the plant's growth and development. Usually the minerals and water are taken up by the root system and conveyed throughout the plant, including the sites of photosynthetic activity.

Plants have evolved to utilize all available habitats such as arid and semi-arid regions, moist and waterlogged areas, full sunlight to complete shade, from tropical to Arctic climates. Thus, it would be logical to expect that plants would evolve to survive in nutrient-poor soils and/or water.

The evolution of carnivorous plants is speculative due to the paucity of the fossil record. Flowering plants (angiosperms) began to evolve during the Cretaceous period of the Mesozoic Era. The flowering carnivorous plants, the topic of this book, therefore, cannot be older than 136 million years. The oldest carnivorous plant fossil is *Aldrovanda* pollen found in rock of the Eocene period that began 53 million years ago and ended 37 million years ago. The earliest Droseraceae pollen is found in the Miocene period, 26 to 12 million years ago.

Many plants today are adapted to foliar feeding. That is, when a nutrient (fertilizer) solution is sprayed on the leaves, the plant can absorb the nutrients through the leaves into the plant body. The beginning of carnivory could have taken place when some leaves formed shallow depressions in which rain water was retained for a period of time after a rain shower. These leaves would be ideal water reservoirs for insects. In the process of obtaining a drink, some insects would drown and eventually be decomposed by bacteria living in the water. The nutrients released into the water could have been absorbed by the leaf into the plant body. This process, similar to foliar feeding, would provide a distinct advantage to plants growing in nutrient-poor soils barely able to provide sufficient nutrients for growth. It would have provided them with a distinct survival advantage. The deeper the depression in the leaf, the more insects could be drowned and decomposed. In times of stress or overcrowding the plants that could derive nutrients through their leaves would be better able to compete in nutrient-poor soil. The plants able to obtain additional nutrients from their leaves would be stronger and healthier and more likely to produce offspring. As time passed, those plants that evolved more effective traps, means of attracting insects and directional guides—that is, the arrangement of nectar-producing glands and hairs that lead the prey into the trap— would be better able to survive in nutrient-poor soils.

The characteristics that distinguish carnivorous plants—such as visual and odiferous lures, directional guides, secreting glands, absorbing glands, trapping, and rapid movement—are found in various plants not considered carnivorous. Some non-carnivorous plants trap insects to effect pollination. Plants such as *Mimosa pudica* and the Telegraph plants (*Desmodium*) have leaves that exhibit rapid motion. Some tree leaves secrete a sticky substance that falls to the ground. While all of the individual characteristics of carnivorous plants can be found in other plants, when they are all combined in the same plant the organism is truly unique, a carnivorous plant whose modified leaves can trap and digest prey lured to the plant. The digested materials are utilized by the plant for its growth and development. The fascination with carnivorous plants partly stems from the ability of these plants to reverse the order we expect to find in nature. Carnivorous plants are the predators rather than the passive prey.

PLANT NAMES

Common names used for plants usually are descriptive but confusing because the same plant may be called by different names in different geographic areas. One common name used for carnivorous plants, Fly Catcher, can refer, for example, to a member of the genus *Sarracenia* or the genus *Dionaea*. Another disadvantage of using common names is that they are not easily recognizable by people speaking other languages. In addition, plants from widely separated genera may have the same common name; common names may suggest relationships that do not exist; and there is no international body for governing common names. To remedy these problems a Latinized binomial system was adopted about a century ago. For the reasons noted in this paragraph binomial names are used in this book.

The binomial system had its beginnings in the sixteenth century and was used by the botanists Brunfels and Dodonaeus. Carolus Linnaeus, in the eighteenth century, standardized and popularized the binomial system, which was adopted in 1867 by the First Botanical International Congress in Paris. The system (*International Code of Botanic Nomenclature*) is under constant review, and changes are made when necessary. Even though the system is not perfect, it does provide only one name for each species of plant. No two plants can have the same genus and species name.

In the binomial system plant names are Latinized because at the time of its development, Latin was the universal language of scholars. The name consists of two words: the first word, the genus name, is capitalized; and the second word, the species name, is not. These terms often describe some characteristic of the plant. For example, *Drosera*, a genus name, is derived from a Greek word meaning dew and refers to the droplet of mucilage on the ends of the tentacles. In the binomial name, *Drosera rotundifolia*, the species name *rotundifolia* refers to the plant's round leaves. Genus and species names are italicized when in print and when written or typed, the binomial is underlined. In technical writing the binomial name is followed by the name or standard abbreviation of the person's name who officially described the plant. If there has been controversy over the plant and its name has been changed, there may be more than one person's name following the binomial name—for example, *Sarracenia purpurea* f. *heterophylla* (Eaton) Fernald. The names of individuals are not italicized.

A genus consists of a group of plants which have very similar characteristics. For example, the genus *Felis* includes all cats, which have many common features. In the cat population there are cats that are sufficiently different from the other cats to be subdivided into a smaller group; this is done with a species name. Thus, the household cat is *Felis catus,* while the tiger, another member of the cat family, is *Felis tigris* and the cougar is *Felis concolor.*

There are finer subdivisions than species. These are in order of decreasing distinction, along with their abbreviations in parentheses, as follows: subspecies (ssp.), form (f.), and variety (var. or v.).

The members of a species have many similar characteristics, but in some cases there are enough minor differences to divide the members into two or more groups called subspecies. An example is *Sarracenia purpurea* ssp. *purpurea* and *Sarracenia purpurea* ssp. *venosa.*

Within the population of *Sarracenia purpurea* ssp. *purpurea* there are members distinguished from the rest by the absence of red coloration. This group is a division of a subspecies and called a form. The correct name for the plants lacking red coloration is *Sarracenia purpurea* ssp. *purpurea* f. *heterophylla.* If there are some differences in the members of a form, they are designated as a variety.

Subdivisional names are italicized but the reference names or abbreviations are not. Either reference names or their abbreviations can be used. This is illustrated by the following examples, *Sarracenia purpurea* subspecies *purpurea* form *heterophylla,* or *Sarracenia purpurea* ssp. *purpurea* f. *heterophylla.*

Once the full name of a plant is used in a discussion and as long as the genus discussed is not changed, the genus name can be abbreviated in further references. For example, after the binomial *Drosera binata* is used once, its further use in the same document is written *D. binata.*

Even though one genus may be quite distinct from another there are groups of genera (plural of genus) which have enough similarities that they are grouped into families. This is illustrated in chart 1, where the 7 families and 15 genera of carnivorous plants are listed.

HYBRIDS

Hybrid plants are produced from two different species or hybrids. Hybrids may occur spontaneously in the wild as the result of natural agents carrying the pollen from the flower of one species to another. Or, hybrid crosses may be made by plant breeders.

Hybrids are identified by one or both of two names: the formula name, or the collective epithet. For example, the formula name of one *Sarracenia* hybrid is *Sarracenia minor* X *Sarracenia psittacina.* This formula indicates the parentage of the hybrid. In usual practice the female parent producing the seed is listed first in the formula name. If this information is unknown, then the parental species are listed alphabetically.

The collective epithet for all hybrid plants resulting from the cross between *S. minor* and *S. psittacina* is *Sarracenia* X *formosa.* The "X" before the second name indicates that the plant is a hybrid. When *Sarracenia* are under discussion, the formula name is often written *S. minor* X *S. psittacina,* and the collective epithet as *S.* X *formosa.*

The collective epithet may also be a word or a phrase of not more than three words in a modern language. The hybrid designation for the cross *S. alata* X *S. psittacina,* for example, is *Sarracenia* (Robin Louise). In this case the "X" is omitted and the collective epithet placed in parentheses following the genus name.

Cultivars

A hybrid which shows exemplary characteristics that distinguish it from the other hybrids of the same parentage may be designated as a cultivar. "Cultivar" is a term which indicates a plant created by man. The term was formed from the two words "cultivated" and "variety." It is used to denote a group of cultivated plants that are distinctive from other members of the same group (grex), whether it be a species, subspecies, variety, or a hybrid of plants in cultivation or in the wild. The difference between a cultivar and other members of the same group resides in such characteristics as color, shape of leaves, size, or floral configuration.

Cultivars may arise or be developed by hybridizing species or hybrids; selecting the best seedling of a self-pollinating cultivar; inbreeding; and propagating natural and/or induced mutations. A cultivar may be derived from cultivated plants or may be found in a natural population of plants. The cultivar must be propagated by seed if it is an annual; but if a perennial, vegetative means of propagation are used in order to maintain its distinguishing characteristics. Sometimes a characteristic that was distinctive in a plant is not heritable; that is, it does not show up in plants propagated from a selected plant. Such a plant cannot be considered a cultivar. In order for a plant to be the basis of a cultivar, its particular identifying traits must be named according to the rules codified in the *International Code of Nomenclature for Cultivated Plants* (latest edition, 1980). Such cultivars must have fancy names; that is, not a botanical name in Latin form. (But cultivar names published prior to 1959 may be botanical names in Latin form.) A cultivar from a hybrid is designated by adding a fancy name to the hybrid's collective epithet or the formula name. The fancy name is preceded by 'cv.' or is enclosed in single quotation marks. For example, if a plant from the cross *S. alata* × *S. psittacina* displayed inheritable vivid red blotches, it could be designated as the cultivar 'Red'. The proper name would be *Sarracenia* (Robin Louise) cv. Red, or (*Sarracenia alata* × *S. psittacina*) 'Red'.

Discretion should be exercised in the naming of new cultivars so that the distinctions are not based on minor or trivial differences.

To make new cultivar names legal or valid, the name and a description of the plant indicating its difference from other plants in the same group, along with the parentage and history and, if possible, a diagram or photograph, must be published and distributed to the public. Publication is accomplished by having it appear in a dated catalog, book, periodical, or by photocopy, ditto, or mimeograph, with distribution to a significant number of people.

The cultivar name should also be registered with the registration authority designated for the genus. The job of the registration authority is to catalog cultivar names and descriptions to prevent both duplication of names and the same cultivar being assigned more than one name. For example, suppose you develop a cultivar and decide to call it *Sarracenia alata* cv. Yellow Gem. You send the description of the plant, along with the name, to the registration authority. The registrar checks previous registrations to determine if the name has already been used by someone else, and also if the cultivar you "developed" has already been registered by someone else. If the former, you simply choose another fancy name and resubmit your application. If the latter, you have no choice but to drop your cultivar name and work on developing another cultivar.

Unfortunately, at this time there is no designated registration authority for carnivorous plants.

For additional information on cultivar naming and registration, consult the *International Code of Nomenclature for Cultivated Plants—1980*, which is in many libraries and available through the American Horticultural Society, Mt. Vernon, Virginia, 22121.

While the foregoing section may seem complicated and pedantic, it is the simplest and most accurate way to deal with plants.

CLASSIFICATION OF CARNIVOROUS PLANTS

Of the one-quarter of a million species of flowering plants about 600 are carnivorous. They are divided into two groups based on corolla structure, Choripetalae and Sympetalae. The group of plants categorized as carnivorous belong to 7 families and 15 genera. Family names can be recognized by their suffix, which is 'aceae.' This classification is illustrated in Chart 1.

Chart 1

Choripetalae Group	**Sympetalae Group**
Byblidaceae	Lentibulariaceae
Byblis	*Genlisea*
Cephalotaceae	*Pinguicula*
Cephalotus	*Polypompholyx*
Dioncophyllaceae	*Utricularia*
Triphyophyllum	
Droseraceae	
Aldrovanda	
Dionaea	
Drosera	
Drosophyllum	
Nepenthaceae	
Nepenthes	
Sarraceniaceae	
Darlingtonia	
Heliamphora	
Sarracenia	

The plants in the Sympetalae group have flowers which are personate. Personate flowers have petals that are joined or fused together forming a two-lipped corolla terminating in a tube. They exhibit bilateral symmetry, having only one plane that can be drawn through the flower that will divide it into two parts that are mirror images of each other.

The plants in the Chloripetalae group have flowers in which the petals are not joined together and the flowers exhibit radial symmetry, meaning the flower parts are arranged around a circle and can be divided into mirror images by any plane that passes through the center of the circle.

Chart 2: List of genera, with their type of trapping mechanism and geographic range.

Genus	Number of species	Geographic Distribution	Type of Trap
Aldrovanda	1	Europe, Asia, Africa, and Australia	Active
Byblis	2	Australia	Passive flypaper
Cephalotus	1	S.W. Australia	Passive pitfall
Darlingtonia	1	California & Oregon, U.S.A. Western Canada	Passive pitfall
Dionaea	1	North & South Carolina, U.S.A.	Active
Drosera	120	Omnipresent	Passive flypaper
Drosophyllum	1	Morocco, Portugal, and Spain	Passive flypaper
Genlisea	14	Tropical Africa & Tropical South America, Madagascar	Passive lobster

Genus	Number of species	Geographic Distribution	Type of Trap
Heliamphora	6	Northern South America	Passive pitfall
Nepenthes	71	Area surrounding and including the East Indies	Passive pitfall
Pinguicula	50	Northern Hemisphere and South America	Passive flypaper
Polypompholyx	2	Australia	Active mousetrap, suction type
Sarracenia	9	North America	Passive pitfall
Triphyophyllum	1	West Africa	Passive flypaper
Utricularia	ca. 300	Omnipresent	Active mousetrap, suction type

TRAPPING MECHANISMS

The trapping mechanisms of carnivorous plants can be categorized as either active or passive with subdivisions in each group.

Active Trapping Mechanisms

An active trap is one in which rapid movement is an integral part of the trapping mechanism. There are two kinds of traps in this category, active "steel" trap and active "mousetrap" suction type.

Active steel type trap: Found in *Dionaea* and *Aldrovanda*. The trap consists of two lobes, which are rectangularly shaped, joined at the midrib and normally open. When stimulated the two lobes move rapidly toward each other and entrap the prey. The opening of the trap is a growth process and, therefore, much slower than the split-second closure.

Active mousetrap suction type: Found in *Polypompholyx* and *Utricularia*. The bladders or leaves which are roughly egg-shaped are the traps. At one end of the bladder is an opening with a door that opens into the trap. When the trap is set, the pressure inside the trap is lower than on the outside. The trigger hairs on the door set the trap off when touched by insects. Since the pressure inside the trap is less than the pressure outside the trap, the prey and water are sucked inside the trap. This is a purely mechanical trap, as distinguished from *Dionaea* and *Aldrovanda* traps which involve growth processes.

Passive Trapping Mechanisms

In passive trapping, rapid movement is not an integral part of the trapping mechanism. There are three types of passive traps: pitfall, lobster, and flypaper.

Pitfall: Found in *Cephalotus, Darlingtonia, Heliamphora, Nepenthes,* and *Sarracenia*. Trapping is accomplished when insects are lured by various methods to a cylindrically-shaped tube, which has been aptly called the stomach of the plant but is more often called the pitcher. The shape and embellishments of the pitchers vary considerably in the five genera and their species.

Lobster trap: Found in *Genlisea*. The prey is led into the trap by two spiral arms which have hairs that guide the prey. Once inside the trap the prey cannot get out.

Flypaper type (1): Found in *Drosera*. Prey is captured by becoming mired in the sticky mucilage produced by the tentacles that cover the upper surface of the leaves. The tentacles bend over to touch and force the prey down against the leaf surface. In many species prior to digestion the leaves will bend around and enclose the prey.

Flypaper type (2): Found in *Pinguicula*. Here as in the *Drosera*-type trap, the prey is entrapped by the sticky mucilage produced by the tentacles on the leaves, but in *Pinguicula* there is no movement of the tentacles. The margins of the leaves can roll up, forming a shallow basin.

Flypaper type (3): Found in *Byblis, Triphyophyllum* and *Drosophyllum*. The prey here is mired in the sticky mucilage as it is in *Drosera* and *Pinguicula* except there is no movement of either tentacles or leaves.

USE OF CARNIVOROUS PLANTS

Carnivorous plants have been used extensively for medication and other purposes. In the past, plants were virtually the only source of medicinal preparations. A plant such as *Drosera* that was able to retain its droplet of mucilage during the day without evaporation was believed to have extraordinary medicinal powers.

Drosera

Macerated *Drosera* leaves or extracts of leaves were used externally to treat warts, corns, and sunburn. Extracts or teas made from the leaves were used to treat internal disorders including tuberculosis, asthma, whooping cough, catarrh of the lower respiratory tract, arteriosclerosis, eye and ear inflammations, liver pain, morning sickness, dropsy, various stomach maladies, syphilis, toothaches, intestinal problems, as a tranquilizer, diuretic, and it was believed to have some aphrodisiacal power. When homeopathy was in vogue, the extract was also used to cause irritation of the skin because it was believed that if the skin was inflamed, an agent which caused inflammation would cure it. This is the theory behind producing and using vaccines for disease control. Scientists have discovered an anti-spasmodic agent in some *Drosera* species.

Pinguicula

The leaves were applied to cattle sores. Mixtures of extract of the leaves and linseed oil were used for treating wounds. Leaves or their extracts have been used to curdle milk and to make a milk-type dessert.

Nepenthes

The fluid in the unopened leaves was used to cure bed-wetters by pouring the fluid of the unopened pitchers on the head of the individuals, who later also drank some of it.

PRESERVING CARNIVOROUS PLANTS

Some species of carnivorous plants are in danger of extinction. Many people attribute this outcome to man's activity. This fundamentally is a false view. Evolution has been going on for eons. True, man has in some cases accelerated the process, but if man were not around, all bogs would eventually become dry land with trees growing in them. Natural geological processes will result in lakes becoming swamps and then dry land. Some of man's activities have certainly reduced populations of carnivorous plants, but the inevitable outcome of natural processes is another cause for diminishing plant numbers.

The prime human activity responsible for the reduction in numbers of some species of carnivorous plants is the alteration of the environment. To many people, wet lands such as bogs and swamps are worthless and a waste of land. As a consequence, they often become sites for dumping trash. With the increase in the "standard of living" many of these areas have been drained for housing developments, shopping plazas, industrial complexes and for recreational activities such as golf courses. With the decrease of available land due to increased demand and cost, farmers have drained wetlands for agricultural purposes. As a consequence of these activities the water table of vast areas has been lowered, adversely affecting the carnivorous plants in those areas.

The advent of modern agricultural and forest management has resulted in the reduction of wild fires and controlled burning. Fire is necessary for the health of certain groups of carnivorous plants. In some species, such as most of those that grow in the United States, fire removes some of the detritus, the dead plant remains, and competing plants which inhibit the reproduction and growth of carnivorous plants. Wild fire is necessary to release the nutrients bound up in other plants. In Australia, for example, periodic burns are required by some *Drosera* plants in order to flower. Others will flower more prolifically if their habitat is burned. Some seeds of Australian *Drosera* species will not germinate until they have been subjected to the heat or gases generated by fire.

Pollution is another factor that leads to the demise of carnivorous plant stands. The extensive use of fertilizers and pesticides produces residues which alter the habitats of carnivorous plants. Waste products from industrial processes also have an effect. Waterways in the Pine Barrens of New Jersey, U.S.A., home of several carnivorous plant species, exhibit oil slicks. One wonders what other chemicals may be dissolved in the water which are not visible.

Field collection of plants has been pushed to the foreground by many as the chief cause for the reduced numbers of some carnivorous plants. It is true that over-collection is detrimental, but it is also obvious to anyone acquainted with native populations of carnivorous plants, that the plant stands often become overcrowded, resulting in substantial mortality. Judicious field collection of plants can be helpful, particularly in overcrowded stands. Wise collecting benefits the total plant population by distributing plants to other suitable habitats.

Laws have been enacted to protect this group of plants. These laws, based on sound scientific premises, have proved cumbersome and, in some situations, notably difficult to enforce.

A growing awareness for the need to preserve carnivorous plants has developed in recent years. As a consequence, many groups have been unselfishly working to preserve and manage natural bogs and wetlands inhabited by carnivorous plants. While these activities are commendable and succeed in preventing man-initiated change, the path of nature is plant succession which means that eventually wetlands will become dry land. We may be able to slow down this natural process but it's doubtful that we can stop it.

Preservation of carnivorous plants for the long-term enjoyment, thousands of years hence, will have to be by means of cultivation by as many people as possible. It is vital that knowledge of the cultural and propagation requirements for this fascinating group of plants be accumulated and disseminated to as many interested people as possible. An ideal way to do this is to join and participate in any of the carnivorous plant societies which publish newsletters.

Another unexplored potential for preserving the plants for the future is to carry on breeding programs to produce carnivorous plants that will grow in less demanding or restrictive environments.

2

Dionaea—Venus Fly Trap

HISTORY

Governor Arthur Dobbs of North Carolina, U.S.A., was the first person to describe the plant which he named the "Fly Trap Sensitive" and which later became known as the Venus Fly Trap. In 1760 he communicated this discovery, and in particular the plant's ability to close and trap objects, to Mr. P. Collinson of England. Later Mr. J. Bartram of Philadelphia sent specimens of these plants, which he knew as "Tipitiwitchet," to Mr. P. Collinson. Study of these plants by Mr. J. Ellis and Dr. D. Solander led to their observation of the similarity of the new plant to the already familiar *Drosera*. Ellis was the first to have an inkling of the possible carnivorous nature of the Venus Fly Trap and conveyed this idea to Linnaeus, the famous eighteenth century biologist, by letter, a portion which reads:

But the plant, of which I now enclose you an exact figure, with a specimen of its leaves and blossoms, shews, that nature may have some view towards nourishment, in forming the upper joint of the leaf like a machine to catch food: upon the middle of this lies the bait for the unhappy insect that becomes its prey. Many minute red glands, cover its inner surface, and which perhaps discharge sweet liquor, tempt the poor animal to taste them; and the instant these tender parts are irritated by its feet, the two lobes rise up, grasp it fast, lock the row of spines together, and squeeze it to death. And, further, lest the strong efforts for life, in the creature thus taken, should serve to disengage it, three small erect spines are fixed near the middle of each lobe, among the glands, that effectually put an end to all its struggles. Nor do the lobes ever open again, while the dead animal continues there.

Despite this letter, which contains inaccuracies, Linnaeus was not convinced of the carnivorous habit of this plant and merely regarded the movement as another case of irritability similar to that of the sensitive plant *Mimosa pudica*, and believed that the insects were later released. Ellis' erroneous belief in the function of the three erect spines, which were discovered to be trigger hairs on the inner surface of the trap, was also shared by Erasmus Darwin who wrote:

In the *Dionaea muscipula* there is a still more wonderful contrivance to prevent the depredations of insects: the leaves are armed with long teeth, like the antennae of insects, and lie spread upon the ground around the stem, and are so irritable, that when an insect creeps upon them they fold up and crush or pierce it to death. Ellis named the plant *Dionaea*. The origin of the name *Dionaea muscipula*, Venus Fly Trap, has its roots in Greek and Roman mythology. In Greek Dione is the mother of Aphrodite or sometimes used as another name for Aphrodite goddess of love. To the Romans, Venus was their goddess of love.

NATURAL HABITAT

The Venus Fly Trap is endemic to the coastal plains of North and South Carolina, but attempts are under way to establish a stand of them in suitable sites in such states as New Jersey and Virginia. They usually grow in semi-pocosin or semi-savannah areas which are intermediate between the wet evergreen bogs and the dry sandy regions in the longleaf pine area. A pocosin is a swamp or a marsh and a savannah is a grassland with scattered trees. The region in which they grow is better known as an ecotone, the transition area between two types of habitats. Often they are found in the company of other carnivorous plants such as Sundews, Butterworts, Bladderworts, and Pitcher Plants. Venus Fly Traps inhabit relatively flat surfaces, avoiding depressions where excess water may accumulate, but thrive along the upper portions of the depressions. Even though they grow in damp soils, these soils may become desiccated during the dry season without any apparent harm to the plants.

Fire appears to be an important ecological factor in the survival of *Dionaea* in nature. The invigorating effect of fire may be due to the release of nutrients in a more available form and/or the elimination of competing plants and detritus, on accumulated plant remains. Results from studies to date favor the latter conclusion. Even though the rhizomes are usually found within 4 in. (10 cm) of the soil surface, the heat from fire does not injure the larger and deeper rhizomes. The moist nature of the soil tends to keep the soil temperatures lower.

The natural soil in which the Venus Fly Traps grow consists of a surface layer of thin peaty material underlaid with mineral soil. About 8% of the soil is organic matter and about 95% of the remaining mineral matter is sand. The bulk of the Venus Fly Trap's roots are usually confined to the upper 4 in. (10 cm) of the soil with some extending to a depth of 1 ft. (30.5 cm). Chemical testing of the soil reveals it has a low fertility with a low pH which ranges from 3 to 5.

DESCRIPTION OF PLANT

The plant consists of a short unbranched rhizome, which is a bulb-like structure formed by the overlapping basal portions of leaves surrounding the growing point. The root system is not extensive. The blade portion of each leaf is modified into a trap, by which the plant captures its prey, while the basal portion, the petiole which supports the trap, is fleshy and stores food. The total length of the leaf may be up to 8 in. (20 cm) long. The leaves are arranged in a rosette, forming a circular pattern around the growing point. New leaves originate from the growing point at the center of the rosette and are protected by the overlapping expanded basal portions of the older leaves. (Fig. 2-1)

Leaves (Traps)
Leaf characteristics vary with the season. Spring leaves tend to be green with broad petioles, whose lateral extensions are referred to as wings. The spring leaves reach lengths of 2¾ in. (7 cm) with a width of ¾ in. (2 cm) at their broadest point. They are either erect or prostrate. Red coloration is absent or relatively limited, but when present it is usually restricted to the glands on the inner surface of the traps. Production of spring leaves is terminated by flowering during late spring or early summer. After

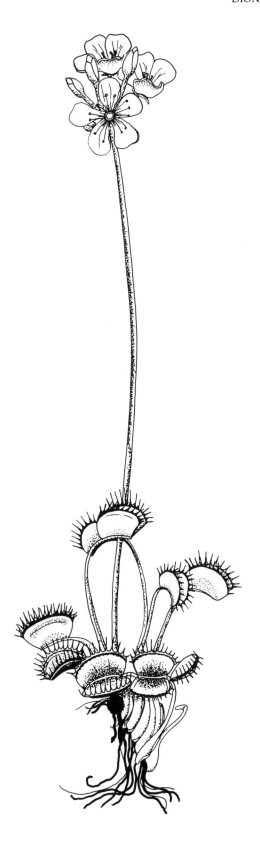

Fig. 2-1 *Dionaea* plant with inflorescence.

flowering is complete, summer leaves are produced which are easily differentiated from spring leaves, as they can be as long as or longer than the spring leaves but are very narrow and almost wingless. The traps produced by a plant usually are largest on the summer leaves and smallest on the winter leaves. Summer leaves tend to grow vertically. Plants growing in intense light, either natural or artifical, develop traps whose inner surfaces, and at times even the marginal spines, are a solid deep maroon-red color. (Photo 2-1) Light intensity controls red coloration in a majority of the Venus Fly Trap plants, although in some it is genetically controlled. When these plants are growing side by side, exposed to the same high-intensity light, most will develop a deep red coloration, but a few may not. With the beginning of fall, winter-type leaves with smaller traps are produced. These leaves tend to be prostrate and the width of the petioles tends to be between that of the spring and summer leaves.

In protected areas of their natural habitat the plants tend to be evergreen, but in other areas frost can kill the leaves during the winter.

Flowers

In the spring, May and June, the plant produces a tall scape (flower stalk), with white flowers. The scape bears from 1–15 white flowers. Each flower consists of 5 green sepals, 5 white petals, usually 15 stamens and 1 compound pistil. (Fig. 2-2) Terminal flower buds open first, followed by the sequential opening of the others further down toward the base of the scape with up to 4 flowers open at one time. Plants grown from bulbs that were kept in cold storage usually will bloom within 2–3 months of planting, regardless of the season. If seed is not desired, remove the scape as soon as it is visible so that energy consumed by the flowering process can be diverted to vegetative plant growth and development.

TRAPPING

Prey is captured by the rectangularly-shaped trap which consists of two lobes united along the midrib of the leaf blade. The trap has been compared to a hinge, but this analogy is inaccurate because a hinge has an articulated joint, and the trap has no such joint. Under normal conditions the angle formed by the open trap is in the neighborhood of 40 to 50 degrees. The margins of the trap are studded with bristles which are sometimes referred to as cilia. On each of the two inner lobes of the trap are three trigger hairs arranged in a triangular pattern with the apex of the triangle directed toward the midrib. (Photo 2-2) In rare cases there are four trigger hairs on each surface and in some cases the hairs bifurcate. On the outer, abaxial surfaces of the trap lobes there is an abundance of star-shaped structures known as stellate trichomes. Covering most of the inner, adaxial, surface of the trap lobes are two kinds of glands: the alluring and digestive-absorptive glands. These glands are structurally identical. The digestive-absorptive glands are conspicuous because of their red coloration due to the water-soluble pigment, anthocyanin, which is present in the cell fluid. The alluring glands, which produce a sugary substance that has a pleasing odor to insects, are arranged along the outer margins of the trap. It has been proposed that this arrangement is by design to prevent insects which are too small from effecting closure, thus enabling the plant to conserve energy for trapping larger meals. According to this theory an insect which is less than ¼ in. (0.6 cm) long is too short to set off the trap as it dines on the nectar produced by the alluring glands.

In nature, trap closure is effected by insects touching the trigger hairs. Observations indicate that a single hair must be stimulated twice or two hairs stimulated in succession for closure to occur. Normally the interval of time between the two stimulations cannot be too short or too long. This time interval has been found to be from about 1 second to about 20 seconds; if the interval is longer, then, additional stimulations are necessary to initiate closure. There are other factors that influence the number of

STAMEN

PISTIL

Fig. 2-2 *Dionaea* flower has 5 sepals, 5 white petals,
numerous stamens and one compound pistil.

stimulations necessary to effect closure such as: age of plant, ambient temperature, length of time since last closure and general health of plant. The higher the temperature the more likely that a single stimulation is sufficient. Some research indicates that at 59°F (15°C) two stimulations are needed, at 95°F (35°C) often one stimulation is sufficient, and at 104°F (40°C) only one stimulation is necessary in half of the cases. As temperature decreases the action becomes sluggish and eventually ceases. The temperature at which trap action ceases is quite variable.

Closure of traps can also be effected by electrical stimulation, hot water 149°F (65°C), chemicals such as ether and chloroform, and by rubbing, pinching or cutting the area above the midrib on either the adaxial or abaxial surfaces of the trap. Virtually the entire surface of the trap is sensitive to stimulation of one sort or another. The closure produced by chemical agents is slower and has a prolonged effect, resulting in the trap being less responsive to later physical stimulation. The trigger hairs are by far the most sensitive or receptive to stimulation. Studies indicate, when electricity is used to set off the traps, that as the strength of the electrical impulse increases, the number of impulses required decreases.

It has been known since the late 1800s, that when the trap is stimulated an electrical voltage is produced. This electricity is produced regardless of whether the trap closes or not. Recent studies involving the electrical phenomenon of Venus Fly Traps have been conducted by Stuhlman and Daren. One of their conclusions is: "The action potential (voltage) runs a course characteristic of mammalian nerves in normal physiological condition."

Under ideal conditions the trap closes with an alarming speed, a second or less. The rapidity of motion can be startling. Upon suitable stimulation a healthy trap will close. This initial closing is known as the closing or shutting phase. (Fig.2-3A) The marginal spines become loosely interlocked, turning the trap into a jail cell with spines for bars. Small insects are able to escape through the open spaces between the interlaced marginal spines. If the trap has been mechanically stimulated to close or if the prey is small enough to escape, the trap will reopen in about 24 hours without further waste of time and energy. If, on the other hand, suitable prey has been placed in the trap or small animals such as insects, mollusks (snails and slugs) and arachnids (spiders and daddy long legs) have sprung the trap, the trap progresses to the narrowing phase which commences about half an hour after stimulation. (Fig.2-3B) By comparing the diagrams of the two traps, (Fig.2-3A and 2-3B), the differences between the phases become evident. The change that occurs in the positioning of the trap and marginal spines is analogous to the difference between interlacing the fingers of your right and left hand in a relaxed position with the thumbs overlapping and the bases of the palms touching as compared to both palms being tightly pressed together with the fingers out straight. During the narrowing phase considerable energy is expended. Often the lobes become so tightly pressed together that the outline of the captured prey is visible, and soft-bodied insects are crushed. (Photo 2-3) Following trap closure, fluids containing digestive enzymes are secreted. The tissue just below the marginal spines forms a secure seal so that prey along with the digestive enzymes that are secreted by the trap intermingle within the confines of the trap interior. It is probable that the digestive fluids drown the prey, putting an end to their struggle if they were not previously crushed. After digestion and absorption have taken place, the trap opens, exposing the chitinous remains from insects and small crustaceans and other undigestable materials.

Traps will remain closed for 1–2 weeks, if suitable prey has been captured. Otherwise they usually open within a day. Reopening of the trap has been attributed to a differential rate of growth of the trap surfaces. The adaxial surface of the trap grows more than the abaxial surface resulting in the opening of the trap.

Even though studies do not indicate that the Venus Fly Trap must have prey to survive, some show that plants which are fed are healthier and produce more seed. A

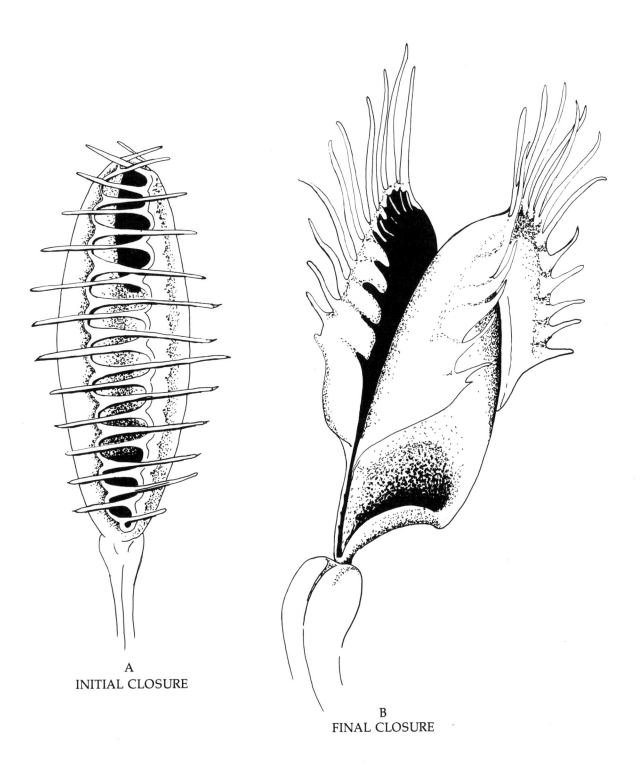

A
INITIAL CLOSURE

B
FINAL CLOSURE

Fig. 2-3 Initial closure is evidenced by interlacing of spines. During final closure the sides of the trap become tightly pressed together.

single trap can usually capture prey 3–4 times before the trap ceases to function. An artifically stimulated trap can close and open many more times.

When the captured prey is of the correct size for the trap, digestion proceeds without decay. The formic acid present in the digestive fluid is believed to be a bactericide. If prey is too large or if fat is placed in the trap, the trap commences to decay and turns black instead of opening. The death of a trap does not mean the death of the plant, as new traps are constantly being formed at the center of the rosette during the growing season.

SPECIES OF THE GENUS *DIONAEA*

There is only one species in this genus, making it monotypical.

CULTURAL INFORMATION

Planting Media
Sphagnum peat moss, sphagnum moss (living or non-living), sand (preferably acidic, pH less than 7) and mixtures of the above media.

Temperatures
Growing season 70–100°F (21–38°C). Dormant season 35–50°F (1.7–10°C). Plants are often subjected to light frost in their native habitat.

Dormancy
A rest period from active growth for 3–5 months is required. During this period the temperature is lowered to 35–50°F (1.7–10°C) and soil moisture is maintained at a lower level than during active growth.

Water & Humidity
During the growing season a relatively high humidity is necessary and the soil must be kept moist. Pots with plants can be left standing in an inch (2.5 cm) or so of water during the growing season, but kept drier during the dormancy period.

Light
Dionaea plants thrive in bright light. In most plants red coloration of the inner lobes of the traps increases with more intense light, whereas insufficient light will result in green plants with little or no red color and spindly growth. Avoid direct sunlight when growing plants in enclosed containers. Artifical light—start with 900 foot candles. Photoperiod (length of time lights are illuminated) Summer: 12–16 hours, winter: 8–12 hours.

Pests
Aphids and foliar blight. See Chapter 8 for control of pests.

Feeding
See Chapter 7 for directions.

PROPAGATION

Sexual Reproduction

In a *Dionaea* flower the pollen is usually mature before the pistil of the same flower is receptive to pollen. When the flower bud opens the anthers are smooth as is the stigma of the pistil. When the pollen is mature and ready for dissemination the anther appears rough and granular and is covered with yellow powder, the pollen. The end of the pistil, the stigma, divides into sections, usually five, when it is receptive to pollen. Transfer of mature pollen to a receptive pistil is necessary for subsequent fertilization and seed production. These plants can be self- or cross-pollinated.

The pollen may be transferred by removing a stamen with a pair of tweezers and rubbing the anther on the receptive stigma of the pistil or by using a small camel's hair brush that is rubbed on the pollen of an anther and then on a receptive stigma or by rubbing the anthers of one flower gently on the stigma of an adjacent flower on a nearby plant. Transfer the pollen 2 or 3 times, each on a different day to insure pollination. Seed matures in 4–6 weeks following pollination.

The black, shiny, pear-shaped seeds are encased within the remaining floral parts, the ovary and sepals, which turn jet black along with the scape as the seed matures. Seeds can be planted immediately or stored in sealed vials or bottles under refrigeration.

Viability decreases with increased storage time so that by the end of a year viability is usually less than 30%. To germinate seed, sprinkle it on a suitable medium, maintain high humidity and bright light. Sow the seed very thinly on the medium so that the seedlings will be able to grow a full season in the same container without being overcrowded or transplanted. This procedure results in larger plants and reduced incidence of fungus diseases which are very common in overcrowded seedlings. The seed can be covered by a thin layer of medium if desired, but this is not necessary. Germination is hastened by maintaining temperatures of 80–85°F (26.7–29.5°C).

When seedlings have at least four leaves they can be transplanted if they are crowded. Seedlings are spaced a minimum of 1 in. (2.5 cm) apart when transplanted.

Asexual Reproduction

1. Leaf cuttings: The entire leaf, including the basal portion, is removed. Older, more mature leaves produce the best results. (Photo 2-4) The leaf cuttings are placed on damp medium such as sphagnum peat moss or preferably sphagnum moss (living or dead) and kept in bright light with a photoperiod of about 14 hours and at a temperature of about 80°F (26.7°C). An alternative method is to insert the cuttings into medium for about ½ their length.

A convenient method of providing an ideal environment is to place the soil and cuttings in a plastic bag in which a stake or piece of glass tubing has been placed in the medium to prevent the collapse of the bag. The bag is twisted shut and secured to the top of the stake or glass rod. (Fig. 9-1)

Buds that look like little bumps appear within two months and plants will develop from the buds. The number of plants produced from each leaf varies from one to as many as 30. When plantlets have developed substantial root systems they can be transplanted and kept under regular growing conditions.

2. 'Bulb' scales: Carefully peel off the 'bulb' scales which are in reality the basal portions of the leaf petioles. The structures that are sold as bulbs are not true botanical bulbs, but rather *Dionaea* plants with the tops of their leaves removed. A few of the scales can be removed from a 'bulb' and then the rest of the 'bulb' can be planted, or all the scales can be removed and utilized for asexual reproduction. Follow the same procedure as detailed for leaf cuttings.

3. Vegetative apomixis: Small plants may develop on the flower stalk and/or in the infloresence. Why this occurs is not known and it is also not known how to induce this reproductive activity. When the plantlets have developed roots they can be removed and planted.

3

The Pitcher Plants

This chapter includes genera from 3 families. *Darlingtonia, Heliamphora* and *Sarracenia,* belong in the Sarraceniaceae, *Nepenthes* in the Nepenthaceae, and *Cephalotus* in the Cephalotaceae. These genera are grouped together in this section because they all have modified leaves that form hollow vessels, referred to as pitchers, which capture prey. The structure, shape, color and embellishments of the pitchers vary considerably from genus to genus.

Sarracenia

HISTORY

Native Americans were probably familiar with *Sarracenia* or Pitcher Plants for a considerable length of time before European explorers discovered them sometime during the early 1500s. The earliest known illustration of *Sarracenia* was published in 1576 in De L'Obel's, *Nova Stirpium Adversaria.* The Canadian physician, Dr. M. S. Sarrazin, sent plants, presumably *Sarracenia purpurea,* to a Mr. Tournefort in Europe. Tournefort's description of the plants became the basis of the genus which was named in honor of Dr. Sarrazin. Although numerous early authors suggested the possible carnivorous nature of these plants, none pursued the subject. Goebel and Higley demonstrated that *Sarracenia* plants can absorb materials through the pitcher walls. Zipperer in 1885 detected digestive enzymes in the plants' secretions. In 1918 Hepburn, St. John, and Jones demonstrated categorically that the plants are capable of digesting prey.

NATURAL HABITAT

Pitcher Plants are native to North America. They are found in bogs, swamps, low wetlands, open pinelands and sometimes in wooded areas. (Photo 3-1) Burning over their range benefits their survival by removing debris and competing plants, and releasing nutrients from organic matter.

DESCRIPTION OF PLANT

There are nine known species in the genus at the present time; the status of one of the nine is currently contested. In addition, there are numerous varieties and hybrids.

Sarracenia plants are herbaceous perennials consisting of a rhizome with fibrous roots and hollow tube-like ascidiform leaves, which are called pitchers. There is an extension of the leaf that forms a canopy-type structure, called a hood, covering the opening of the pitchers, except in one species. In *Sarracenia purpurea* the hood does not cover the pitcher opening. The leaves, or pitchers, are decumbent in two species and erect in the remainder. The pitchers ususally form a rosette around the growing point on the rhizome. The lower portion of the pitcher corresponds to the petiole and the upper portion to the leaf blade. (Fig. 3-1)

Leaves

When *Sarracenia* seeds germinate, the first leaves to appear are the cotyledons. The leaves produced thereafter are almost identical in all species and resemble miniature mature leaves of *Sarracenia minor*. These leaves are known as juvenile leaves and are produced for a year or two by plants grown from seed. Juvenile leaves are often the first leaves produced during asexual propagation. In addition to these leaves, some *Sarracenia* species produce two types of adult or mature leaves. The adult leaf-type produced during the summer is ascidiform. Identification of *Sarracenia* species is essentially based on the characteristics of the ascidiform leaves. The second type of mature leaf, produced during the fall, is sword-shaped or ensiform and called phyllodia. Since phyllodia usually last throughout the cold season, they are also called winter leaves.

Flowers

Flowers are borne singly on scapes, which may attain heights of 30 in. (76 cm). Flower color varies considerably between individual species, but each species has a distinctive color. Flowers have from 50 to 80 stamens and a 5-carpellate compound ovary. (Fig. 3-4 A) The style divides into 5 sections forming an umbrella-type structure, with each section terminating in a stigma. There are 5 sepals and 5 petals in the flower.

Leaf Zones

The inner surface of the pitcher is divided into four zones based on the function and structure of the surface. These four general zones are common to all species of *Sarracenia*. The first zone encompasses the area on the undersurface of the hood. It is called the attractive zone and contains the nectar glands intermingled with stiff, downward pointing hairs which direct the insect's movement toward the bottom of the pitcher. Zone 2, containing numerous nectar-producing glands, is smooth and is located just below zone 1. The digestive glands are located in the smooth waxy walls of zone 3. While the first two zones offer a precarious foothold for the insect, zone 3 offers none. Moving downward in the pitcher, zone 4 is distinguished from zone 3 by the appearance of downward pointing hairs. This is the digestive and absorptive area. The digestive enzymes and bacteria in the fluid in this region of the pitcher are responsible for digestion of prey. The function of the downward pointing hairs in this zone is to prevent prey from leaving the fluid. Indigestable insect remains are often found as a blackened mass in this region at the end of summer. (Fig. 3-2)

TRAPPING

Presumably, luring of prey is accomplished by secretion of nectar, coloration, odor, and fenestrations of the leaves. (Photo 3-2) Although not all of these enticements are

Fig. 3-1 *Sarracenia alata* plant.

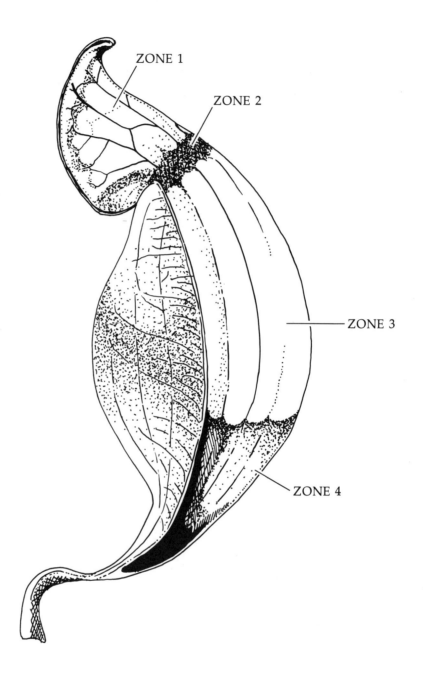

ZONE 1

ZONE 2

ZONE 3

ZONE 4

Fig. 3-2 *Sarracenia purpurea* ssp. *purpurea* showing the interior zones.

utilized by every species, secretion of nectar is universal among *Sarracenia*. In fact, in some cases the nectar secretion is so copious that the nectar is found in globules, particularly in zones 1 and 2 of the pitcher. Nectar glands occur on the outside surface of the pitcher, the upper inner surfaces of the pitcher and hood, as well as on the floral parts.

After an insect discovers the nectar and begins feeding on it, it will work its way to where the nectar is most abundant, in the vicinity of the pitcher's opening. As the insect feeds on the nectar produced on the rim of the opening, it may be enticed into the pitcher by the accumulation of nectar on the surface below the rim, inside the pitcher or along the underside of the hood. On the underside of the hood nectar glands are intermingled with hairs which point down toward the bottom of the pitcher. These downward pointing hairs do not provide a stable footing for the insects. It almost seems that some insects sense the possible danger and, rather than attempt to walk on the hairs, will stand on the rim and stretch as much as possible to reach the nectar. In the process they may lose their balance and tumble to the bottom of the pitcher. Other insects will attempt to carefully work their way around the hairs, feeding on the nectar, unaware that the path they are taking is leading them to the bottom of the pitcher. It is much easier for the insects to walk in the direction that the hairs are pointing than to walk against them. If the insect continues, it will reach zone 2 which, being smooth and waxy, offers no foothold. Hence, the insect falls to the bottom.

Sarracenia minor, S. leucophylla, and *S. psittacina* have visual lures known as fenestrations to attract insect prey. (Photo 3-3) Fenestrations are areas located on the hood and/or upper part of the pitchers which lack pigmentation and thus are translucent. The fenestrations allow light to enter the pitcher. Insects are apparently more likely to enter the lighted pitchers than if they are dark. When an insect reaches the rim it may see these translucent areas and, believing them to be openings, will fly from the rim to one of these "openings," only to smash into the fenestration and tumble down to the bottom of the pitcher. Alternatively, insects feeding on the nectar may follow a path which leads them to one of these "openings." Once there, the insect usually has no recourse, but to continue down into the pitcher because to get back to the rim it must walk against the pointed hairs.

Words cannot adequately describe the behavior of insects as they feed on the nectar and are unwittingly led to their death. At times during their feeding, the insects stop their activity as if they sense something ominous.

OBSERVING TRAPPING

There is a simple way to observe and study insects as they feed on and become trapped in the pitchers. A plant or preferably a single pitcher is covered with a transparent container, such as a wide mouth gallon mayonnaise jar, bell jar, or a plastic bag. A single pitcher is more suitable than a whole plant because if a whole plant is used, a larger container is necessary. Also the insect has more plant area to investigate and, therefore, it may take longer for the insect to settle down and the activity of the insect may be harder to follow. A pitcher should be selected which has a relatively large supply of nectar. The nectar appears on the pitcher as small droplets of liquid which are sticky to the touch. *Sarracenia* produce the most copious nectar flow in the spring of the year. Often in the fall and winter the pitchers are devoid of nectar.

The pitcher is anchored in a vertical position in a pot of sand or soil and covered with a suitable container. This entire set-up is placed in a sunny area, but not in direct sunlight because the temperature inside may become excessive. (Fig. 3-3)

Now the set-up is ready for insects. We have used houseflies, honeybees, ants, millipedes, centipedes, hornets, grasshoppers, and small beetles. The fastest results are obtained with honeybees, which may be trapped within 10 minutes. The live, captured insect is put in a container which, in turn, is placed in a freezer for 3–5 minutes. This treatment slows the activity of the insect so that it can be handled easily. Care should be taken not to freeze it. The insect is then placed in the container with the pitcher. Within 5–10 minutes after removal from the freezer, the insect is usually active again. If a hole of suitable size is cut through one side of the pitcher near ground level, the trapped insect will have a means of escape. On one occasion we had a honeybee which was trapped and escaped 20 times in one afternoon. There are numerous variations to the set-up. For example, to follow the activities of an insect more easily with species such as *S. flava,* the hood can be cut off, thus revealing more of the inner surface. In the case of *S. minor,* a small opening may be cut in the back of the hood, enabling one to follow the activities of the insect inside the hood. Sometimes the insect will fly out of this opening but this may be prevented by taping transparent material over the hole.

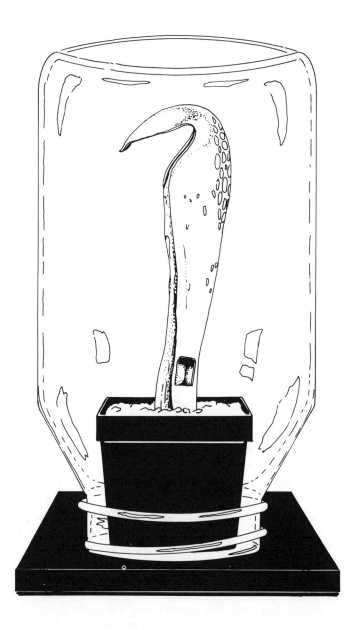

Fig. 3-3 Set-up for observing insect capture in *Sarracenia.*

DIGESTION OF PREY

The bottom of the hollow pitcher, zone 3, is lined with glands which secrete digestive enzymes and zone 4 with absorptive glands. These enzymes are effective in the chemical breakdown of prey, except for the more resistant portions of the insect's body, such as chitin. Numerous organisms exist and thrive in the liquid that accumulates in the base of the pitchers. Among these denizens are yeast cells and bacteria which assist in the digestion of the prey, although the full extent of their role has not been ascertained. In any case, digestion does occur and protein is broken down into amino acids, which are absorbed by the plant along with minerals. The efficiency of *Sarracenia* pitchers is attested to by the numerous insects and their remains that accumulate in the base of the pitchers. Some of the more common victims are ants, beetles, crickets, wasps, spiders, flies of various kinds, and occasionally small toads.

INHABITANTS

While *Sarracenia* is famous for its carnivory, not all insects succumb to the lures which lead most prey to their death. In fact, many insects feed on the plants' pitchers and rhizome, while others live in the fluid bath and still others make use of the pitchers to capture insects in their own way and for their own use.

One of the most intriguing members of *Sarracenia* society is a group of moths of the genus *Exyra*. Depending on the species, they lay one or more eggs in each pitcher. If more than one egg has been laid in the pitcher, upon hatching, one of the larvae will kill the others or drive them off so that only one larva of the species remains per pitcher. Thus, a single plant with five pitchers supports a maximum of five larvae. Another species in this group lays its eggs in the area surrounding the mouth of the pitcher. When the eggs of the moths hatch, the emerging larvae eat the superficial tissue of the pitcher, causing eaten areas to become translucent.

Eggs from another species of *Exyra* hatch into larvae which feed on the pitcher walls and produce a tent of silk. Members of this group often spin a net or webbing across the opening of the pitcher, forming a home with protection against rain and other insects. An even more ingenious species of *Exyra* forms a home for its eggs in a unique way. Shortly before the larva pupates, it eats the superficial material from a narrow zone encompassing the whole circumference of the inside of the pitcher, at about one third the distance from the bottom of the pitcher. This results in a groove being produced, in effect girdling the pitcher. The pitcher above this groove dies, dries out and becomes somewhat leathery. Since the grooved area of the pitcher is considerably weakened because part of the wall has been removed, the weight of the pitcher above the groove, aided by wind, will cause the pitcher to fold over, effectively barring rain and unwanted visitors from the pitcher chamber.

Larvae of another species of this group of moths plan ahead for their escape after pupating into a moth by eating an opening in the pitcher wall through which they can escape. Another hole is eaten below the escape hatch so that if rain enters the chamber, it will not flood because the water can drain out through the lower hole. This group of moths, whose larvae not only use the pitchers as a dwelling place but also derive nourishment from the tissues of the walls, does not limit its appetite to the pitcher but will also devour the flower and even the rhizome.

Creatures such as spiders inhabit the mouth of the pitcher and some build webs and catch prey in the mouth area. Often the web will completely cover the opening. We have observed a small toad waiting just outside the mouth of the *Sarracenia purpurea* pitcher for some prey to come along.

The caterpillar (larvae) of *Papaipema appassionata* lives on rhizome tissue that it bores out of *Sarracenia* rhizomes, thereby forming hollow tubes. This larvae leaves its tell-tale evidence at the surface, a pile of debris which is colored light brown, granular, and resembles earthworm castings.

SPECIES OF THE GENUS *SARRACENIA*

Species	Common Name
*S. alabamensis**	Alabama Canebrake Pitcher Plant. Species designation is being contested at this time. Some taxonomists feel it is a subspecies of *S. rubra*.
*S. alata***	The Pale Pitcher, formerly named *S. sledgei*.
*S. flava***	Huntsman's Horn, and Yellow Pitcher. There are at least five color variants in this species.
*S. leucophylla***	White Trumpet, formerly named *S. drummondii*.
S. leucophylla var. *alba***	—
S. minor	The Hooded Pitcher Plant.
*S. oreophila***	The Green Pitcher Plant.
S. psittacina	Parrot Pitcher
S. purpurea ssp. *purpurea*	Purple Pitcher, Pitcher Plant, and Northern Pitcher Plant. Formerly named *S. purpurea* ssp. *gibbosa*.
S. purpurea ssp. *purpurea* f. *heterophylla*	—
S. purpurea ssp. *venosa*	Southern Pitcher Plant
S. rubra ssp. *rubra*	Sweet Trumpet
S. rubra ssp. *alabamensis**	—
S. rubra ssp. *gulfensis*	—
S. rubra ssp. *jonesii*	—
S. rubra ssp. *wherryi*	—

*These two are the same plant. Some botanists consider this plant a species, whereas others consider it a subspecies.

**Species which produce ensiform or winter leaves known also as phyllodia.

DESCRIPTION OF THE SPECIES

S. alabamensis Case & Case. Erect leaves with narrow wings which are trumpet-shaped and reach lengths of 20 in. (51 cm). The orifice is covered with an ovate suberect hood which has wavy margins. Two types of leaves and occasional phyllodia are produced. Early spring leaves tend to be curved with summer leaves tending to be straighter and usually larger with a more pronounced taper. The pitcher is green with maroon venation and in strong light has a reddish hue. Faint fenestrations or areoles are present.

Scapes tend to be a few inches (cm) taller than the pitchers and bear reddish-colored flowers. Plants flower in April and May.

S. alata (Wood). Leaves are erect, trumpet-shaped usually with a narrow wing, and measure up to 35 in. (89 cm) in length with a suberect ovate hood with a flat or slightly revolute edges. Leaves usually appear at flowering or shortly thereafter. Pitcher color varies from greenish to pale yellow and in strong light there is red to purple veining with diffuse red coloration on the upper part of the pitcher. Few, if any, sword-shaped ensiform phyllodia are produced. When present they are usually less than ⅔ the length of the summer leaves. Flowers vary from yellow to whitish yellow color and have a musty odor. Scapes may reach heights of 30 in. (76 cm). Plant blooms about mid-March.

S. flava L. Summer leaves are erect, trumpet-shaped with a wide flaring orifice subtended by a rounded hood which is almost flat with revolute edges and has a prominent keel. The leaves can reach lengths of 39 in. (99 cm) and those produced after flowering have a narrow wing. Numerous sword-shaped ensiform phyllodia which are usually 20 in. (51 cm) or less in length are produced during late summer and winter. Leaf color is quite variable ranging from light green to yellow with red splotches and in some plants the whole pitcher is a solid red or maroon color. Often there is red or maroon venation in the leaves. Flowers are bright yellow color and have a pronounced musty odor. Usually it is the first *Sarracenia* to bloom in a given location. Blooming starts in mid-March at the southern limit of its range to mid-May in North Carolina. Scape is shorter than the summer leaves.

S. leucophylla Raf. Leaves appear at the same time as flowers and measure 37 in. (94 cm) with a narrow wing. They are trumpet-shaped with an erect to suberect ovate hood with wavy margins. This plant is distinguished from other *Sarracenia* by extensive white coloration of the upper part of the pitcher. The distinctive leaves are mistaken for the bloom. There is red or green veining in the white area with a red or maroon suffusion. In late summer and fall a few ensiform phyllodia or ascidiform leaves with greatly reduced pitchers are formed. Scapes are usually shorter than the leaves and red to maroon-colored flowers are produced which have a sweetish odor. Flowering takes place from March to April. The upper ½–⅔ of the leaves of var. *alba* are almost solid white with red venation.

S. minor Walt. Leaves are up to 28 in. (71 cm) long, gradually expand from base to orifice, are erect and have a wing which is widest in the middle. An ovate hood arches closely over the orifice. The leaves appear before flowering. Pitcher color is mainly green with a coppery red and/or yellow coloration in strong light. There are numerous fenestrations on the upper part of the pitcher. No phyllodia are produced. Flowers which are yellow color and odorless are borne on scapes which are shorter than the leaves. Flowering occurs from mid-March to mid-May.

S. oreophila (Kearney) Wherry. Summer leaves appear before or at flowering, usually have no wing and measure 30 in. (76 cm) in length. The trumpet-shaped leaves have a suberect rounded hood whose base is strongly constricted, colored green to yellow-green with a diffused red or maroon coloration in strong light. Ensiform, falcate phyllodia are usually less than 20 in. (51 cm) long. The numerous scythe-shaped phyllodia are characteristic of this species and distinguish it from *S. flava* and *S. alata*, the two species often confused with *S. oreophila*. These leaves are produced during late summer and fall. The flower scape is as long as the summer leaves. Flowers are greenish yellow to yellow color and bloom from mid-April to early June. The lack of odor and the lighter color of the flower helps to distinguish it from *S. flava*.

S. purpurea ssp. *purpurea* Wherry. Pitchers which may reach lengths of 18 in. (46 cm) are curved, decumbent to ascending with considerable expansion at the orifice which is not covered because the hood is erect. The hood has prominent lateral wings and the edges are wavy. Pitchers are green in shaded habitats, otherwise they have varying degrees of red or maroon variegation. In full sunlight the plants are often a solid red or maroon color. Flowers which are borne on scapes that may reach lengths of 28 in. (71 cm) vary in color from yellowish green to shades of maroon to light pink. Flowering is from March to May.

S. purpurea ssp. *venosa* Raf. This plant is similar to *Sarracenia purpurea* ssp. *purpurea* except that its pitchers are shorter and wider and their exterior surfaces tend to be pubescent. This subspecies occurs in the southern portion of its range whereas *S. purpurea* ssp. *purpurea* exists in the northern part. The distinction between these subspecies is not clear where their ranges merge in the New Jersey, Pennsylvania and Carolina regions.

S. purpurea ssp. *purpurea* f. *heterophylla* Eaton. Plants are the same as *S. purpurea* ssp. *purpurea* except they have no red or maroon coloration in the pitchers or flowers. (Photo 3-4)

S. psittacina Michx. Evergreen leaves 2–12 in. (5–30 cm) long are usually decumbent forming a basal rosette. The wing is 0.4–1.6 in. (1–4 cm) wide, being widest near the fenestrated globose hood. The orifice or opening is small, round and has a collar. Leaves are green with varying degrees of red to purple coloration the extent of which is determined by light intensity. Flowers appear from March to May. Flower color ranges from red to maroon with lighter areas often appearing on the ends or throughout the petals. Scapes vary from 4–14 in. (10–36 cm) in length. (Photo 3-5)

S. rubra ssp. *rubra*. Pitchers are erect, have a narrow wing and are dull green with a profuse reddish to purple veining near the upper part of the pitcher. This is the smallest of the erect Pitcher Plants with the narrowest pitchers having a rather uniform expansion of the pitcher. Sometimes there is a difference between the early leaves of the season, often called spring leaves which are curved, whereas the later or summer leaves tend to be straight. An ovate, suberect hood arches over the orifice of the pitchers which may measure up to 11 in. (28 cm). Scapes are taller than leaves reaching lengths of 22 in. (56 cm). Flowers are sweet-scented and of various shades of maroon. It has been reported that a yellow flowered variety has been discovered. Flowering takes place from mid-April to June.

S. rubra ssp. *jonesii*. The pitchers are longer, 28 in. (71 cm), than those of *S. rubra* ssp. *rubra* with a more pronounced expansion of the pitcher near the orifice. The hood is higher over the orifice and the hood is wider than in any of the ssp. of *S. rubra*. The veining is much more prominent and there are faint areoles on the pitchers.

S. rubra ssp. *wherryi*. Very closely resembles *S. alabamensis*. Its hood is shorter than that of *S. alabamensis* and almost as long as wide. The pitchers have faint areoles and more venation in the area of the orifice and column and are 18 in. (46 cm) long. The pitchers are dark green whereas in *S. alabamensis* they are yellow-green.

S. rubra ssp. *gulfensis*. This subspecies has the longest pitchers, 26 in. (66 cm), which proportionally do not expand as much as the pitchers of other ssp. The external veining is darker and more prominent, whereas the internal area of the orifice and column is less developed.

SARRACENIA HYBRIDS

Listed below are the simple *Sarracenia* hybrids. Since *Sarracenia* hybrids cross very easily with each other, producing viable seed, there are numerous crosses between hybrids and between hybrids and species.

Sarracenia Hybrids

Interspecies Cross	Collective Name
S. alata × *S. minor*	
S. alata × *S. psittacina*	*S.* (Robin Louise)
S. alata × *S. rubra*	*S.* × *ahlesii*
S. flava × *S. alata*	*S.* (Tricia)
S. flava × *S. leucophylla*	*S.* × *mooreana*
S. flava × *S. minor*	*S.* × *harperi*
S. flava × *S. oreophila*	
S. flava × *S. purpurea*	*S.* × *catesbaei*
S. flava × *S. psittacina*	*S.* (Darcy Ann)
S. flava × *S. rubra*	*S.* × *popei*

Interspecies Cross	Collective Name
S. leucophylla × *S. alata*	*S.* × *areolata*
S. leucophylla × *S. minor*	*S.* × *excellens*
S. leucophylla × *S. psittacina*	*S.* × *wrigleyana*
S. leucophylla × *S. rubra*	*S.* × *readii*
S. S. minor × *S. psittacina*	*S.* × *formosa*
S. oreophila × *S. alata*	
S. oreophila × *S. leucophylla*	
S. oreophila × *S. minor*	
S. oreophila × *S. purpurea*	
S. oreophila × *S. psittacina*	
S. oreophila × *S. rubra*	
S. purpurea × *S. alata*	*S.* × *exornata*
S. purpurea × *S. leucophylla*	*S.* × *mitchelliana*
S. purpurea × *S. minor*	*S.* × *swaniana*
S. purpurea × *S. rubra*	*S.* × *chelsoni*
S. purpurea × *S. psittacina*	*S.* × *courtii*
S. rubra × *S. minor*	*S.* × *rehderi*
S. rubra × *S.* psittacina	*S.* × *gilpini*

CULTURAL INFORMATION

Planting Media

Sphagnum moss, living or dead, sphagnum peat moss, acid sand and mixtures of the above ingredients. *Sarracenia purpurea* ssp. *purpurea* will grow in a slightly alkaline medium.

Temperatures

Summer 70–95°F (21–35°C) Winter 35–45°F (1.7–7°C) All *Sarracenia* can take light frosts. *S. purpurea* ssp. *purpurea* and *S. purpurea* ssp. *purpurea* f. *heterophylla* can withstand temperatures well below freezing.

Dormancy

Sarracenia purpurea ssp. *purpurea* and *S. purpurea* ssp. *purpurea* f. *heterophylla* require at least 5 months dormancy and all the others 3. Providing a longer period of dormancy is not harmful, but on the contrary is beneficial. Ideally Pitcher Plants should be provided with a dormant period that is of a length that will allow them to grow during the spring and summer and rest during the fall and winter. Many of the species will start to produce flower buds when their internal rest period is over, a fact we observe every year when plants in cold storage at 38°F (3.3°C) start growing flower stalks.

Water & Humidity

High humidity and wet soil are necessary during the growing season. Soil should be much drier during the dormant season.

Light

Sarracenia thrive in full or direct sunlight. *Sarracenia purpurea* ssp. *purpurea* will tolerate full sunlight as long as the soil remains cool. When growing under artificial light start with about 1200 foot candles of illumination and a photoperiod of 12–14 hours during the growing season. They need no light during the dormant season, but will tolerate it. Intensity of illumination is below that of the growing season with a photoperiod of 6–8 hours.

Pests

Aphids, rhizome borer, larvae and fungus. See Chapter 8 for remedies.

Feeding

Feeding suggestions are given in Chapter 7.

Miscellaneous

All of the *Sarracenia* species are relatively easy to grow. In choosing species, the height of the mature plant should be considered relative to the height of the container it is to be grown in.

PROPAGATION

Sexual Reproduction

Flowers should be cross-pollinated for maximum seed production, as self-pollination usually results in limited seed set. (Fig. 3-4 A-C) Within a week after flowers open, pollen is shed from the anthers. At this time the pollen is transferred to the receptive pistils. The pistil is not receptive until the flower sheds its pollen. After pollination and fertilization the ovary swells and in 3–5 months the seed matures. At maturation the former ovary, now the seed pod, will dehisce (split). Seeds are plump and their color varies from tan to purplish.

Once mature, the seed is dried at room temperature for about one week and then sealed in bottles or vials and stored under refrigeration. Stored in this fashion, viability will remain high for 3–5 years. Seed from plants that grow in the southernmost states of the United States such as Florida and Georgia will germinate if planted immediately upon maturation, but the percentage of germination is much lower than if they are given a cold treatment, called stratification. For maximum percentage and uniformity of seed germination, stratify seed as per directions given in Chapter 9. Uniformity of germination refers to the number of seeds sown that will geminate within a few weeks of each other. Some unstratified seed will germinate over a period of several months but some won't germinate until the following year. Provide all species except *Sarracenia purpurea* ssp. *purpurea* with at least 2 months of stratification. *S. purpurea* ssp. *purpurea* germinates best with at least a 4 month period of stratification.

Sow the seed on the appropriate medium and dust lightly with fungicide, keeping the environment humid, and warm, 70–85°F (21–29°C). Seedlings can be transplanted when they have produced 2 or 3 leaves in addition to the cotyledons.

This genus is physically easier to hybridize than most because of its large floral parts. After the flower has opened, the progress of pollen development can be followed by lifting a petal and looking inside the flower. When mature and ready for pollination, the yellow pollen grains are shed and accumulate in the cup of the umbrella-shaped style. A small brush or flat toothpick can be used to transfer the pollen to a receptive stigma. The brush is dipped in the pollen and then rubbed gently on the stigma of a flower. The stigma is receptive after pollen release. When flowers of 2 plants are cross-pollinated, they must shed their pollen at about the same time. To ensure a successful cross, transfer of pollen should be repeated once a day for 3–5 days. The procedure for hybridizing early and late flowering *Sarracenia* is explained in Chapter 9.

Before the flower opens, it is important that the flowers be covered with a piece of muslin, cheesecloth, paper bag or gauze to keep out insects that may be carrying pollen from other Pitcher Plants. Also, vitally important is good record-keeping. The crossed plants should be identified with a label made of permanent material such as plastic markers which should be attached directly to the plant if possible.

Asexual Reproduction

1. Leaf cuttings: Remove the leaf (pitcher) with a small piece of the rhizome attached, dip end in Rootone powder and place in damp sphagnum moss. Dust the cutting and medium with a fungicide. Keep humidity high and provide bright light. Keep the temperature in the 70–85°F (21–29.5°C) range. Transplant when leaves and roots have developed.

Success rate is fair for cuttings without roots. It is 100% for cuttings with roots. (Fig. 3-5)

2. Rhizome cuttings: Cut a rhizome into 1 in. (2.5 cm) lengths, being careful not to sever any roots. Dust the cut surfaces with a fungicide. Repot the rhizome pieces in a horizontal position and cover with about ½ in. (1.25 cm) of sphagnum moss. Treat them in the same manner as leaf cuttings. A very successful technique.

3. Crown separation: Some rhizomes have multiple crowns or growing points. Carefully divide the rhizome into separate plants by cutting the rhizome apart between crown regions. Dust cut surfaces with a fungicide. Then repot each crown separately. Very successful technique. (Fig. 3-6)

4. Bud induction (removal of growing point): Carefully remove all the pitchers including their petioles from a rhizome. Next cut off about 1 in. (2.5 cm) from the terminal end of the leafless rhizome and dust the cut surfaces with a fungicide. Plant the rhizome horizontally in the soil so that the top of the rhizome is at or just above soil level. Small buds in the leaf axil that were inactive will now develop into plants.

Plant the terminal rhizome section that was initially cut off the rhizome with the cut surface which has been dusted with a fungicide in the soil deep enough so that about ½ of it is buried below soil level. The tip will develop into a plant. Treat the tip cutting the same as leaf cuttings. By this procedure you can obtain up to 15 buds (the maximum we have ever obtained) or more which will eventually develop into individual plants from the horizontal rhizome. When several leaves and roots develop, the individual plants can be cut from the rhizome. (Fig. 3-7 A-C)

This procedure can be carried out on a growing plant, without uprooting it. This is best done during spring or early summer. Cut off an inch (2.5 cm) from the growing end and carefully remove all the pitchers including the petiole and the soil from the upper surface of the rhizome. In situations where the rhizome is erect, the same procedure is followed except, in this case, the whole upper portion of the rhizome will be above soil level. In many cases the plants with erect rhizomes do not have enough length to the rhizome to cut off an inch (2.5 cm). In this situation remove the pitchers and scrape off the growing tip with a knife or your fingernail.

5. Bud induction (without removal of growing point): There is a variation of the above technique in which the tip is not cut off. Instead, after the leaves have been removed, with a sharp, clean knife or razor blade slits about ¾ of an inch (2 cm) apart are cut into the upper surface of the rhizome if it is horizontal, or on one side if it is growing vertically. The cuts should penetrate to about ½ the thickness of the rhizome. (Fig. 3-8)

In the first procedure the source of auxin that inhibits the development of axillary buds is removed, whereas in the latter procedure the cuts prevent the auxin produced by the growing shoot tip from reaching all of the lateral buds and therefore, does not suppress their growth. The former method will yield more plants per rhizome. Both techniques are very successful.

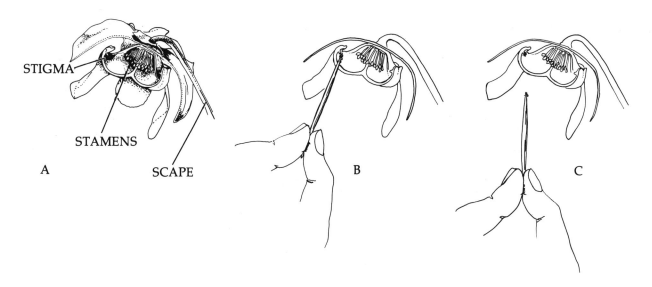

STIGMA

STAMENS

A   SCAPE   B   C

Fig. 3-4 A-C Cross pollination of flower.

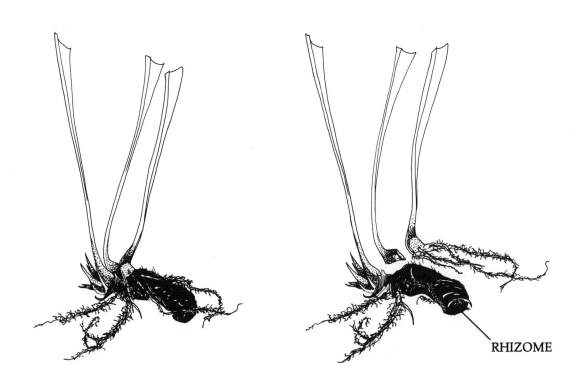

RHIZOME

Fig. 3-5 Procedure for making leaf cuttings.

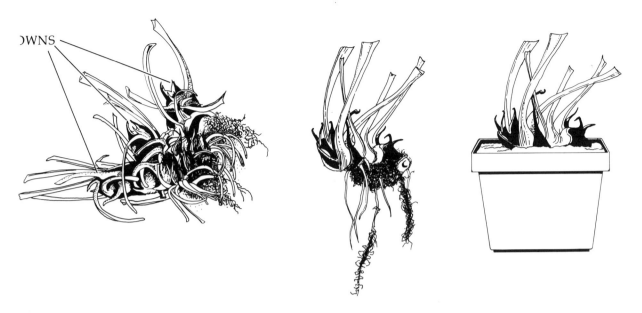

Fig. 3-6 Separating multiple crowns in *Sarracenia* into individual plants.

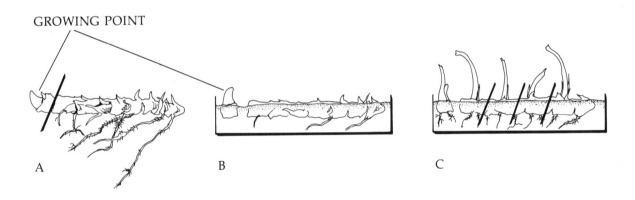

Fig. 3-7 Dormant bud growth in *Sarracenia* encouraged by removal of growing point.

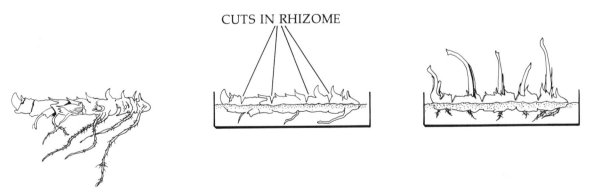

Fig. 3-8 Vertical incisions in *Sarracenia* rhizome encourage dormant bud growth.

Nepenthes _____

HISTORY

E. de Flacourt, the Governor of Madagascar when it was under French rule during the mid-17th century, was the first to write about these tropical pitcher plants, of which there are more than 70 species. In 1689 J. P. Breyne described the plants and was the first to use the name *Nepenthes*. Digestion in *Nepenthes* was reported by J. D. Hooker to the British Association for the Advancement of Science in 1874. In 1875 L. Tate discovered the presence of a digestive enzyme in *Nepenthes* secretions. Thereafter the tide of opinion swept back and forth between digestion caused by enzymes and digestion by bacterial decay. Today it is recognized that both processes contribute to digestion. *Nepenthes* is derived from the Greek word "nepenthes" meaning the removal of sorrow and grief. It is also the name of a plant that is used with wine to make a potion or drug to relieve sorrow and grief and produce exhilaration.

NATURAL HABITAT

The distribution of *Nepenthes* is restricted to tropical areas of the Old World. They grow in an area bounded by Madagascar, northward to the Seychelles Islands, Sri Lanka and northeastern Australia and includes the Malayan Archipelago (Indonesia and Malaysia area).

The habitats of *Nepenthes* species are quite diverse. They grow on limestone cliffs which are continually damp, in sand fields having both a wet and dry season, in swamps which are under water part of the year, on sea shores, as epiphytes growing on other plants (particularly trees), and as creepers on the surface of the soil.

DESCRIPTION OF PLANT

Nepenthes are herbaceous perennials whose stems are quite coarse, having diameters exceeding 2 in. (5 cm). In some species the length of the stem exceeds 66 ft. (20 m). The stems either climb on nearby bushes and trees or are prostrate, creeping on the ground. Arising from the stems, which vary in cross section from circular to triangular are the long narrow leaves which in some species are over 2 ft. (.6 m) in length. (Fig. 3-9)

The fluid of unopened pitchers has been used as a laxative, a remedy for burns, coughs, inflamed eyes and various skin disorders. Open pitchers are used to carry water and as pots for cooking food, while the vines are used for cordage. Pitcher color varies from shades of green to yellow with red and/or purple variegation.

Leaves

The long leaf blades are green to yellow-green with midribs that extend beyond the leaf blade apex to form a cylindrical tendril which is as long or longer than the leaf blade. The tips of the yellow-green tendrils develop into pitchers in an appropriate environment.

Nepenthes plants tend to have two types of pitchers. While pitcher shape varies with the species, generally pitchers close to the ground are cylindrical with two parallel wings extending from the top to bottom on the front of the pitcher. Pitchers on the upper parts of the plant are roughly funnel-shape, tapering toward the tendril end. These tendrils coil around adjacent structures and plants to provide the means of support. The tendrils supporting the lower pitchers do not coil.

The mouth of the opening to the pitcher is edged with a ridged collar, the peristome. The ridges in the peristome terminate in sharp points on the inner side of the pitcher. They are believed to aid in preventing escape by presenting a barrier to prey trying to climb out of the pitcher.

Fig. 3-9 *Nepenthes* plant with inforescence, upper and lower leaves with traps.

Overhanging the mouth of the pitcher is a lid whose size varies considerably between species. The lid is attached to the back side of the pitcher orifice. It separates from the front of the pitcher as the pitcher matures, forming a flap or hood over the mouth which in some species prevents water from entering the pitcher. (Fig. 3-10) It was once erroneously believed that the lid was capable of motion and involved in trapping prey. Protruding from the area of attachment of the lid to the pitcher body is a finger-like projection called a spur. Pitcher color varies from green to green mottled with deep red or purple.

Flowers

Nepenthes plants are dioecious. Therefore, to produce seed two plants are needed, one bearing male flowers and the other female flowers. Neither male nor female flowers are showy. They are small, lack petals, have four sepals, and their reproductive structures, either stamens or pistils, are located centrally in the flower and look quite similar to each other. Female flowers can be distinguished by the swollen superior ovary just above the sepals. The flowers are borne in panicles or racemes. (Photo 3-6)

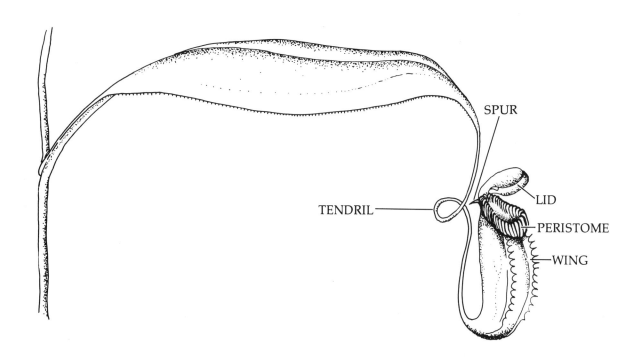

Fig. 3-10 *Nepenthes* leaf with trap.

TRAPPING

The glands producing nectar are found at the base of each inner projection of the peristome and the inner surface of the lid. Capture occurs when prey, feeding on the nectar near the opening of the pitcher, slips and falls into the liquid bath in the trap. (Photo 3-7) The viscosity of the digestive fluid, a mixture of rain water and enzymes, combined with the sharp peristomes tend to prevent the prey from escaping. The struggling prey is reportedly tranquilized by an unidentified agent in the liquid.

Digestive and absorbing glands are located in the lower, inside walls of the pitchers. Digestive enzymes are secreted into the liquid that accumulates in the pitcher. Bacterial decomposition aids the digestive enzymes in the breakdown of the captured prey.

Nepenthes plants possess the largest trap of any of the carnivorous genera. *Nepenthes merrilliana* from the Philippines produces the largest pitchers exceeding 20 in. (50 cm) in length and 10 in. (25 cm) in diameter. Allegedly, small birds, rats and other such animals have been caught by the pitchers, which are locally known by a variety of names such as Monkey Pitchers and Monkey's Rice Pots.

SPECIES OF THE GENUS *NEPENTHES*

Contrary to common belief, *Nepenthes* are not all jungle plants and shade-loving, but usually seek open, sunnier areas. While most grow in an area designated as tropical, many species grow at high elevations where temperatures are lower. For cultural purposes *Nepenthes* can be divided into two groups. The highland types, which account for about two-thirds of the species, grow at elevations greater than 3281 ft. (1000 m) where temperatures range from 50–70°F. (10–21°C.). The remaining third of the species are the lowland type growing at elevations below 3281 ft. (1000 m) with a temperature range of 70–85°F. (21–29°C.).

Highland Type

N. alata	N. lowii
N. anamensis	N. macfarlanei
N. bongso	N. madagascariensis
N. boschiana	N. maxima
N. burbidgeae	N. mollis
N. burkei	N. muluensis
N. carunculata	N. paniculata
N. clipeata	N. pectinata
N. deaniana	N. pervillei
N. densiflora	N. pilosa
N. dentata	N. rajah
N. distillatoria	N. rhombicaulis
N. dubia	N. sanguinea
N. edwardsiana	N. singalana
N. ephippiata	N. spathulata
N. fusca	N. spectabilis
N. geoffrayi	N. stenophylla
N. gracillima	N. tentaculata
N. gymnamphora	N. tobaica
N. hirsuta	N. treubiana
N. inermis	N. veitchii
N. klossii	N. ventricosa
N. khasiana	N. vieillardii
N. leptochila	N. villosa

Lowland Type

N. albo-marginata	N. mirabilis
N. ampullaria	N. neglecta
N. bellii	N. neoguineensis
N. bicalcarata	N. northiana
N. campanulata	N. papuana
N. decurrens	N. petiolata
N. globamphora	N. rafflesiana
N. gracilis	N. reinwardtiana
N. insignis	N. thorelii
N. kampotiana	N. tomoriana
N. merrilliana	N. trichocarpa
	N. truncata

DESCRIPTION OF COMMERCIALLY AVAILABLE SPECIES

Nepenthes are identified mainly by pitcher characteristics. The pitcher description provided is for the lower pitchers which are always found on cultivated plants. Upper ones may not form in cultivation.

N. alata Pitchers are funnel-shaped with a ventricose base, narrowing in the middle and having 2 fringed wings.

N. ampullaria Pitchers are small ellipsoidal, green to red, with some purple spots. The lid is small and reflexed. (Photo 3-8)

N. albo-marginata Pitchers tend to be tubular, green and purple in color. The collar is white and the lid is inclined over the opening.

N. burkei Pitchers are gibbous and cylindric. Color is green with purple splotches.

N. distillatoria Pitchers are tubular at the top and gibbous below with fringed wings. Pitchers tend to be green to yellow-green.

N. fusca Pitchers are cylindrical with 2 fringed wings and erect lids. Color is green with purple to blackish areas.

N. gracilis Pitchers are gibbose cylindric in shape, with reduced wings. Color is green with some purple spots. (Photo 3-9)

N. kampotiana Pitchers gibbous at base narrowing at top with a large lid and a pair of fringed wings. Color is greenish red.

N. khasiana Pitchers are tube-like with a slight bulge below the midpoint. Wings are fringed. Lid is reddish green on its underside.

N. maxima Pitchers cylindrical, enlarged at the base and have 2 fringed wings. Color green with red-purple blotches.

N. mirabilis Pitchers ventricose at the base and cylindrical toward the top. Color is light green sometimes with red.

N. rafflesiana Pitchers tend to be ellipsoidal with fringed wings. Color is green with purple splotches.

N. sanguinea Leaves are sessile. Pitchers are ventricose, cylindrical in shape. Color varies from green to reddish green to red. Peristome is red.

N. thorelii Pitchers are gibbous below, cylindrical above with an enlarged lid and fringed wings. Color is reddish green.

N. trichocarpa Pitchers basically cylindrical, slightly gibbous at base with 2 fringed wings. Color mainly green with some red.

NEPENTHES HYBRIDS

The naming of *Nepenthes* hybrids is an area of great confusion due to use of incorrect names and synonymy. Identical crosses made by different people and/or at different times were often given distinct names. This state of confusion could have been eliminated if there were a clearing house to keep track of hybrids and cultivars. Poor record keeping resulted in misnaming some hybrids.

The names listed here are those researched by Ron Fleming, and appeared in the March 1979 issue of the *Carnivorous Plant Newsletter*. The names are followed by the breeder's name when known, date of the cross or when it was offered for sale, the "hybrid group," and its supposed lineage. The "hybrid group" indicates that the plant is almost identical to other named hybrids. The "hybrid group" name used is usually the earliest hybrid of the group.

'Amabilis' (, 1886, Excelsior Group) = (*rafflesiana* × *ampullaria*) × *rafflesiana*

'Allardii' (Allard, 1897, Tiveyi Group) = *veitchii* × *maxima*

'Amesiana' (Veitch, 1893, Excelsior Group) = *rafflesiana* × (*rafflesiana* × *ampullaria*)

'Dr. Edgar Anderson' (Pring, 1950, Chelsonii Group) = [(*rafflesiana* × *gracilis*) × (*rafflesiana* × *ampullaria*)] × [*rafflesiana* × *gracilis*]

'Atropurpurea' (,   , Nobilis Group) = *sanguinea* × *maxima* 'superba'

'Alliottii' (,   , Mixta Group) = *northiana* × *maxima*

'Atro-sanguinea' (Taplin, 1882) = (*distillatoria* × *gracilis*) × *khasiana*

'Balfouriana' (Tivey, 1899, Balfouriana Group) = (*northiana* × *maxima*) × (*sanguinea* × *khasiana*)

'Bohnickii' (Bonstedt, 1931, Mixta Group) = [(*northiana* × *maxima*) × *maxima*] × [(*northiana* × *maxima*) × *maxima*]

'Boissiana' (Jarry-Desloges, 1905) = [*maxima* × *veitchii*] × [*mirabilis* × (*rafflesiana* × *ampullaria*)]

'Boissiense' (Lecoufle-Bert, 1955, Henryana Group) = *gracilis* × [(*gracilis* × *khasiana*) × (*rafflesiana* × *ampullaria*)]

'Caroli-schmidtii' (Bonstedt, 1931, Deslogesii Group) = (*northiana* × *maxima*) × (*veitchii* × *maxima*)

'Chelsonii' (Seden, 1872, Chelsonii Group) = (*rafflesiana* × *gracilis*) × (*rafflesiana* × *ampullaria*)

'Chelsonii excellens' (Tivey, 1900, Chelsonii Group) = *rafflesiana* × [(*rafflesiana* × *gracilis*) × (*rafflesiana* × *ampullaria*)]

'Coccinea' (Taplin, 1882, Wrigleyana Group) = (*rafflesiana* × *ampullaria*) × *mirabilis*

'Compacta' (Taplin, 1881, Wrigleyana Group) = (*rafflesiana* × *ampullaria*) × *mirabilis*

'Courtii' (Court, 1877, Dominii Group) = *gracilis* × (*rafflesiana* × *gracilis*)

'Joseph Cutak' (Pring, 1950, Chelsonii Group) = [(*rafflesiana* × *gracilis*) × (*rafflesiana* × *ampullaria*)] × [*rafflesiana* × *gracilis*]

'Cylindrica' (Tivey, 1887) = *distillatoria* 'rubra' × *veitchii*

'Deslogesii' (Jarry-Desloges, 1905, Deslogesii Group) = (*maxima* × *veitchii*) × (*northiana* × *maxima*)

'Dicksoniana' (Lindsay, 1888) = *rafflesiana* × *veitchii*

'Dominii' (Dominy, 1862, Dominii Group) = *rafflesiana* × *gracilis*

'Dormanniana' (Taplin, 1882, Dormanniana Group) = *mirabilis* × (*gracilis* × *khasiana*)

'Dyeriana' (Tivey, 1900, Dyeriana Group) = (*northiana* × *maxima*) × (*rafflesiana* × *veitchii*)

'Edinensis' (Linsay, 1888, Chelsonii Group) = *rafflesiana* × [(*rafflesiana* × *gracilis*) × (*rafflesiana* × *ampullaria*)]

'Excelsa' (,   ) = *veitchii* × *sanguinea*

'Excelsior' (Taplin, 1885, Excelsior Group) = *rafflesiana* × (*rafflesiana* × *ampullaria*)

'Eyermanni' (Siebrecht, 1889, Wrigleyana Group) = *mirabilis* × (*rafflesiana* × *ampullaria*)

'Dr. D C Fairburn' (Pring, 1950, Chelsonii Group) = [(*rafflesiana* × *gracilis*) × (*rafflesiana* × *ampullaria*)] × [*rafflesiana* × *gracilis*]

'Formosa' (Kew Garden, 1897) = [(*rafflesiana* × *gracilis*) × (*rafflesiana* × *ampullaria*)] × *distillatoria*

'Fournieri' (Gautier, 1903, Mixta Group) = *northiana* × *maxima*

'Gamerii' (Jarry-Desloges, 1905, Deslogesii Group) = (*maxima* 'superba' × *veitchii*) × (*northiana* × *maxima*)

'Gautieri' (Gautier, 1903, Mixta Group) = *northiana* × *maxima*

'Goebelii' (Bonstedt, 1931, Mixta Group) = (*northiana* × *maxima*) × *maxima*

'Goettingensis' (Bonstedt, 1931, Dyeriana Group) = (*northiana* × *maxima*) × (*rafflesiana* × *veitchii*)

'Grandis' (Jarry-Desloges, 1906, Deslogesii Group) = *maxima* 'superba' × *northiana* 'pulchra'

'Harryana' (natural hybrid complex) = *edwardsiana* × *villosa*

'Henryana' (Taplin, 1881, Henryana Group) = (*gracilis* × *khasiana*) × (*rafflesiana* × *ampullaria*)

'Hibberdii' (Taplin, 1883, Henryana Group) = (*rafflesiana* × *ampullaria*) × (*gracilis* × *khasiana*)

'Hoeischeri' (Bonstedt, 1931) = (*northiana* × *maxima*) × ([*gracilis* × (*rafflesiana* × *gracilis*)] × *distillatoria* 'rubra')

'Hookerae' (Taplin, 1895) = *rafflesiana* × *mirabilis*

'Hookeriana' (H. Low) (natural hybrid complex) 1847 = *rafflesiana* × *ampullaria*

'Nel Horner' (Pring, 1950, Chelsonii Group) = [(*rafflesiana* × *gracilis*) × (*rafflesiana* × *ampullaria*)] × [*rafflesiana* × *gracilis*]

'Hybrida' (Dominy, 1866, Hybrida Group) = *khasiana* × *gracilis*

'Hybrida maculata' (Dominy, 1866, Hybrida Group) = *khasiana* × *gracilis*

'Hybrida maculata elongata' (Court, 1877, Dominii Group) = *gracilis* × (*rafflesiana* × *gracilis*)

'Intermedia' (Court, 1877, Dominii Group) = *gracilis* × *rafflesiana*

'Kinabaluensis' (natural hybrid complex) = *rajah* × *villosa*

'Krausii' (Bonstedt, 1931, Deslogesii Group) = (*northiana* × *maxima*) × (*veitchii* × *maxima*)

'Ladenburgii' (Bonstedt, 1931, Mixta Group) = (*northiana* × *maxima*) × *maxima*

'Lawrenciana' (Taplin, 1880, Wrigleyana Group) = *mirabilis* × (*rafflesiana* × *ampullaria*)

'Longicaudata' (Jarry-Desloges, 1906, Mixta Group) = *maxima* 'superba' × *northiana* 'pulchra'

'Lyrata' (Court, 1877, Lyrata Group) = (*khasiana* × *gracilis*) × *rafflesiana*

'Dr. John MacFarlane' (Veitch, 1909, Nobilis Group) = *sanguinea* × *maxima* 'superba'

'Maria-Louisa' (Gautier, 1903, Mixta Group) = *northiana* × *maxima*

'Mastersiana' (Court, 1881) = *sanguinea* × *khasiana*

'Mercieri' (Gautier, 1903, Mixta Group) = *northiana* × *maxima*

'Merrilliata' (natural hybrid complex) = *merrilliana* × *alata*

'Mixta' (Tivey, 1892, Mixta Group) = *northiana* × *maxima*

'F. W. Moore' (Tivey, 1904, Dyeriana Group) = (*northiana* × *maxima*) × (*rafflesiana* × *veitchii*)

'Director G. T. Moore' (Pring, 1950, Chelsonii Group) = [(*rafflesiana* × *gracilis*) × (*rafflesiana* × *ampullaria*)] × [*rafflesiana* × *gracilis*]

'Katharine Moore' (Pring, 1950, Dominii Group) = [(*rafflesiana* × *gracilis*) × (*rafflesiana* × *ampullaria*)] × [*rafflesiana* × *gracilis*]

'Morganiana' (Taplin, 1881, Wrigleyana Group) = *mirabilis* × (*rafflesiana* × *ampullaria*)

'Neufvilliana' (Bonstedt, 1931, Mixta Group) = (*northiana* × *maxima*) × *maxima*

'Nobilis' (Veitch, 1910, Nobilis Group) = *sanguinea* × *maxima* 'superba'

'Outramiana' (Taplin, 1879, Henryana Group) = (*gracilis* × *khasiana*) × (*rafflesiana* × *ampullaria*)

'Paradisae' (Taplin, 1883, Wrigleyana Group) = *mirabilis* × (*rafflesiana* × *ampullaria*)

'Patersonii' (Saul, 1889, Wrigleyana Group) = *mirabilis* × (*rafflesiana* × *ampullaria*)

'Paullii' (Jarry-Desloges, 1906, Deslogesii Group) = (*maxima* 'superba' × *veitchii*) × (*northiana* × *maxima*)

'Petersii' (Bonstedt, 1931, Deslogesii Group) = (*northiana* × *maxima*) × (*veitchii* × *maxima*)

'Picturata' (Tivey, 1903, Dyeriana Group) = (*northiana* × *maxima*) × (*rafflesiana* × *veitchii*)

'Pitcheri' (Pitcher & Manda, 1895) = [*mirabilis* × (*rafflesiana* × *ampullaria*)] × [(*gracilis* × *khasiana*) × (*rafflesiana* × *ampullaria*)]

'Leutenat R B Pring' (Pring, 1950, Chelsonii Group) = [(*rafflesiana* × *gracilis*) × (*rafflesiana* × *ampullaria*)] × [*rafflesiana* × *gracilis*]

'Rafflesiana pallida' (Court, 1877, Lyrata Group) = (*khasiana* × *gracilis*) × *rafflesiana*

'Ratcliffiana' (Court, 1880, Wrigleyana Group) = *mirabilis* × (*rafflesiana* × *ampullaria*)

'Remilliensis' (Jarry-Desloges, 1905, Deslogesii Group) = (*northiana* × *maxima*) × (*veitchii* × *maxima*)

'Reutheri' (Bonstedt, 1931, Balfouriana Group) = (*northiana* × *maxima*) × (*sanguinea* × *khasiana*)

'Robusta' (Taplin, 1880, Wrigleyana Group) = *mirabilis* × (*rafflesiana* × *ampullaria*)

'Roedigeri' (Bonstedt, 1931, Mixta Group) = (*northiana* × *maxima*) × *maxima*

'Rubro-maculata' (Court, 1887) = (*khasiana* × *gracilis*) × *veitchii*

'Rufescens' (Court, 1888) = [*gracilis* × (*rafflesiana* × *gracilis*)] × *distillatoria* 'rubra'

'Rutzii' (Bonstedt, 1931, Deslogesii Group) = (*northiana* × *maxima*) × (*veitchii* × *maxima*)

'Saint Louis' (Pring, 1950, Chelsonii Group) = [(*rafflesiana* × *gracilis*) × (*rafflesiana* × *ampullaria*)] × [*rafflesiana* × *gracilis*]

'Sedenii' (Seden, 1872, Hybrida Group) = *gracilis* × *khasiana*

'Henry Shaw' (Pring, 1950, Chelsonii Group) = [(*rafflesiana* × *gracilis*) × (*rafflesiana* × *ampullaria*)] × [*rafflesiana* × *gracilis*]

'Siebrechitiana' (Siebrecht, 1889, Dormanniana Group) = *mirabilis* × (*gracilis* × *khasiana*)

'Siebertii' (Bonstedt, 1931, Deslogesii Group) = (*northiana* × *maxima*) × (*veitchii* × *maxima*)

'Simonii' (Gautier, 1903, Mixta Group) = *northiana* × *maxima*

'Shinjuku' (, Shinjuku Group) = [*northiana* × *maxima*] × [*mirabilis* × (*rafflesiana* × *ampullaria*)]

'Sprendida' (Pitcher & Manda,   , Wrigleyana Group) = *mirabilis* × (*rafflesiana* × *ampullaria*)

'Stammieri' (Bonstedt, 1931, Mixta Group) = [(*northiana* × *maxima*) × *maxima*] × [(*northiana* × *maxima*) × *maxima*]

'Stewartii' (Court, 1879, Wrigleyana Group) = mirabilis × (rafflesiana × ampullaria)

'Superba' (Taplin, 1880, Henryana Group) = (*gracilis* × *khasiana*) × (*rafflesiana* × *ampullaria*)

'Tiveyi' (Tivey, 1897, Tiveyi Group) = *maxima* 'superba' × *veitchii*

'Gerald Ulrichi' (Pring, 1950, Chelsonii Group) = (*rafflesiana* × *gracilis*) × (*rafflesiana* × *ampullaria*)

'Vallierae' (Jarry-Desloges, 1905, Deslogesii Group) = (*maxima* 'superba' × *veitchii*) × (*northiana* × *maxima*)

'Ventrata' (natural hybrid complex) = *ventricosa* × *alata*

'Williamsii' (Taplin, 1880, Henryana Group) = (*gracilis* × *khasiana*) × (*rafflesiana* × *ampullaria*)

'Wittei' (Witte, 1897) = *maxima* × *stenophylla*

'Wrigleyana' (Court, 1880, Wrigleyana Group) = *mirabilis* × (*rafflesiana* × *ampullaria*) (Schnell, 197-) = *thorelii* × (*maxima* × *stenophylla*)

Nepenthes hybrids of Japanese origin before 1978 as compiled by Mr. Isamu Kusakabe. The hybrid name is followed by the breeder and date.

'Accentual Koto' (Kawase, 1974) = *thorelii* × (*rafflesiana* × *ampullaria*)

'Aichi' (Kondo & Sakai,   ) = *thorelii* × [(*northiana* × *maxima*) × (*sanguinea* × *khasiana*)]

'Ambrosial Koto' (Kawase, 1974) = *trichocarpa* × (*rafflesiana* × *ampullaria*)

'Arakawae' (Toyoshima, 1970) = (*northiana* × *maxima*) × *alata*

'Balmy Koto' (Kawase, 1975) = *thorelii* × *maxima*

'Dreamy Koto' (Kawase, 1977) = *thorelii* × *veitchii*
'Ecstatic Koto' (Kawase, 1978) = *thorelii* × *maxima*
'Effulgent Koto' (Kawase, 1978) = *mirabilis* × *thorelii*
'Fukakusana' (Toyoshima, 1964) = *rafflesiana* × [(*northiana* × *maxima*) × (*rafflesiana* × *veitchii*)]
'Fushimiensis' (Toyoshima, 1970) = *globamphora* × *thorelii*
'Hachijo' (Okuyama, 1978) = *thorelii* × *mirabilis*
'Kikuchiae' (Okuyama, 1967) = [(*northiana* × *maxima*) × *maxima*] × *maxima*
'Masahiroi' (Kondo,   ) = *albo-marginate* × *thorelii*
'Masamiae' (Toyoshima, 1970) = *thorelii* × *maxima*
'Minamiensis' (Naito, 1964) = [(*northiana* × *maxima*) × *maxima*] × [*mirabilis* × (*rafflesiana* × *ampullaria*)]
'Mizuho' (Kondo, 1965) = *rafflesiana* × [(*northiana* × *maxima*) × (*rafflesiana* × *veitchii*)]
'Nagoya' (Kondo, 1967) = (*northiana* × *maxima*) × *thorelii*
'Oisoensis' (Ikeda, ca 1935) = (*northiana* × *maxima*) × *maxima*
'Princeps' (Kondo, 1966) = (*northiana* × *maxima*) × [(*northiana* × *maxima*) × (*rafflesiana* × *veitchii*)]
'Prosperity' (Kubo, 1978) = *mirabilis* complex × [(*northiana* × *maxima*) × (*rafflesiana* × *veitchii*)]
'Rokko' (Yamakawa, 1977) = *thorelii* × *maxima*
'Shioji' (Kondo, 1966) = (*northiana* × *maxima*) × [(*northiana* × *maxima*) × (*rafflesiana* × *veitchii*)]
'Suzue Kondo' (Kondo,   ) = (*northiana* × *maxima*) × *thorelii*
'Takayuki Sakai' (Kondo & Sakai,   ) = *tobaica* × *thorelii*
'Tokuyoshi Kondo' (Kondo & Sakai,   ) = ([(*rafflesiana* × *gracilis*) × (*rafflesiana* × *ampullaria*)] × [*rafflesiana* × *gracilis*]) × *rafflesiana*
'Toyoshimae' (Toyoshima, 1970) = *truncata* × *thorelii*
'Tsujimoto' (Takarazuka B.G., 1951) = (*sanguinea* × *khasiana*) × [*mirabilis* × (*rafflesiana* × *ampullaria*)]
'Yatomi' (Kondo & Sakai,   ) = *thorelii* × *veitchii*

CULTURAL INFORMATION

Planting Media
The medium should be well drained. Common media used are living or non-living sphagnum moss, sphagnum peat moss, mixtures of sphagnum peat moss with sphagnum moss, sphagnum peat moss mixed with coarse sand (about equal volumes of each), and chopped osmunda fiber. Some *Nepenthes* grow in sandy to clayey soils in their native habitat. We have not used nor do we know of anyone using these soils for growing them.

Temperatures
The highland type 50–70°F (10–21°C). The lowland type 70–85°F (21–29°C). Both types of *Nepenthes* can be grown at a temperature of about 70°F (21°C), but most plants grow best when maintained at a temperature that is not at either extreme but somewhere near the middle of their range.

Dormancy
Apparently none. Rate of growth may be depressed during the winter.

Water & Humidity
Generally speaking, *Nepenthes* need high humidity for proper trap development, but we know of at least one exception. We have grown a plant of *Nepenthes anamensis* in our bedroom for 2 years. It was planted in a plastic pot which was placed on a saucer to catch excess water. The plant was watered when the soil was dry and never misted. It grew prolifically and pitchered well. Contrary to accepted views, it did well even

though the house is heated with forced hot air. In light of this experience, we wonder how many of the other species will grow well in a low humidity environment. The soil should be wet during the growing or warm season and drier during the winter or cool season.

Light

Nepenthes tend to grow in open areas in their native habitat, receiving direct sunlight for at least part of the day. When grown in adequate light the pitchers have a colorful variegation. They grow well under artificial light at an illumination of about 1300 foot candles and a photoperiod of 12–14 hours.

Pests

The only pest with which we have had any trouble is aphids. See Chapter 8 for control of pests.

Feeding

Follow directions in Chapter 7.

Miscellaneous

Smaller and slower growing species such as *Nepenthes gracilis, N. ampullaria,* and *N. madagascariensis* can be grown in containers as small as ½ gal. (2 l). We have used both sphagnum moss and sphagnum peat moss as the medium. Under our conditions the plants grew slower in sphagnum peat moss and, therefore, needed less pruning to contain them. Care must be exercised when growing in containers without drainage. The soil should be kept moist, but not water logged. If too much water is supplied, leave the top off the container to allow the excess water to evaporate. When the soil is moist in a covered container, the plants often will go months, in one case 8 months, before another watering is necessary. Once the plant reaches the top of the container, it is cut back by ½–⅔ of its height and the plant will send up a new stem. The removed portion is used for cuttings to produce additional plants.

Nepenthes are excellent candidates for hanging baskets and side board planting. By side board we mean growing them on boards as Staghorn ferns are often grown. (Fig. 3-11)

Unless you have a very large growing area the plant will eventually outgrow its space. As *Nepenthes* grow in length, the older pitchers and leaves near the bottom of the stem die off, leaving an empty space which detracts from the beauty of the plant. To control this problem the stem is cut back to within 1–2 in. (2.5–5 cm) of the medium. The plant will then send up a new stem. Often a plant will send up new shoots even though the old stem has not been removed. The removed plant material can be used for cuttings to propagate more plants. The easier species to grow depend upon your local temperatures. The highland species are usually very difficult because they require year-round temperatures of 50–70°F (10–21°C). A few of the highland species will grow well at temperatures suitable for the lowland species. For most growers the lowland species are best. Some of the easier species are:

Nepenthes alata, N. albo-marginata, N. ampullaria, N. bicalcarata, N. burkei, N. decurrens, N. fusca, N. gracillima, N. gracilis, N. khasiana, N. maxima, N. mirabilis, N. rafflesiana, N. reinwardtiana, N. sanguinea, N. thorelii, N. tobaica, and *N. ventricosa.*

PROPAGATION

Sexual Reproduction

Since the male and female flowers are on different plants, the chances of having

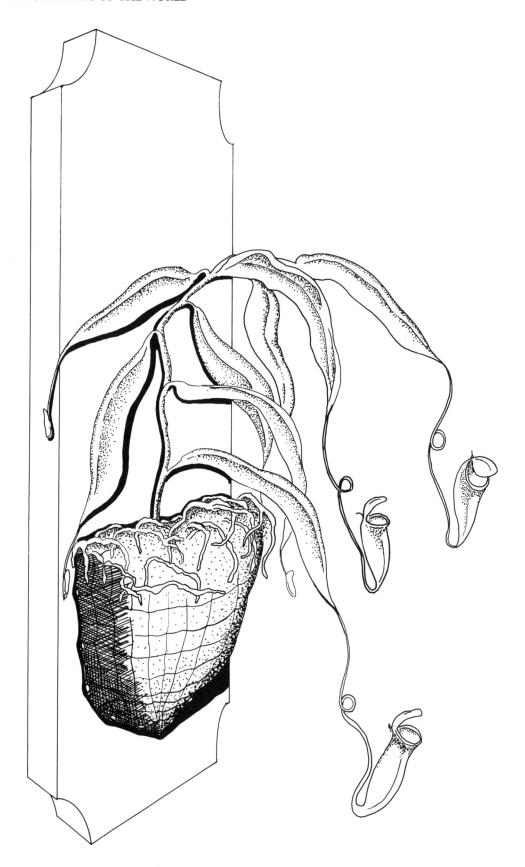

Fig. 3-11 *Nepenthes* plant grown as a side board planting.

both types of flowers in bloom at the same time are better if you have several plants. (Fig. 3-12) An alternative is to use stored pollen. A method for storing pollen is described in Chapter 9. If you are using stored pollen follow directions given in the hybridization section. The long, slender seeds develop within the ovary which matures into a slender capsule. Seed stores well under refrigeration and is viable for at least one year in all species of which we are aware. Store seed at 38°F (3°C).

Sow the seed by sprinkling it on the soil surface, followed by a dusting of a fungicide on both the seed and soil. Keep the humidity high with a temperature of 70–85°F (21–29°C) for the lowland type and 50–70°F (10–21°C) for the highland type. Germination usually occurs within 6 weeks. When seedlings have produced 2 or 3 leaves with pitchers, they can be transplanted, if necessary, to provide adequate space to grow. Seedling plants should have a minimum spacing of 1 in. (2.5 cm) between them.

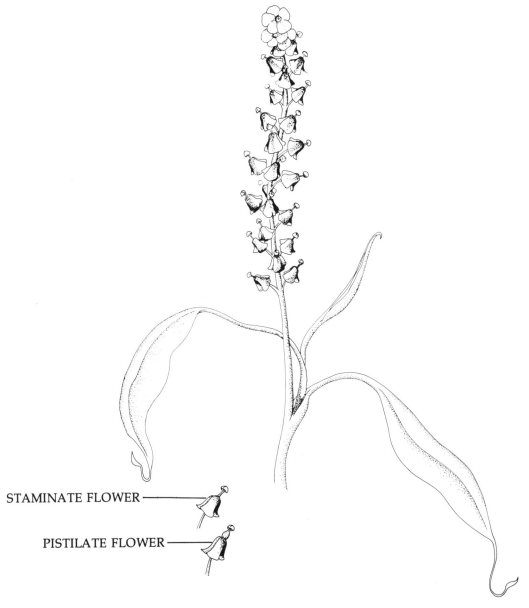

STAMINATE FLOWER

PISTILATE FLOWER

Fig. 3-12 Staminate inflorescence of *Nepenthes*. Insert illustrates staminate (upper) and pistilate (lower) flowers.

Asexual Reproduction

1. Stem cuttings: When determining the length of the cutting two factors must be considered: the number of plants desired and ease of handling cuttings. Shorter stem cuttings will provide more plants from a given quantity of material. Long stem cuttings have more leaves which the newly-developing root system must support and which can stress the cutting, resulting in poor growth or even death. But longer sections are easier to handle. With some experience at rooting cuttings, 1-node cuttings become quite manageable. For a first attempt however, 2–3 node cuttings are recommended.

To make stem cuttings, use a clean, sharp tool such as a pair of heavy duty scissors, knife or a razor blade. The cut should be made perpendicular to the stem. After the sections have been cut, the bottom of each section is tapered diagonally to expose a maximum amount of cambium for most effective rooting and about ½ to ⅔ of the length of each leaf is cut off. If 1-node cuttings are used, the cutting from the apex of the stem should include the growing tip with the next node below it. The growing tip is tender and very susceptible to decay. Therefore, including an extra node provides insurance that the cutting will root.

Treat all the cuts with a fungicide to help prevent decay and treat the bottom diagonal cut of each stem cutting with both a fungicide and a rooting hormone such as Rootone to hasten rooting. (Fig. 3-13) Place the cutting in a pot. If a 1-node cutting, the node should be at soil level, whereas in a 2–3 node cutting, the bottom node is placed below soil level. (Fig. 3-14) Living or non-living sphagnum moss placed around the cutting will hold it securely in position so that the cutting will not move after it has rooted and cause damage to the roots. Some growers place the cuttings in a well-drained sandy soil. To help reduce root damage wrap the end of the cutting with sphagnum moss, secure it with a rubber band or string and place it in a container. (Fig. 3-15) This technique, permits the placing of several cuttings in the same container for rooting to save space until they have rooted. The cuttings are maintained under high humidity, bright light, and at temperatures of 70–85°F (21–29°C) for the lowland types and 50–70°F (10–21°C) for the highland types. Successful rooting will be evidenced by new leaf and stem growth. When the cuttings have produced at least 2 new leaves they can be removed, potted if necessary, and placed in the regular growing area.

Another method used to propagate *Nepenthes* with stem cuttings is illustrated in Fig. 3-16. First, cut off the growing tip with the first node below it and handle the stem section as a cutting as per directions given in the preceding paragraphs. After several weeks the bud(s) in the leaf axils of the leaves on the original plant will start to develop and grow. When the buds produce leaves that are about 1–1½ in. (2.5–4 cm) long, cut the node off and treat it as a cutting.

Dip the lower end in fungicide and Rootone and wrap sphagnum moss around the node so that the top of the node is at moss (ground) level with the young leaves extending above the moss. As each succeeding node develops it is cut off, providing that the bud in the node below it has started to swell. Leave at least one node on the plant to produce another plant or stem on the existing root system. In some species, cutting off the top node stimulates several of the remaining buds to develop simultaneously. Each can be removed and rooted.

2. Air layering: Select a mature branch or stem and make a ringing cut, that is, make a cut into the stem that encircles it or cut a notch on one side so that about ¼ of the stem's diameter is removed or make a cut that penetrates the stem about ½ its diameter and then insert a toothpick in the cut to keep the surfaces apart. (Fig. 3-17) In some species the space between the leaves is adequate to do this, but in others a leaf or two must be removed to expose the stem.

Dust the cut or notch with Rootone and fungicide, then wrap at least a 1 in. (2.5 cm) layer of damp sphagnum moss around the wound, enclosing the entire section of stem between the leaves. Cover the moss with a piece of transparent plastic that will prevent

NODE

A

B

FUNGICIDE AND ROOTING HORMONE ⎯⎯⎯ ◯

FUNGICIDE ⎯⎯⎯ ◯

Fig. 3-13 Stem cuttings are made by cutting the stem into one or two node sections. One-half to two-thirds of each leaf is removed (A). Cut ends are treated with fungicide and the bottom cut of each stem cutting is treated with a rooting hormone (B).

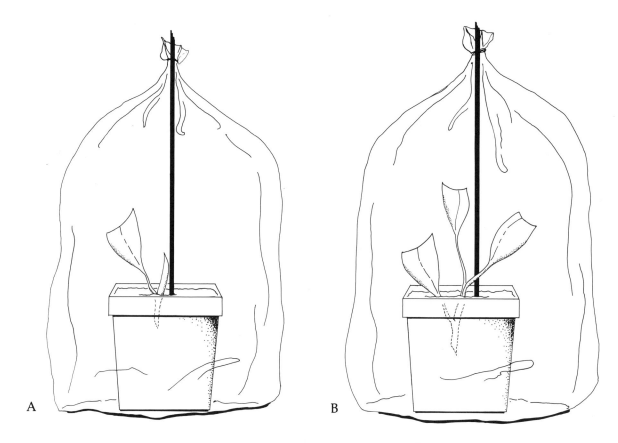

Fig. 3-14 One (A) and two (B) node cuttings of *Nepenthes*.

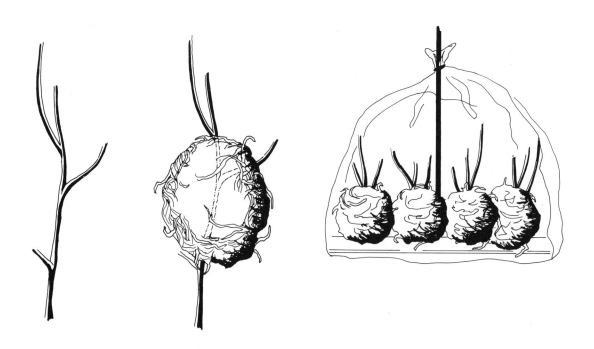

Fig. 3-15 Stem cuttings are wrapped with sphagnum moss to prevent root damage. They are placed in a plastic bag to insure a high humidity.

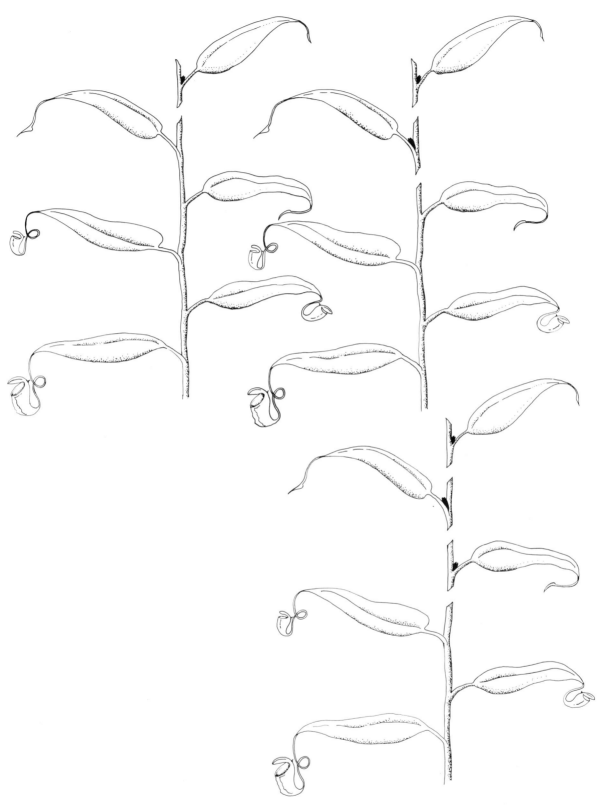

Fig. 3-16 Induction of axillary bud growth. As a one node cutting is removed from the top of the plant, the dormant bud in a lower leaf axil will develop. The developed bud and stem section are removed and rooted.

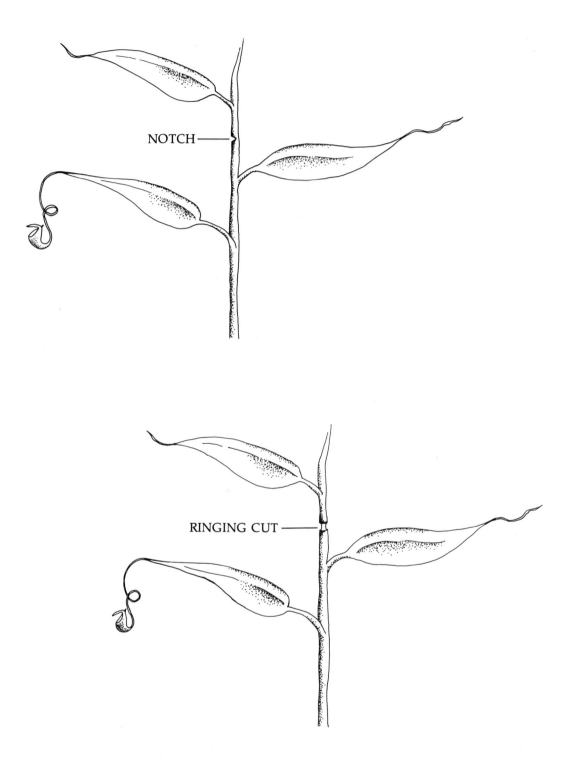

NOTCH

RINGING CUT

Fig. 3-17 Air layering of *Nepenthes* is accomplished by notching or ringing the stem, dusting the cut with a rooting hormone and layering damp sphagnum around the wood.

the moss from drying out while allowing monitoring of root development without disturbing the air layer. Some growers like to cover the moss with opaque plastic to keep the light out. If plants are in direct sunlight then transparent plastic should be covered with black plastic or a piece of metal foil to keep out the sunlight and prevent heating of the roots. If the moss should dry out before rooting is evident, add water to keep it moist.

Rooting should take place in 2–4 months. When a good root system has developed sever the stem and carefully pot the removed plant. It is best to keep newly-rooted plants or cuttings in sealed plastic bags for a month or so to give the roots time to adjust. If the rooted cutting is placed in a low-humidity environment the root system may be stressed and the plant can die.

3. Ground layering: This method is similar to air layering except that the branch or stem must be supple or flexible enough so that it can be bent down to place the wounded area of the stem in contact with the medium. In this method the notch is cut on the side of the stem that touches the medium when placed into position or a ringing cut may be made as was suggested for air layering.

The wound is dusted with Rootone and fungicide. The stem is bent down into the medium and is covered in the area of the cut with a mound of medium. (Fig. 3-18) The stem must be secured by some means to keep it anchored. Weights may be used or a piece of string or wire that runs through the pot out the bottom and up around the side to the top and around the stem and tied to the other end. Occasionally check for root development by gently moving the soil away from the wounded area.

When adequate roots are formed, sever the stem to remove it from the mother plant and follow the procedures as outlined for cuttings. It is best not to transplant cuttings, ground or air layered, for at least one year after rooting to allow them to become well established.

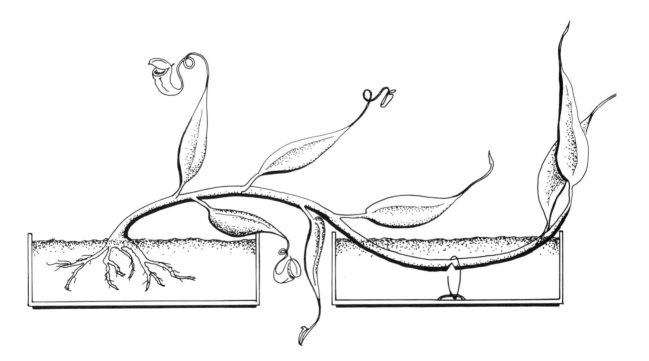

Fig. 3-18 Ground layering of *Nepenthes*. After notching or ringing the stem is bent down and secured so the wounded area is in contact with the growing media.

Darlingtonia _____

HISTORY

J. D. Brackenridge, a botanist accompanying an expedition in the Mt. Shasta area of California, U.S.A., is credited with discovering *Darlingtonia*. After studying some specimens, J. Torrey concluded that there were sufficient differences between them and *Sarracenia* plants to warrant the formation of a new genus, which was named in honor of Torrey's friend and outstanding biologist Dr. W. Darlington. Later the name *Darlingtonia californica* was discovered to be invalid according to the international rules for naming plants and it was changed to *Chrysamphora californica*. This name was subsequently changed back to *Darlingtonia californica* because of widespread usage of the original name. Common names include Cobra Lily, California Pitcher Plant, and Cobra Plant.

NATURAL HABITAT

The native habitat of *Darlingtonia* is the mountainous region from western Oregon southward to northern California, U.S.A., and in British Columbia, Canada. Plants grow in bogs or wet areas with high water tables such as borders of springs and streams.

DESCRIPTION OF PLANT

Darlingtonia are herbaceous perennials. The leaves, which usually grow upright, form hollow pitchers that terminate in a dome from which 2 flaps of tissue, the fangs, project. The domed pitchers arise from a fibrous rooted rhizome. When the plants are mature the rhizome sends out stolons from which new plants develop. (Fig. 3-19) The pitchers have an unusual growth feature in that they twist just enough as they grow so that the opening of the pitcher is facing outward from the center of the plant. Each plant has from 5–15 leaves and usually 1 scape bearing a solitary flower.

Leaves

The pitcher-shaped leaves may exceed lengths of 1 yd. (0.9 m) and terminate in a dome whose opening is to the front and below the dome. From the front edge of the opening hangs a fang-like appendage which presumably acts as a landing ramp for the prey. There are translucent areas on the dome called fenestrations which, to an insect inside the pitcher, may look like openings to the outside. (Photo 3-10) Juvenile leaves which are produced by seedlings, by side shoots from a rhizome and by cuttings lack the forked appendage and dome. Leaf color varies from green to yellowish-green mixed with red and maroon. In intense light the whole plant may be a solid maroon color.

Flowers

The *Darlingtonia* flower consists of 5 long yellow-green sepals, 5 purple-pink petals, about 15 stamens and a 5-lobed compound pistil. It is pendulous on a tall scape which has numerous pink-lavender bracts that become papery and abscise as the ovary of the flower matures into a dry fruit containing seeds. (Fig. 3-20)

TRAPPING

Coloration and the production of nectar are probably the most effective lures for attracting insects. The efficiency of the plants' trapping ability is attested to by its leaves or pitchers which are, more often than not, full of insects and their remains. Once the insect stumbles into the bottom area of the pitcher the downward pointing hairs that line the inside surface hinder the prey from climbing out. (Fig. 3-21)

Fig. 3-19 *Darlingtonia californica* plant with young plant developing from stolen.

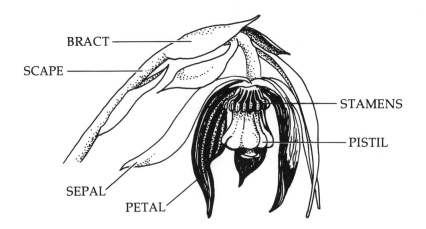

Fig. 3-20 Flower of *Darlingtonia californica*. Some petals and sepals have been removed to expose the five-lobed compound pistil surrounded by stamens.

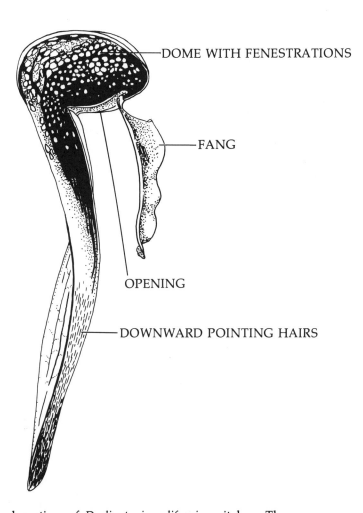

Fig. 3-21 Longitudinal section of *Darlingtonia californica* pitcher. The downward pointing hairs hinder prey from climbing out of the pitcher. Insects trying to fly through one of the transparent areas find themselves hitting something solid and fall to the bottom of the pitcher.

Insects landing on the fangs are enticed toward the dome opening by the increased abundance of nectar just inside the mouth (opening) of the pitcher. Once inside the insect may try to fly out through one of the transparent areas in the dome, a fenestration, only to slam into it and drop down into the fluid below.

The interior of the *Darlingtonia* pitcher is similar to that of *Sarracenia's* pitchers. In some areas there are downward pointing hairs that direct the path of insects into regions that afford no foothold for them.

Until recently bacterial action was thought to be solely responsible for digestion in *Darlingtonia*, but it was discovered that at least one enzyme is secreted by the pitchers into the fluid bath. Here, as in the case of other Pitcher Plants, there are insects that are able to survive and thrive in the digestive bath living off the plants' captured prey.

SPECIES OF THE GENUS *DARLINGTONIA*

Darlingtonia is a monotypic genus; that is, there is only one species in the genus.

CULTURAL INFORMATION

Planting Media
Sphagnum peat moss, sphagnum moss (live or dead) and various mixtures of sphagnum peat moss with sand and/or perlite.

Temperatures
Temperatures in its native habitat extend from below freezing to about 100°F (38°C). Even though the usual summer air temperature is about 80°F (27°C), the temperature of the soil is usually lower than 68°F (20°C). Greenhouse experience indicates that best growth occurs when soil temperatures range from about 60–68°F (16–20°C). During the winter the plants will have an adequate dormant period with temperatures ranging from 35–50°F (2–10°C).

To keep soil temperature at reasonable levels, grow plants out of direct sunlight and plant them in large pots. The more medium there is in the pot, the longer it will take for the soil temperature to increase during the day. Lower ambient night temperatures will allow the soil temperature to also drop at night and, therefore, be cool at the start of the next day. Copious watering during hot periods will help keep soil temperatures low. Some growers use ice water to keep the temperature under control. If plants are grown in an outdoor greenhouse, they should be placed on the floor where it is cooler than at bench level.

Dormancy
Darlingtonia require a rest period of 4–6 months at 35–50°F (2–10°C).

Water & Humidity
During the growing season the growing medium can be quite wet, almost waterlogged, as long as the water is not stagnant. Keep the medium drier during the dormant period. The plants thrive best in a high humidity environment.

Light
Plants grow best in strong light in which they will develop a beautiful red pigmentation. Plants do well in direct sunlight except when sunlight heats the soil to temperatures that are detrimental to growth. If provisions can be made to keep the soil cool, some direct sunlight is beneficial.

Pests
The only pests with which we have had problems are aphids and the fungus *Botrytis*,

particularly on seedlings and young plants. See Chapter 8 for control measures.

Feeding
See Chapter 7 for directions.

PROPAGATION

Sexual Reproduction

Flowers can be either self- or cross-pollinated for viable seed production. When pollen is mature the anther surface changes from smooth to rough, which is the result of maturation of the pollen grains. Since the pollen grains tend to stick to the anther, the whole stamen can be removed with a pair of tweezers and then rubbed on the pistil of a flower. Seeds will mature about 2 months later.

If seeds are to be stored they should be dried at room temperature for about one week and then stored in a refrigerator in sealed containers.

Darlingtonia seed must be stratified for at least 2 months for germination to occur. After cold treatment, sow the seed thinly on the medium surface, followed by a dusting of fungicide. Keep seeds damp and in strong light at a temperature of 70–85°F (21–29°C) until the seed germinates and produces 2–4 leaves. Then maintain temperature at about 70°F (21°C). Seedling plants do not transplant very easily. Best results are obtained by transplanting them in the spring just before active growth resumes.

Asexual Reproduction

1. Rhizome division: Planting the plants in large (wide) pots will encourage the formation of secondary rhizomes or stolons whose ends will produce plants which, when they have developed a root system, can be severed from the mother plant.

2. Rhizome cuttings: Cut the rhizome into 2 in. (5 cm) sections and lay them on damp sphagnum moss. Dust cut surfaces with fungicide. Keep the humidity high, light bright, and the temperature at about 70°F (21°C). New shoots will develop in about 3–6 weeks.

3. Leaf cuttings: Not very reliable. Remove the whole leaf with a small piece of the rhizome and maintain under the same conditions as outlined for rhizome cuttings. Rooting may take several months.

Cephalotus

HISTORY

Cephalotus follicularis, commonly known as the Australian Pitcher Plant, was first collected by Archibald Menzies, a naturalist with the Vancouver expedition of 1791. In 1792 La Billardiere, a naturalist with a French expedition, encountered the same plant on the Island of Esperance Bay and mainland Australia whereupon he described the plant and named it *Cephalotus follicularis*. *Cephalotus* is derived from the Greek word "kephalotus" meaning headed, referring to the open anthers of the stamen. The term "follicularis," referring to a small bag or pod, relates to the modified leaf structure.

NATURAL HABITAT

In nature *Cephalotus* grows exclusively along the southwestern coastal areas of Australia in swampy or boggy areas. The acid soil is peaty, having a high organic matter content. During the rainy season the plants may be partially submerged for short periods of time.

DESCRIPTION OF PLANT

Cephalotus follicularis is a herbaceous perennial with a rosette of leaves arising from a stout and sometimes surmounting rhizome. In older, mature plants secondary rhizomes emerge from the primary rhizome to form secondary plants. In summer (December through February in Australia) white pubescent flowers, which can number up to 100, are borne on flower stalks that often exceed 2 ft. (61 cm) in length. (Fig. 3-22) In the Northern Hemisphere plants flower during July and August.

Leaves

Cephalotus is evergreen and tolerates light frosts with no apparent ill effects. With the arrival of spring and warmer temperatures, longer days and more intense sunlight, new growth is initiated and a rosette of green, flat, oval-shaped leaves which are foliage or vegetative leaves develop. Toward the end of the active growing season (September to October) pitchered leaves are produced on the ends of long, pubescent petioles that extend beyond the rosette of foliage leaves so that the pitchers form a ring around the foliage leaves. Often leaves of intermediate form develop. They tend to be flat with a depression of varying depth at the tip. In some cases these intermediate leaves will form a pitcher which, instead of the usual oval-shaped hood, has a deeply incised hood, resulting in a hood with two pointed projections. In shade the plants, pitchers and foliage leaves tend to be large and green, whereas in full sunlight colors ranging from brilliant reds to purples decorate both types of leaves. Pitchers can reach 3 in. (8 cm) in length with a diameter of 1.2 in. (3 cm).

The pitchers are jug-shaped with a hairy lid over the orifice of the pitcher. (Photo 3-11) The lid presents a corrugated appearance resulting from the red to purple colored ridges which radiate from the attachment outward in a fan shape. The grooves are translucent. When light shines through them they appear as openings to insects inside the pitchers.

The openings of the pitchers are oriented outward from the center of the plant. It was once erroneously thought that the lid was capable of motion and could close over the mouth of the pitcher to incarcerate prey.

The pitcher is supported in the back by its petiole while its base usually rests on the soil. The hollow pitcher is given rigidity by 3 pubescent ribs on its front surface. The central rib extends the length of the front of the pitcher while the other 2 start at the mouth and extend to either pitcher side.

The mouth of the pitcher has a prominent rim which is reinforced by numerous ridges that terminate inside the pitcher as sharp, pointed spines. Below the interior rim of the pitcher is a collar about half the length of the lid, containing numerous nectar secreting glands, that overhang the cavity of the pitcher. The collar is differentiated from the cavity of the pitcher both in color and texture. The collar is pale, almost white, with a velvety texture while the cavity of the pitcher in mature specimens is streaked with dark red blotches and is shiny-wet looking.

The sides of the pitcher's cavity are glossy with digestive glands in the upper region. The digestive glands are concentrated in 2 symmetrical regions between the central rib and the rib to either side of it just above the bottom front of the pitcher. Internally these 2 regions are darker in color, usually deep maroon in mature pitchers. Externally they are lighter colored than the surrounding areas of the bottom region of the pitcher.

Flowers

The flower clusters are borne on a tall scape that may reach 26 in. (66 cm) in length. (Photo 3-12) Individual flowers are small, usually less than 0.2 in. (0.5 cm) in diameter and lack petals. (Fig. 3-23) The 6 greenish white sepals are attractive and appear very waxy. There are 6 long and 6 short stamens; all 12 are shorter than the sepals. Seeds are borne, usually singly, within each of the 6 free carpels. (Photo 3-13) The entire panicle is rather inconspicuous.

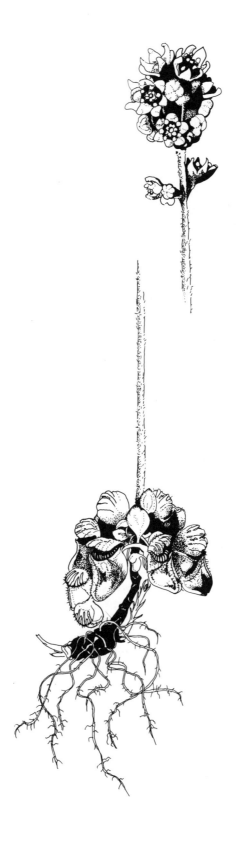

Fig. 3-22 *Cephalotus* plant with flowers.

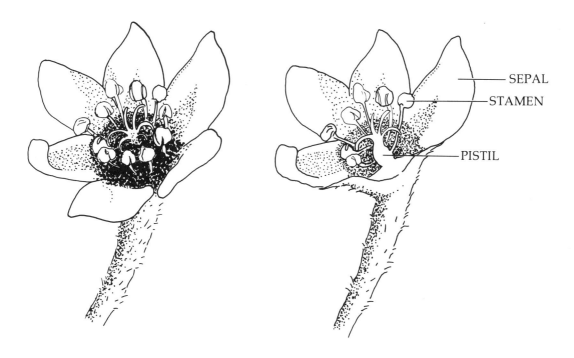

Fig. 3-23 *Cephalotus* flowers are small and lack petals. The sepals are waxy. Of the 12 stamens, 6 are long and 6 are short.

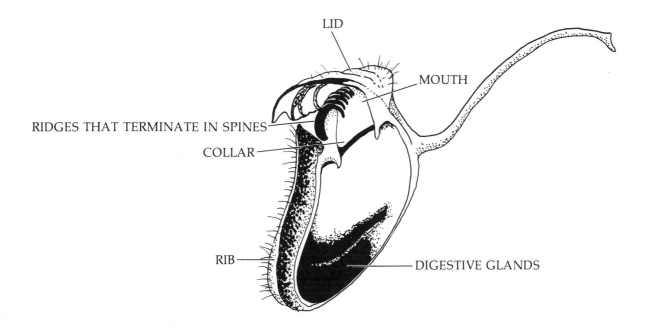

Fig. 3-24 Longitudinal section of *Cephalotus* pitcher. Once inside the pitcher insects find that the smooth walls offer no foothold and the spines, which line the opening, present a formidable barrier.

TRAPPING

The frontal ridges have been likened to ramps leading insects to the trap. Insects are attracted to the nectar in the collar region. Once inside the pitcher, it is difficult for the insect to escape. The collar is surmounted by the spines of the rim of the mouth which present a formidable barrier. If the insect slips, it winds up in the watery bath within the cavity of the pitcher. The walls in and above the water are smooth and offer no foothold. Should the victim manage to scale the walls after extricating himself from the digestive bath, he encounters the rim of the collar which is similar to a lobster trap in that it allows entrance but prohibits exits. The rim of the collar overhangs the walls of the pitcher virtually preventing an insect from climbing out. (Fig. 3-24) Flying insects may try to fly out through the transparent areas in the lid only to fall in the pitcher's enzyme and bacterial bath. Some believe that the transparent areas in the lid allow light to pass through and shine on the liquid below attracting insects to the pitcher's depths. Both theories are supportable.

SPECIES OF THE GENUS *CEPHALOTUS*

Cephalotus is a monotypic genus. The only species is *C. follicularis* Labill.

CULTURAL REQUIREMENTS

Planting Media
Sphagnum moss (living or non-living), sphagnum peat moss, mixtures of sand with sphagnum peat moss. Living sphagnum moss tends to overgrow *Cephalotus* plants when they are young; therefore, the moss needs regular pruning. But it does provide a beautiful green background for the reddish maroon pitchers and leaves.

Temperatures
Range from 38–95°F (3–35°C). Plants can survive a light frost. *Cephalotus* will grow well at constant temperatures of 70–85°F (21–29°C) the year around. We keep our plants at 38–40°F (3–4°C) during the winter while summer temperatures reach 95°F (35°C) or more. In their native habitat, temperatures are lower in winter than in summer. Our plants are thriving and produce flowers each year.

Dormancy
There seems to be no dormancy requirement.

Water & Humidity
Keep soil damp or wet during the growing season or summer and if, during the winter, the plants are maintained at low temperatures such as in the 40–60°F (4–16°C) range, keep the soil drier.

Light
Plants grown in full sunlight are smaller than those grown in shade or indirect sunlight, but they have a beautiful red to maroon coloration which is absent on those grown in diffuse light. To get large plants with red coloration, grow the plants in indirect light to obtain large robust plants and then, gradually expose plants to stronger light to develop the dramatic coloration.

When growing *Cephalotus* under artificial lights start with 1000–1500 foot candles with a 12–16 hour day.

Pests
The only pests we have had are aphids and *Botrytis*. See Chapter 8 for treatment.

Feeding

Feed as per instructions in Chapter 7.

Miscellaneous

Plant *Cephalotus* in wide pots. If given plenty of space horizontally they are more likely to send out secondary rhizomes which produce more plants.

PROPAGATION

Sexual Reproduction

The flowers must be cross pollinated in order to produce viable seed. Using the procedure given below we have harvested considerable seed from our plants, even though some individual flowers produce none. The flowers open a few at a time over a period of time of up to a month or more. Begin pollinating when 2 or more flowers are open by gently rubbing a small camel's hair brush over the pistil and stamens of all the open flowers. This procedure is repeated every other day as long as the flowers are open. When pollination and subsequent fertilization has been effected, the ovules will start to swell. The ovaries will be visible as a green, hairy structure growing out of the flower. When the swelling is visible stop transferring pollen to these flowers. About 6 weeks after cessation of flowering the first seed should be mature. The seeds are egg-shaped and brown. Each seed is enclosed in a pubescent fruit. (Photo 3-13)

Seed does not seem to store well so it should be stratified and sown as soon as possible. Our experience indicates that a stratification period of 2–3 months at temperatures of 40–50°F (4–10°C) is required for seed to germinate. Stratified seed is spread thinly on the appropriate planting medium for germination. The seed can be covered lightly with medium or left uncovered. Seed is kept moist and at a temperature in the range of 70–90°F (21–32°C). Seed usually germinates within 8 weeks, but we have had some germinate almost a year after planting.

Asexual Reproduction

1. Rhizome: Cut rhizomes into pieces about 1 in. (2.5 cm) and place them horizontally on the medium if a maximum number of plants is desired, or place them vertically if you prefer fewer but larger plants. Dust the cut surfaces with fungicide. Cover the rhizomes with about ½ in. (1.75 cm) of medium. Keep the medium damp, the humidity high, and the light bright with temperatures in the range of 70–90°F (21–32°C). Leaves should appear in about 1 month. Several plants will emerge from each cutting. When roots have formed the plants can be severed from each other and replanted.

2. Leaf cuttings: Both types of leaves can be used; the older, more mature leaves produce best results. (Photos 3-14,3-15) Remove the leaves carefully so that the leaf and petiole or the pitcher with its petiole is removed intact. Dip the cut or broken end of the stalk in Rootone and fungicide, shake off the excess powder and insert the severed end in planting medium so that about ½ of the petiole is buried. Some growers prefer to lay the leaves flat on the surface of the medium without covering them. Our experience indicates that the best results are obtained when the petioles are buried in the medium. Treat these cuttings in the same manner as outlined for rhizome cuttings.

3. Decapitation: Cut the plant off at ground level or just below ground level without uprooting it. Treat the cut off plant as a cutting. The rhizome remaining in the medium will send up new shoots.

Heliamphora _____

HISTORY

R. H. Schomburgk, a German naturalist, discovered these plants in 1839, while surveying the Guayana Highlands for The Geographical Society of London. G. Bentham, in 1840, established the genus on the basis of specimens collected by Schomburgk on Mount Roriama, which he named *Heliamphora nutans.*

The genus name is derived from two Greek words meaning "marsh" and "vessel." Since the prefix *heli,* also refers to the sun, the name has been interpreted to mean sun pitcher. The common names for *Heliamphora* are South American Pitcher Plant, Sun Pitcher Plant, and the Marsh Pitcher Plant, with the latter being preferred.

NATURAL HABITAT

Heliamphora are native to and grow only on the summits of the "tepui" or mesas of the Guayana Highlands of southern Venezuela, Guayana, and northern Brazil. The mesas are very high 5,000–10,000 ft. (1,524 to 3,048 m), flat-topped features isolated from one another by deep valleys with steep walls. One of the largest mesas called Auyan-tepui has an area of 286 sq. miles (750 sq. km.). Angel Waterfalls, the highest in the world, plummets 3,300 ft. (1,006 m) down the sheer wall of Auyan-tepui. The "tepui" form islands of vegetation which are adapted to much lower temperatures than the tropical jungles at their bases. The Guayana Highlands have an extremely high annual rainfall, often exceeding 100 in. (254 cm). The mesas are often shrouded by clouds and mist which keeps the humidity high. Weathering and erosion have carved valleys and canyons on the mesa tops and walls. The plateaus are remote and extremely difficult to reach, therefore, few people have seen *Heliamphora* plants growing in their native habitat.

So isolated is the area that it was almost 100 years after the discovery of the first species before others were found. The plants are confined to the top of sheer-sided mesas where they grow in acid soils in swampy savannahs exposed to the brilliant equatorial sun.

DESCRIPTION OF PLANTS

Heliamphora are herbaceous plants consisting of rhizomes from which arise simple, branched or dendroid stems. Both ensiform (phyllodia) and ascidiform leaves are produced and occur in rosettes in some species. Flowers which may be green, white or pink are borne on scapes that are longer than the leaves. (Fig. 3-25)

Leaves

The pitchers are roughly cone-shaped and in some species there is a constriction, of varying degree, which produces a bulging region below it with a flare-out above it, called the bell. The leaves appear to have been produced by rolling the sides of the lamina around a thin funnel and then securing the structure down the front along the leaf margins, leaving an external seam allowance that flares out forming two "keel-like" wings or ala.

The margins are either fused along their entire connective length or only in the lower region of the pitcher leaving a slit partway down the front of the pitcher. The slit maintains a constant level of water in those pitchers that do not have a pore below the slit, acting as an overflow for the water but not an escape hatch for insects. Some pitchers also have a pore which is located further down the front of the pitcher keeping the water level even lower.

A prominent midrib extends the length of the back of the pitchers. At the apex of the

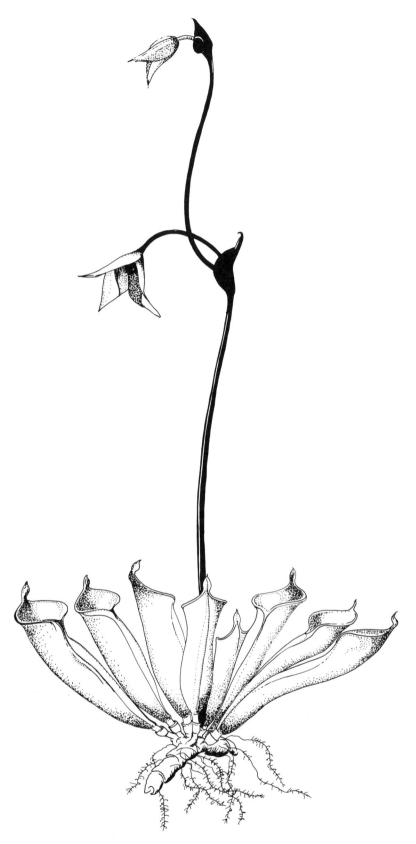

Fig. 3-25 *Heliamphora* plant, including rhizome with roots, pitchers and flower stalk with flowers.

pitcher, in most species, is a hood, a spoon-like structure, with the concave surface facing into the hollow leaf. Glands and V-shaped hairs are located on the outer surface of the pitchers. In cultivation leaves are usually green, but with a hint of reddish coloration when grown in strong light.

Flowers

Several flowers are borne in a racemose inflorescence held above the leaves by a long peduncle. The ovary is densely pubescent and the glabrous stigma and style are surrounded by 10 or more stamens. The perianth is composed of 1 whorl of petal-like appendages, usually 4 in number, but occasionally 5–6. Flower color is not the same in all species and varies from shades of green, to pink or white with color darkening sometimes to deep maroon during fruiting. (Fig. 3-26)

TRAPPING

In most species the inside of the pitcher is zoned similarly to the ascidiform leaves found in most pitcher plants. The hood, when present, is plentifully strewn with nectar glands. Just below it, in the region of the opening and below, are numerous long, flexible, downward pointing hairs intermingled with nectar glands. This region attracts insects, offering them an unstable foothold. The next lower region is distinguished by smooth pitcher walls which prevent insects from maintaining a foothold. The walls of the lowermost region of the pitcher have sharp, stout, downward pointing hairs that prevent the upward movement of prey. (Fig. 3-27) Digestion, according to current knowledge, is due to bacterial activity in the watery bath that is maintained within the pitcher in nature by heavy rainfalls.

SPECIES OF THE GENUS HELIAMPHORA

Heliamphora nutans, H. neblinae, H. ionasi, H. tatei, H. minor, and *H. heterodoxa* are the 6 recognized species. *Heliamphora minor* is the most diminutive of the genus [2–3 in. (5–8 cm)] while *H. tatei* var. *tatei* is the largest, with a dendroid growth habit reaching 3–5 ft. (0.9–1.5 m), and in sparsely populated areas climbs to heights of 13 ft. (4 m).

DESCRIPTION OF THE SPECIES

H. heterodoxa Steyermark. Pitchers up to 12 in. (30 cm) long on stems with a pronounced constriction just above the center.
    var. *exappendiculata* has a vestigial hood and pink flowers.
    var. *glabra* has no pubescence on the upper internal surface of the pitcher and has white flowers.
    var. *heterodoxa* is pubescent on the upper internal surface of the pitcher. Flowers white to pink, pitchers with some red coloration.
H. ionasi Maguire. Pitchers up to 20 in. (51 cm) long, reddish in color and forming rosettes. They have a definite constriction near the top. Flowers first white then turning red.
H. minor Gleason. Pitchers 2–3 in. (5–8 cm) tall with a constriction near the top and a small apical cap or hood whose inner surface is red.
H. neblinae Maguire.
    var. *neblinae* Pitchers usually exceeding 10 in. (25 cm) in length. Leaves pubescent with short hairs and having a prominent pore and weakly developed hood. Perianth frequently 5–6 parts, white turning pink.
    var. *viridis* Same as var. *neblinae* except perianth is greenish and has 4 segments.
    var. *parva* Pitchers usually less than 8 in. (20 cm) long, externally glabrous with an inconspicuous pore. Plants usually have a red-tinge. Perianth white with some pink later turning maroon.

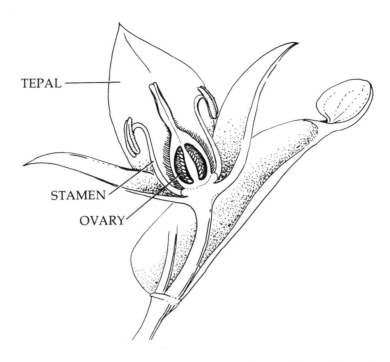

Fig. 3-26 Longitudinal-section of *Heliamphora* flower. The pubescent ovary is surrounded by 10 stamens.

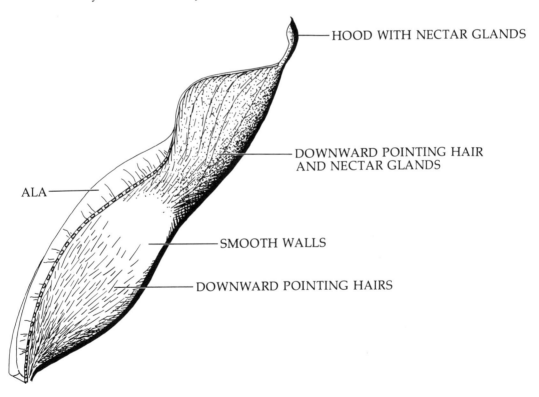

Fig. 3-27 Longitudinal-section of *Heliamphora* pitcher. The lowermost region has sharp downward pointing hairs. The middle region is smooth, offering no foothold to an insect. The uppermost region has long flexible hairs intermingled with nectar glands. The lid contains numerous necta secreting glands.

H. nutans Bentham. Pitchers 4–6 in. (10–15 cm) long with a constriction near the top. Internal surface of hood is red. Flower white turning red.

H. tatei Gleason.

var. *tatei* Dendroid growth reaching heights of 3–5 ft. (0.9–1.5 m) in dense populations, growing to 13 ft. (4 m) in open areas. Pitchers reach 14 in. (36 cm) in length growing from shrubby stems. Pitchers internally pubescent, perianth 4 parted, white turning red.

var. *macdonaldae* Same as var. *tatei* except pitchers are internally glabrous save at the mid-zone.

CULTURAL INFORMATION

Planting Media

Living or non-living sphagnum moss, a mixture of sphagnum peat moss and sphagnum moss, or a mixture of sphagnum moss and perlite. Yearly repotting is recommended.

Temperatures

The range in their native habitat is 38–78°F (3–26°C). Temperatures in cultivation should not be allowed to go above 78°F (26°C) for any length of time. Recommended: summer 55–75°F (13–24°C), winter 40–60°F (4–16°C).

Dormancy

There is no true dormancy period, but in cultivation the rate of growth is considerably reduced and few are leaves produced during the winter.

Water & Humidity

Heliamphora plants require high humidity and daily watering during the summer. During periods of high temperatures, the plants may need watering several times a day to prevent temperatures from reaching the upper limit. Keep the soil drier during the winter season.

Light

Heliamphora require strong light for maximum growth and will tolerate full sunlight, producing vigorous healthy plants. In their native habitat, the soil and air remains relatively cool under full sunlight because of the high elevation, whereas in a greenhouse, exposed to full sunlight, soil and air temperatures rise considerably above the level to which the plants are adapted. Make provisions for maximum light with soil and air temperatures not exceeding 78°F (26°C). Under artificial light provide an intensity of at least 1500 foot candles with a summer photoperiod of 13–14 hours and a winter photoperiod of 12–13 hours.

Pests

Known pests are aphids and *Botrytis*. See Chapter 8 for control.

Feeding

Many growers have indicated that fertilizing *Heliamphora* often results in death of the plant.

Miscellaneous

The easier species of *Heliamphora* to grow are *H. heterodoxa*, *H. nutans*, and *H. minor*.

PROPAGATION

Sexual Reproduction

The stigma is receptive to pollen for a few days immediately following the opening of the flower, while the anthers produce mature pollen about one week after the stigma has ceased to be receptive. Because of the timing of pollen maturation and stigma receptivity, the pollen from one flower cannot pollinate a pistil in the same flower. Therefore, two or more flowers must be mature at about the same time or the pollen from one flower must be stored for a few days until a stigma in another flower is receptive. There are no reports of anyone trying to store *Heliamphora* pollen for later use. It may well be that this pollen can be stored under refrigeration as can that of *Sarracenia*.

When the anthers are mature they will swell and split to release their pollen. Sometimes the anthers will swell and become yellowish green, indicating that pollen has formed but will not release the pollen. In this situation, try teasing the anthers with a pair of forceps or with a pin-point to open the cavity and release the pollen. If this fails, pull the anther apart to free the pollen. An alternative is to remove the anthers and allow them to dry for a day or two and then gently take them apart if drying does not induce dehiscence.

The oval-shaped seed, is sown on the medium surface and maintained in a humid environment out of direct sunlight and within a temperature range of 68–72°F (20–22°C). Germination will usually occur within three months. Growth of plants from seed is a slow process which may indicate that there are some special growing requirements that have not yet been ascertained.

Asexual Reproduction

Crown or rhizome division:

Heliamphora plants develop growing points on the rhizome or stem that will produce new plants. The new plants can be separated by cutting them apart from the mother plant. This is most successfully done during the spring or early summer. It is particularly important with this genus to avoid damaging the roots when making the separation of crowns and transplanting them. Plant the crown divisions in the medium and maintain a high humidity under strong light within a temperature range of 55–75°F (13–24°C).

2-1. *Dionaea muscipula* plants. Red
coloration of traps indicates good
lighting conditions in most cases.

2-2. *Dionaea muscipula* leaf. Trigger hairs
are arranged in a triangular pattern on
the inner lobes of the trap. The margins
of the trap are studded with bristles.

2-3. *Dionaea muscipula* leaf with captured insect. During the narrowing
phase of capture, the lobes can become
so tightly pressed together that the
outline of the captured prey is visible.

2-4. *Dionaea muscipula* leaf section with plantlets. Leaf cuttings placed on damp medium, kept in bright light and in moist environmental conditions, produce buds that develop into plantlets.

3-1. *Sarracenia oreophila* growing in natural habitat in southeastern United States.

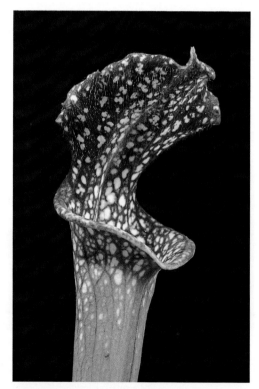

3-2. *Sarracenia leucophylla* leaf. Showing coloration of the leaf, fenestrations and secretion of nectar.

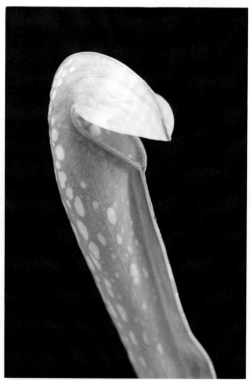

3-3. *Sarracenia minor* leaf. Fenestrations, translucent area lacking pigment, allow light to pass through. Insects on the rim of the pitcher, looking up, mistake the fenestrations for openings, fly into them, and drop to the bottom of the pitcher.

3-4. Flower of *Sarracenia purpurea* ssp. *purpurea* f. *heterophylla.* This form of *S. purpurea* lacks the usual maroon-red coloration in the vegetative parts and in the flower.

3-5. *Sarracenia psittacina* plants with flowers. Petals are maroon with cream apices.

3-6. Staminate flowers of *Nepenthes.* The flowers lack petals, have four sepals and golden colored anthers. The sequence of flower opening is from the bottom of the inflorescence toward the top.

3-7. In nature, the pitchers, filled with rainwater and enzymes, await prey. *Nepenthes ampullaria.* (Photo by Bill Hanna)

3-9. *Nepenthes gracilis* lower pitcher. (Photo by Bill Hanna)

3-8. *Nepenthes ampullaria* pitcher. The small ellipsoidal trap has a deep red collar and a small reflexed lid.

3-11. The jug-shaped pitchers of *Cephalotus* form a ring around the rosette of foliage leaves. The openings of the pitchers are oriented outward from the center of the plant.

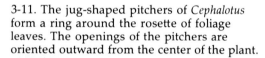

3-10. *Darlingtonia californica* plant. Pitchers twist so that the opening, from which hangs a fang-like appendage, faces outward from the center of the plant. The translucent areas are fenestrations.

3-12. *Cephalotus* flowers are borne in clusters.

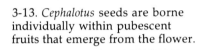

3-13. *Cephalotus* seeds are borne individually within pubescent fruits that emerge from the flower.

3-14. Plant growing from a foliage leaf of *Cephalotus*.

3-15. Plant growing from a pitcher of *Cephalotus*.

4-1. Pygmy *Drosera* with flat, disc-shaped gemmae in the center of the plant.

4-3. *Drosera pulchella* plant with flowers. The leaf blades are circular.

4-2. *Drosera paleacea* plant with flowers. The plant produces layers of new leaves on top of the older ones.

4-4. *Drosera whittakeri.*

4-5. Tuberous *Drosera* tubers. A variety of sizes and colors exists in tubers of different species.

4-6. *Drosera gigantea* tuber. Scales are visible on the tuber. New growth is emerging from the center.

4-7. The leaves of *Drosera rotundifolia* form a prostrate rosette. The leaf blades are almost circular.

4-8. Flower of *Drosera regia*

4-9. *Drosera* × *Nagamoto* winter bud.

Photo 4-10. Plants of *Drosera binata* var. *binata* produce erect, bisected leaf blades.

4-12. *Drosera capensis* leaves are erect with a linear leaf blade.

4-11. *Drosera binata* var. *multifida* leaf blade with many divisions.

4-13. *Drosera adelae* plants.

4-14. *Drosera petiolaris* plants. Leaf color is pale due to heavily pubescent petioles.

4-15. *Drosera prolifera* plantlet and flower produced on the same scape.

4-16. *Drosophyllum* fruit with seeds.

4-17. Uncoiling of *Drosophyllum* leaves with red colored tentacles. Two flower buds are present.

4-18. *Drosophyllum* older plant with new growth developing in leaf axils.

4-19. *Byblis gigantea* plant with flower.

4-20. *Byblis liniflora* flower has 5 petals, 5 sepals and 5 stamens.

5-1. The corolla of *Pinguicula* flowers narrows to form a pointed spur. The palate is the pubescent structure on the lower lip of the corolla. *Pinguicula vulgaris.*

5-3. *Pinguicula caerulea* plant growing in natural habitat.

5-2. *Pinguicula longifolia* plant. Leaves tend to curl up during and after prey capture to form a shallow bowl which contains the digestive fluids and prevents loss of prey.

5-4. *Pinguicula longifolia* flower.

5-5. *Pinguicula moranensis* plant with flower.

5-6. Winter bud of *Pinguicula longifolia* with smaller brood bodies in foreground.

5-7. Leaf of *Pinguicula* with small plantlets.

6-1. Terrestrial *Utricularia* plants. The surface leaves are photosynthetic . Rhizoids which bear bladders anchor the plant in the growing medium. Sometimes grow out of the growing medium.

6-2. *Utricularia alpina* plant with flowers.

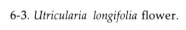

6-3. *Utricularia longifolia* flower.

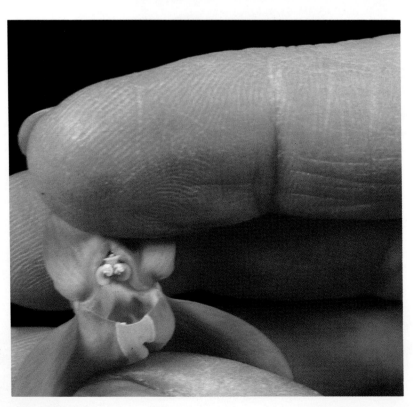

6-4. Reproductive structures of *Utricularia longifolia*. The two curved stamens are below the stigma.

6-5. *Utricularia inflata,* an aquatic bladderwort.
(Photo by O.H. Weiss)

6-6. *Utricularia menzeisii* plants form dormant
structures during the dry season. Many white
rice-like structures are enmeshed within a
fibrous network.

6-7. *Polypompholyx multifida* plants in natural
habitat.

6-8. *Aldrovanda* plant.

9-1. Rhizome proliferation is encouraged by removing leaves from rhizome and cutting off growing tip. The remaining portion of the rhizome is planted halfway into the growing medium. Buds will develop into plants that can later be separated from each other.

4

Sundew Types

This group of plants could well be called living "flypaper." Their leaves are covered with tentacles which terminate in spherical glands which are enclosed in a ball of sticky mucilage. The glistening of their mucilage in sunlight suggests the common name, Sundews. Insects are trapped when they light on the leaf and become entangled in the sticky mucilage. As the insect attempts to pull free it frequently pulls over or accidentally touches other glands and, through struggling, becomes hopelessly mired. There are several types of tentacles on the leaves of the various Sundew species leaves. One type found in several species can, when stimulated, move and so push the struggling prey down onto the leaf surface. Movement of the tentacles can be induced by either mechanical or chemical stimulation. Tentacle bending is usually obvious within a half hour of stimulation. Tentacles of some of the genera in this group exhibit no motion.

This group of plants is quite diverse in shape, cultural requirements, and size. The Sundew group includes the genera *Byblis*, *Drosera*, and *Drosophyllum*.

Drosera

HISTORY

There are more than 100 species of *Drosera* in the world with the greatest concentration of species in Australia. It was Dr. A. W. Roth, a physician and botanist, who discovered in 1779 that the tentacles or stalked glands on *Drosera* were capable of movement. By this time *Dionaea*, the Venus Fly Trap, was well-known and investigators surmised that *Drosera* was a carnivore. Carnivory in *Drosera* was definitely established by Darwin, who conducted several meticulous studies on the digestive ability of these plants. *Drosera* is derived from the Greek words "droseros" which means dewy and "drosos" meaning dew, alluding to the resemblance of the drop of mucilage on the tentacle gland to dew.

DESCRIPTION OF PLANT

Members of this genus are extremely diverse, ranging in size from plants a fraction of an inch (a few mm) high to those that are bushlike and 39 in. (1 m) or more high. While most grow as upright plants, some grow along the ground like vines. Most *Drosera* species are perennials, but a few are annuals. They grow in all climates from tropical to arctic and from wet to dry. (Fig. 4-1)

Leaves

The leaves of *Drosera* plants consist of a leaf blade and either a distinct petiole or one which is continuous with the shape of the blade. Leaf blade shape is extremely variable within the two major categories, broad and thread-like blades. Within the broad blade type, the overall shape varies from circular to spathulate to linear. The thread-like leaf blades are either simple or divided into segments which are long and thin. (Fig. 4-2) In both types the petiole is usually distinguishable from the blade by the absence of tentacles.

Tentacles or stalked glands exist on the adaxial surfaces and margins of the leaf blade and, in some cases, on the leaf petiole. The stalked glands lure, capture and digest prey. The stalkless, sessile glands are found on practically all exposed surfaces including the tentacle stalk and are the structures which absorb digested materials.

The leaves form a rosette in some species while in others they are borne along upright or creeping stems. Some species have both a basal rosette of leaves and leaves borne on an elongated stem.

Above-ground parts of the plants arise from rhizomes, roots or tubers.

Flowers

The flowers are borne singly or in clusters. Petal color varies and includes shades of almost all colors. Petals and sepals usually number 5 per flower, each with 1 compound ovary and 5 stamens. Flowers usually open in bright light during the late morning to early afternoon, closing later in the day. The sequence of flower opening proceeds from the bottom of the scape upward, with the lowest flower on the scape opening first. Usually one or more flowers open each day.

TRAPPING

A spherical gland surmounting a tapering stalk comprises the stalked gland, which is commonly called a tentacle. These glands in healthy plants are enveloped in a layer of mucilage-like material which glistens in the sunlight, hence the common name Sundew. In strong light or sunlight the tentacle glands in most species develop a deep red coloration, whereas in the shade they develop little or no red coloration. The relatively clear and stiff mucilage which surrounds the tentacle gland presumably acts as a visible and odoriferous lure as well as the trapping medium. When an insect alights on a leaf and comes into contact with a gland, it is quickly mired in the thick mucilage. As the insect attempts to pull away one of its appendages, the mucilage is drawn out into thin threads. This commotion induces the glands with which it is in contact to produce impulses which travel to other tentacles. The impulses trigger the secretion process in other tentacle glands, resulting in the release of additional fluids. Simultaneously, the tentacles commence bending toward the prey. Eventually the flexing tentacles reach the prey, forcing it down to the surface of the leaf where it is bathed in fluids. The prey apparently drowns in these fluids. In some species the leaf also folds around the prey after its capture. With the completion of digestion and absorption the tentacles return to a vertical position again and the leaf blade, if folded, opens, exposing the undigestible remains of the prey.

The tentacle gland is exceedingly complex. A few of its multitudinous functions

Fig. 4-1 *Drosera capensis* plant. Older leaves form an apron around the
base of the plant.

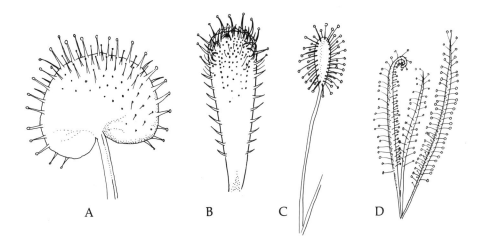

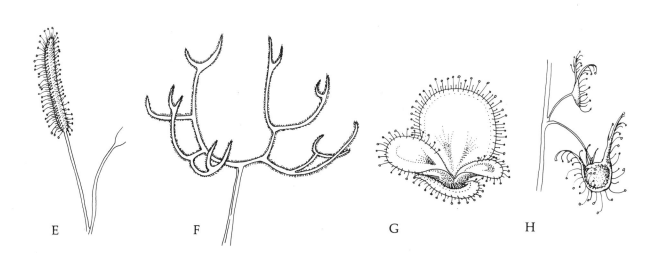

Fig. 4-2 Leaf shape in *Drosera* is variable. Most shapes fit within two major categories; broad or thread-like. *D. prolifera, D. spathulata, D. intermedia, D. filiformis, D. capensis, D. binata* var. *multifida, D. schizandra, D. peltata.*

include: generation, acceptance and conveyance of stimuli resulting in the bending movements of the tentacles and increased secretion of fluids by the tentacle glands. If a deglanded tentacle is directly stimulated no movement results, indicating that the gland is necessary for the generation of an impulse. If a nearby tentacle is stimulated and produces an impulse, the glandless tentacle will bend in response to the stimulus. In addition, the gland secretes digestive enzymes, mucilage, water and probably an odiferous substance, and absorbs the digested materials.

Bending of tentacles is the result of differential growth. For example, if a tentacle flexes to the left, the rate of growth is greater on the right side of the tentacle than on the left side. The increased rate of growth originates at the base of the tentacle and progressively moves toward the top. When digestion and absorption have been completed, the tentacle assumes its former orientation by reversing the differential rate of growth. After tentacles have reached the limit of their growth, they lose their ability to bend in response to a stimulus; a tentacle can usually undergo this process 3–4 times. A *Drosera* leaf can capture and digest more than 3–4 insects because not all the tentacles are involved in capturing and digesting a single insect, particularly on large leaves. It is not unusual to see the remains of half a dozen or more trapped insects on a single leaf.

The number of tentacles involved in the capture of an insect is influenced by the size and strength of the prey. Size and strength of an insect will obviously determine the intensity of its struggle. As the intensity of the insect's struggle increases, the strength of the impulses produced also increases. More tentacles are stimulated as the impulse becomes stronger.

Stimulation of tentacles in nature is usually effected by insects, but tentacles can be stimulated artificially by physical contact with any object. Darwin discovered that as little as 0.000822 milligrams of matter will stimulate a tentacle gland. The crucial factor in stimulation of a gland is the contact of the stimulating agent with the gland surface. The tentacle gland is enveloped in a layer of mucilage: therefore, for stimulation to occur, the stimulating agent must penetrate the mucilage to reach the gland surface. If the gland was not protected by the mucilage, rain and dust could cause stimulation of the gland and result in a waste of energy due to useless bending. The layer of mucilage protects the gland and reduces the incidence of nonproductive responses.

The initiation of the bending of the tentacle is, at times, visible within a few minutes after stimulation. All stimulated tentacles will usually complete their bending within 18 hours of excitation. A tentacle stimulated artificially by physical contact will bend and straighten out within a day, whereas if suitable prey is the stimulating agent, the time interval between bending and straightening out is 1–2 weeks.

In addition to physical stimulation, the tentacles will also respond to both certain chemicals and hot water. Some substances such as creatine, a nitrogenous substance, when placed on the tentacle gland, will be digested without any visible movement of the tentacle.

Based on their response to stimuli and size, the tentacles of *Drosera* fall into three categories: marginal, interzonal and discal. These three general groups of tentacles occur in all species of *Drosera* which have been studied. The marginal tentacles are located along the periphery of the leaf blade and are usually the longest. Those found in the center portion of the leaf are known as the discal tentacles, and are usually the shortest. The interzonal tentacles are located between the marginal and the discal tentacles. They are of intermediate length, longer than the discal but shorter than the marginal.

The three groups of tentacles react differently to stimulation. The marginal tentacles will respond to direct stimulation; that is, the tentacle whose gland is stimulated will bend. It has been reported that they can complete their bending in less than one minute, a speed we have never observed. A stimulated marginal gland does not send an impulse to surrounding marginal tentacles. The initial bending of the marginal tentacles is nastic, which means that upon stimulation they will bend toward the discal gland area. After the nastic response, the bending of the marginal tentacles becomes tropic: the tentacles that were bending toward the discal gland area adjust their bending so that they move toward and touch the struggling insect, the source of stimulation. These responses are best observed on the leaves of *Drosera filiformis* var. *filiformis; D. filiformis* var. *tracyi;* and *D. intermedia.* The function of the marginal tentacles is to bring the prey in contact with the discal glands. At times the marginal tentacles will bend in response to impulses received from stimulated discal tentacles if the impulse is sufficiently intense. Impulses which evoke a response from the marginal tentacles are usually produced by strong and/or large insects. Often when an insect has been captured by the discal tentacles, the marginal ones commence to bend, but before completing their bending they will straighten out. Apparently the impulses generated by the discal glands were not continuous or of sufficient intensity to completely stimulate the marginal tentacles. Marginal tentacles stimulated by impulses from the discal glands respond less rapidly than those stimulated directly. They usually return to their original orientation in about a week.

The interzonal tentacles respond as rapidly to direct stimulation as the marginal tentacles do. In response to indirect stimulation, the interzonal tentacles react faster and more vigorously than the marginal ones. To direct stimulation the reaction of the interzonal tentacles is nastic, whereas to indirect stimulation the reaction is both nastic and tropic.

When stimulated directly by prey the discal tentacles do not respond by bending; they send impulses to surrounding discal, interzonal, and marginal tentacles, thereby stimulating them to bend, and resulting in their glands being forced onto the prey. The reaction of the discal tentacles is always tropic. They bend directly toward the prey after receiving indirect stimulation. These tentacles complete their bending from within 1–24 hours.

In some species such as *D. capensis* the whole leaf will fold to enclose the captured prey, presumably to allow more glands to contact the victim and so maximize the digestive process and as well as to form a saucer to maintain digestive juices in contact with the prey. (Fig. 4-3)

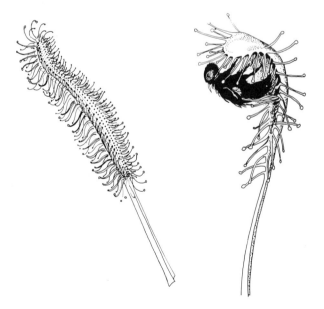

Fig. 4-3 *Drosera capensis* leaves. Leaf on left illustrates the three types of tentacles, the long marginal, medium interzonal and short discal. Leaf on the right shows a response to stimulation by an insect.

Other glands, the sessile or stalkless glands, are found on practically the entire surface of the plant excluding the roots. Apparently these glands are capable of absorption. Those located on the adaxial surface of the leaf and on the tentacle stalk may assist in the absorption of digested prey. Another possible function for these glands is that of guttation, excretion of water.

Drosera secretes enzymes, digests prey and absorbs the products of digestion intrinsically but is assisted by bacterial breakdown of prey.

In order to discuss the culture of *Drosera* in an organized fashion, it is convenient to group the plants according to environmental similarities into pygmy *Drosera*, tuberous *Drosera*, temperate *Drosera*, and tropical *Drosera*.

Pygmy *Drosera*

NATURAL HABITAT

Most of the pygmy *Drosera* species are found in southwestern Australia. The majority of pygmy *Drosera* grow in areas that have hot, dry summers and cool, moist winters with 15–22 in. (38–56 cm) of rain. Typical winter temperatures range from about 40–70°F (4–21°C) with frost occurring on rare occasions. Summer temperatures vary from about 70–100°F (21–38°C).

DESCRIPTION OF PLANT

This group of *Drosera* includes the smallest sundews found anywhere in the world, 0.4 in. (1 cm) in diameter with leaves one half this dimension and is characterized by gemmae formation during the fall and/or winter. Gemmae are small, greenish structures formed in the crown area of the rosette of leaves. Gemma is species specific. For example, *D. paleacea* has spherically-shaped gemmae, while *D. pulchella* has flat, disc-shaped gemmae. (Photo 4-1) Gemmae size varies from 0.04 to 0.2 in. (1–5 mm). (Fig. 4-4) The gemmae, also called brood bodies, develop into plants under appropriate environmental conditions.

The plants tend to form rosettes. The leaves, which have concave leaf blades, vary in shape from almost round to oval to linear. A characteristic feature in this group of *Drosera* is the growth of translucent stipules from the base of the petioles. Stipules are present in other *Drosera* plants but in this group they are showy and quite large in comparison to the leaf blades. Some species can be identified by the cone-shaped structure that the stipules form when the plant is dormant. Many species tend to flower profusely. Flower color varies considerably, including all colors except green and blue. The smallest flowers are the order of 0.08 in. (2 mm) long.

Pygmy *Drosera* grow during the Australian winter which is the wet season and usually go dormant during the hot, dry summer. Plants survive the dry season by forming a bud in the crown area of the plant which is held in place by roots that extend through the parched soil surface into damp subsoil beneath.

SPECIES OF THE PYGMY TYPE OF THE GENUS *DROSERA*

The following list includes all known species of pygmy *Drosera*. The species not yet officially named are listed by the name of the area in Australia where they were discovered.

Pygmy Sundews

D. androsacea
"Bannister Pale Pink"—W
'Brookton Orange Flower"

Pygmy Sundews

D. dichrosepala
D. drummondii
D. glanduligera
"Lake Badgebup White Flower"—W
D. leucoblasta
"Millbrook Road"
D. miniata
"Mt. Manypeak Type"
"Muchea Pink"—W
D. nitidula—W
"North Beermullah Small Pink"—W
D. occidentalis
D. omissa
D. paleacea
D. platystigma
D. pulchella—W
D. pycnoblasta
D. pygmaea—W
"Regans Ford Yellow Flower"
D. scorpioides
D. sewelliae
"Toodyay Pink"
"Walyinga Pink"

W= Soil is wet the year around.

DESCRIPTION OF PLANTS COMMERCIALLY AVAILABLE

"Bannister Pale Pink"   A rosette with 6–10 pink flowers per scape. Petiole about 0.6 in. (1.5 cm) long with an oval blade whose diameter is about 0.08 in. (2 mm).

D. glanduligera   A rosette with 1 or 2 scapes and up to 20 red flowers on each. Leaves yellowish green. Petiole tends to be linear and about 0.3 in. (8 mm) long with an oval blade with a diameter of about 0.2 in. (5 mm).

"Lake Badgebup White Flower"   A rosette with 1–3 scapes with 1 flower on each. Petiole tends to be linear about 0.4 in. (1 cm) long with a roundish blade whose diameter is about 0.08 in. (2 mm).

D. miniata   A basal rosette with 2–5 scapes and 2–8 red flowers on each. Petiole tends to be linear and about 0.3 in. (8 mm) long with a roundish blade whose diameter is about 0.08 in. (2 mm). Stipules whitish or brownish yellow.

D. paleacea   A tight rosette with 1–3 scapes and up to 30 white flowers tightly placed on one side of the scape. Petiole tends to be linear and about 0.8 in. (2 cm) long with a roundish blade whose diameter is about 0.12 in. (3 mm). (Photo 4-2)

D. pulchella   A rosette with 1–3 scapes with about 4 flowers per scape. Flowers may be pink, red or orange. Petiole tends to be linear, tapering near the blade and about 0.8 in. (2 cm) long with a round blade whose diameter is about 0.12 in. (3 mm). (Photo 4-3)

D. pygmaea   A rosette with 1–8 scapes with a single white flower on each. Petiole tends to be linear and about 0.2 in. (5 mm) long with a peltate blade whose diameter is about 0.08 in. (2 mm).

CULTURAL INFORMATION

Planting Media

Sphagnum peat moss, milled sphagnum moss, 1 part sphagnum peat moss to 1 part sand (preferably silica sand) or perlite, 1 part sphagnum peat moss to 1 part sand and 1 part perlite.

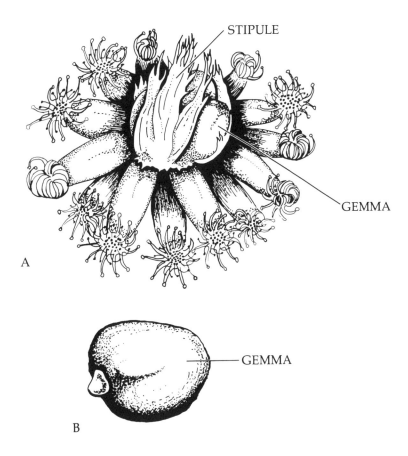

Fig. 4-4 Pygmae *Drosera* are small rosette type plants. Gemmae form in the crown area of the leaves. Some gemmae are roundish. Stipules are prominent and quite large in comparison to the leaf blades. Insert illustrates one gemma.

Plants grow best in deep pots. The pots should be a minimum of 4 in. (10 cm) deep, but preferably deeper, 6–8 in. (15–20 cm) or more.

Temperatures

While most of the pygmy *Drosera* grow in their native habitat during the winter, which is the wet season with temperatures of 40–68°F (4–20°C), and are dormant during the drier summer when temperatures may approach and at times exceed 100°F (38°C), most of them will grow throughout the year if provided with moisture.

Dormancy

Most pygmy *Drosera* go dormant in their native habitat during the dry, hot summer, but apparently this is not a requirement for successful growth as we and many other growers have grown them the year around with no apparent problems. To mimic nature, the soil should be almost dry during the dormant, summer season. In nature the roots extend down to a considerable depth, so that while the surface soil is dry, the root ends are in damp soil. Therefore, the lower layer of soil should be at least slightly damp. During dormancy, the plants will produce a bud in the crown area that will survive the dry season from which growth sprouts when conditions are suitable.

Water & Humidity

All the pygmy *Drosera* require high humidity when actively growing. While only some pygmy *Drosera* species grow in very wet areas, they all do well in moist medium which is not water logged. They should be watered from the bottom to prevent soil from being splashed on the leaves. Since the leaves are generally quite small, many of the tentacles will be needlessly stimulated to move by splashed soil, causing both considerable unneeded expenditure of energy by the plant and a reduction of photosynthetic activity due to screening of light by the medium.

Some growers water plants from above with syringes to avoid splashing medium on the leaves. Others heap the medium into mounds about 1 in. (2.5 cm) or so high and insert the plants on the top of the mounds so that when they are top watered the water will not splash up on the leaves. One drawback to mounding the planting medium is that gemmae fall into the depressions created, and grow there. Since ventilation in the depression is poor, the young plants are subject to fungus infection which can spread to the other plants in the pot.

Another watering technique employed to avoid splashing planting media on the leaves is to place a layer of very coarse sand or small pebbles on top of the medium. The sand or pebbles prevents soil from splashing up onto the plants when they are top watered.

In our judgment the best method is to set the pots in a container with 1–2 (2.5–5 cm) of water. Leave the pot in the container until the water has soaked up to the surface of the medium. We grow pygmy *Droseras* in pots standing in trays of water 1 in. (2.5 cm) deep.

Light

Indirect or filtered sunlight. With adequate light the tentacles of most species display a red coloration. If artificial light is used, start with 900 foot candles of illumination for a photoperiod of 12–14 hours during the growing season and 8 hours during the dormant period.

Pests

The only known pests are aphids and fungus. See Chapter 8 for treatment.

Feeding

See Chapter 7 for feeding instructions.

Miscellaneous

The easier species to grow in this group include "Lake Badgebup White Flower", "Millbrook Road", *D. nitidula*, *D. paleacea*, *D. pygmaea*, *D. pulchella*, "Toodyay Pink", and "Walyinga Pink".

PROPAGATION

Sexual Reproduction

Most of the pygmy *Drosera* flower prolifically, some produce abundant seed, while many do not produce any seed under greenhouse conditions. It might be that those that have not set seed need to be cross-pollinated.

Viability of pygmy *Drosera* seed is quite variable. Perhaps the seeds need some sort of pre-treatment before they will germinate. But neither we nor other growers have pursued this area to date. To our knowledge, no one has produced any hybrids in this group of *Drosera*. The primary obstacle to artificial cross-pollination and/or hybridizing the pygmy group is their small flower size. It is virtually impossible to control pollination by ordinary methods in cultivation.

Sow seed on the soil, dust with a fungicide, keep the soil damp and the humidity high. Light should be strong and temperatures should range from about 70–80°F (21–27°C). It is best to allow the seedlings to grow one season before transplanting.

Asexual Reproduction

1. Leaf cuttings: Propagation by leaf cuttings is not always successful, but works sporadically. Success is enhanced if the whole leaf including the base of the petiole is utilized. Place the removed leaves top side (side with the tentacles) up on damp medium. Keep them in strong light with high humidity and within a temperature range of 70–80°F (21–27°C). Within 4–8 weeks plantlets will be visible. When the plantlets have developed roots they can be transplanted.

2. Gemmae formation: Propagating pygmy *Drosera* by inducing gemmae formation (gemmification) is a far more satisfactory means rather than growing plants from seed or leaves. All species but *D. glanduligera,* (which though included in the pygmy group does not produce gemmae and is an annual) may be successfully propagated by gemmae. *D. glanduligera* produces seed each year which germinates readily.

Gemmification is induced by lowering the growing temperature to between 40–65°F (4–18°C) while the plants are growing in moist soil. The photoperiod should be reduced to about 8 hours. Usually within 2 weeks a swelling in the central area of the rosette where the gemmae are forming can be detected. As the swelling develops and enlarges, individual gemmae will appear as separate structures.

Tweezers may be used to remove the gemmae, but this is tedious work. A simpler method is to drain the pot for a few hours then up-end it over a piece of paper and brush the area where the gemmae are located with a brush or toothpick. The gemmae will fall on the paper. Gemmae should be removed, even if your intention is not propagation. If not removed, they start to grow on and around the mother plant; overcrowding will result in some dying due to lack of growing space. The dead ones become good targets for fungus such as *Botrytis* which will quickly spread throughout the plants in the pot. The removed gemmae should be planted immediately upon a suitable media.

Tuberous Drosera

NATURAL HABITAT

Almost all of the species of tuberous *Drosera* are indigenous to Australia, the vast majority being found in the southwestern part of the country. *Drosera peltata* has the most extensive range extending from Australia to Asia and Japan. They usually grow in sandy soils.

DESCRIPTION OF PLANT

Tuberous *Drosera* grow from underground spherical storage stems called tubers similar to white potatoes. (Photo 4-4) Some tubers have scales. Tuber color varies to include shades of white, red, pink, orange, and yellow. Tuber shape varies between species but is reasonably constant within a species. Tuber size in some species can exceed 1½ in. (3.8 cm) in diameter. (Photo 4-5) The growth habit of tuberous *Drosera* ranges from low growing rosette forms to erect and climbing forms.

Tuber depth is different for each species. If tubers are not planted at the required depth for a particular species, tubers will be formed at progressively lower levels in succeeding years until the appropriate depth is reached. *D. gigantea,* for example, has the deepest tubers reaching depths of 5 ft. (1.5 m) or more.

The new tubers, in some species, are formed within the cavity formed by the previous tuber which eventually forms a 'skin' around the new tuber. Old tubers have been found with up to 50 layers of 'skin'. It is believed that the skins protect the tuber from high temperatures and prevent desiccation. In some species the skin deteriorates and the tubers are naked. (Fig. 4-5)

Brush fires are required for some species to flower, while in other species fire

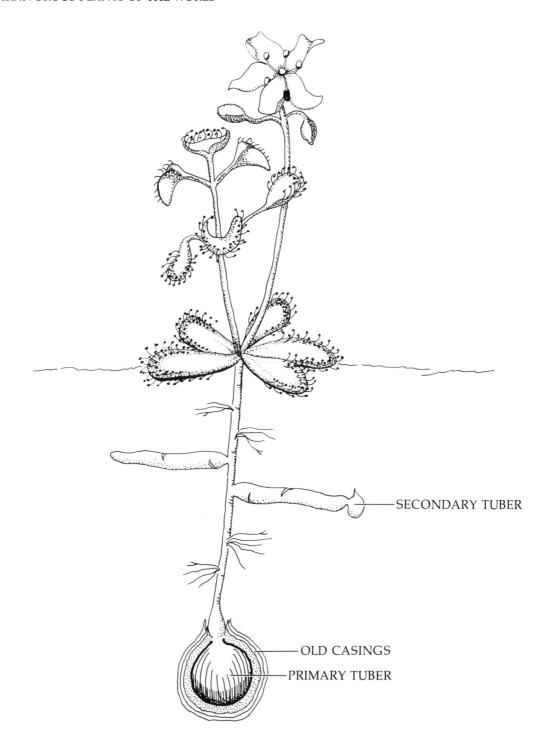

SECONDARY TUBER

OLD CASINGS

PRIMARY TUBER

Fig. 4-5 *Drosera stolonifera* plant showing tuber and development of a secondary tuber which can produce a new plant at the start of the next growing season. The plant utilizes the food reserves in its tuber to establish itself. Later in the growing season excess food produced by photosynthesis is stored in the new tuber. The new primary tuber forms within the casing of the previous years tubers. The old casings form protective layers around the newly stored food.

induces more profuse flowering. It is not known if this response to fire is caused by the temporarily increased soil temperature or higher temperature of the soil for a much longer period of time resulting from the removal of competing plant cover, allowing the sun to shine directly on the soil; or to nutrients released to the soil by the burning of surface vegetation. It does not seem likely that soil temperatures would be much affected at the depths that some of the tubers are found. Another idea that has been advanced is that ethylene produced during burning promotes flowering. Ethylene does induce flowering in such plants as pineapples.

Tuberous *Drosera* have long been considered the most difficult plants of the Sundew group to grow in culture. This unwarranted reputation is attributable to the inadequacy of good cultural information until recently. The want of good information in the past prevented growers from providing the necessary and correct environment for successful growth. The most common outcome with tuberous *Drosera* in culture was a continuing decrease in tuber size with each succeeding year until the plant simply died of starvation.

In their native habitat, tuberous *Drosera* experience a 6-month growing season, during the Australian winter season, when the temperature ranges from 35–79°F (2–26°C) accompanied by 15–22 in. (38–56 cm) of rain. During the Australian summer the plants must endure a 6-month drought relieved only by an occasional thundershower, with temperatures ranging from 70–100°F (21–38°C). During this season the aboveground portions of the plants die back. The below-ground tuber, with its stored food, will resume growth upon the arrival of the wet season.

The problem experienced when growing tuberous *Drosera* in cultivation turned out to be the lack of attention to the plants' natural requirement for 6 months of vigorous growth in temperate, moist conditions. Instead growers, following customary practice, allowed the plants only about 3 bountiful months. As a consequence of the short growing season furnished the plants, the tubers could not store enough carbohydrates to form a tuber as large or larger than the original. Thus each year the tuber produced shrank, resulting in smaller and weaker plants the following year. When provided constant environmental conditions so the plants grow for about 6 months, the tubers and plants become larger each year until their mature size is reached. Upon reaching mature size they maintain their size and also produce the axillary tubers utilized for natural asexual reproduction. In short, the key to successfully growing tuberous *Drosera* is the provision of a sufficiently long growing season, accompanied by strong light with an adequate photoperiod, so that the plants can make and store food reserves to insure vigorous future growth.

SPECIES OF THE TUBEROUS TYPE OF THE GENUS *DROSERA*

Grow well in well-drained medium

D. andersoniana	D. stolonifera
D. bulbosa	D. thysanosepala
D. erythrorhiza	D. zonaria
D. huegelii	
D. macrantha—C	
D. macrophylla	
D. menziesii	
D. microphylla	
D. modesta—C	
D. pallida—C	
D. planchonii	
D. platypoda	
D. ramellosa	

Grow in poorly-drained medium

D. bulbigena
D. bulbosa
D. gigantea
D. heterophylla
D. menziesii
D. myriantha—C
D. neesii
D. subhirtella—C
D. sulphurea

Grow in damp or wet medium the year around

D. auriculata—B
D. peltata—B
D. whittakeri (alpine)

KEY
C=Plant with a climbing habit.
B=Species will grow with a wet and dry season.

DESCRIPTION OF COMMERCIALLY AVAILABLE SPECIES

D. bulbosa   Rosetted plants that occur in two forms. "Hill" form: Leaves become maroon to purplish upon maturity attaining lengths of 2.5 in. (6 cm). Petiole is wedge-shaped with a round blade. White flowers are borne singly on each of several scapes. The orange tuber is heart-shaped with scales.
"Sand" form: Similar to the "Hill" form but is smaller, having fewer leaves. The tuber is spherical lacking scales and may be white, pink, or red.

D. erythrorhiza   A rosetted plant with a circular blade tapering toward the base to a short almost indistinguishable petiole. Blade is about 1.2 in. (3 cm) wide. Numerous white flowers are borne on a single scape. There are 2 forms in this species. The tubers of both forms are red with scales.
"Sand" form: Usually has up to 6 leaves whose blades are not as circular as those of the "Hill" form. "Hill" form: This variety is more robust with plants usually having more leaves than the "Sand" form.

D. gigantea   An erect plant with numerous branches. It can exceed a height of 40 in. (102 cm). Color varies from yellowish green to maroon. The cupped, peltate leaves have upward pointed lobes. Smaller leaves develop later in the season from the leaf axils. Scale-like leaves occur on the lower portion of the stem. Numerous white flowers are terminal on the branches. The red kidney-shaped tuber has scales. (Photo 4-6) When this plant emerges from the soil in the fall it resembles an asparagus shoot.

D. heterophylla   An erect plant growing up to 14 in. (36 cm) high. Leaves are shield- to almost kidney-shaped on short petioles with the blade about 0.2 in. (5 mm) long, occurring singly on the upper part of the stem. Scale-like leaves occur on the lower part of the stem. One or more white or pink flowers are borne on the top of the foliage stem.

D. huegelii   An erect plant whose stem zigzags to a length of 29 in. (74 cm) or more with usually fewer than 8 leaves and at times may have only scale-like leaves. The upper leaves, hanging from long petioles, are round and cupped about 0.4 in. (1 cm) wide with the tentacled surface facing downward. The leaves on the lower part of the stem are of the scale type. Numerous white to pink flowers are borne terminally on the foliage stems. The tubers are white.

D. macrantha   Leaves and stem are yellowish green and have no red coloration. The climbing stem can reach a length of 51 in. (130 cm) and its leaf blades are round, cupped and up to 0.4 in. (1 cm) in diameter. Leaves are arranged in groups of 3 on the stem with 1 of the leaves having a much longer petiole than the others. Scale-like leaves occur on the lower part of the stem. Several white or pink flowers are borne on the top of the foliage stem. The tuber is white and usually kidney-shaped with a bumpy surface.

D. macrophylla   A rosetted plant with a roundish blade tapering to a short petiole. Leaves are up to 2.4 in. (6 cm) across at the widest point and up to 4.8 in. (12 cm) long. Leaves do not develop a red coloration. Usually 2 or more white flowers with black spotted sepals are borne on each of several scapes. The tuber is orange-red.

D. menziesii   There are several varieties of this species which can be erect or climbing or have a stem that zigzags, reaching a length of 40 in. (102 cm) or more. Color ranges from red to purple. Leaves are round and cupped and up to 0.2 in. (5 mm) in diameter. They occur in groups of 3 with 1 leaf having a much longer petiole than the other 2. Several red to pink flowers are borne terminally on the foliage stem. The tuber is pink.

D. modesta   A yellowish green climbing plant that can exceed 40 in. (102 cm) in length. Leaves are cupped and shield-shaped with 2 upward pointed lobes and are about 0.2 in. (5 mm) wide. The 2-lobe leaf distinguishes this plant from *D. macrantha*. Leaves occur in groups of 3 with 1 leaf having a much longer petiole than the other 2. Scale-like leaves occur on the bottom part of the foliage stem. Numerous white flowers are borne on the end of the foliage stem. The tubers are white.

D. platypoda   Erect plant with a skimpy basal rosette of leaves. Leaves are fan-shaped and may tend to become funnel-shaped. This plant can be easily distinguished from *D. stolonifera* which usually has the same shaped leaves in that the leaves are borne singly in the former and in whorls of 3–4 in the latter. Leaves may be up to 0.2 in. (5 mm) across the widest part and 0.6 in. (1.5 cm) long. Numerous white flowers, with black spotted sepals, are borne on a simple or branched stem terminally on the foliage stem or on a scape arising from the basal rosette. The orange tuber is oval-shaped with scales and is pointed on the bottom.

D. ramellosa   The plant consists of a basal rosette of leaves and one or more erect stems. The clasping, fan-shaped yellowish green leaves are alternately arranged on the stem. From 1 to several white flowers are borne on each short scape which can number from 1 to several. The tuber is orange-red.

D. stolonifera   There are several forms that vary from a single erect stem with a basal rosette of leaves to branching forms which may have several semi-erect stems. Leaves are usually fan-shaped with size varying considerably in the various forms. Leaves may be red, purple or orange and occur in whorls of 3 to 4. White flowers are borne on a branching scape and in some forms on the top of the foliage stem. The red tuber has scales and the upper surface is concave. In cross section it is kidney-shaped.

D. sulphurea   A greenish, erect plant with a zigzag stem that can be up to 18 in. (46 cm) long. Leaves occur in groups of 3 with 1 leaf on a much longer petiole than the other 2. They are shield-shaped with 2 pointed lobes about 0.2 in. (5 mm) wide. Scale-like leaves clothe the lower part of the stem. Several bright yellow flowers are borne on the top of the foliage stem. Tuber color is yellow or pink to white.

D. zonaria   A rosetted plant with green, kidney-shaped leaves. The leaf blade is up to 0.6 in. (1.5 cm) wide. The petioles are covered by the overlapping blades. Leaf margins tend to become red to maroon. Numerous white flowers are borne on a single scape. Tubers are red with scales and tend to be spherical.

CULTURAL INFORMATION

Planting Media

Media pH should be in the range of 4.5 to 6.5. For the "well-drained" species 2 parts sand to 1 part sphagnum peat moss. For the "poorly-drained" and "damp medium" species: 2 parts sphagnum peat moss and 1 part sand. Media should be at least 5 in. (13 cm) deep, but preferably 10 in. (25 cm) or more. We have successfully grown *D. gigantea* in a 2 ft. (0.6 m) length of 6 in. drain tile. (Note, tubers of *D. gigantea* can be 5 ft. (1.5 m) deep in nature.) Tubers should be planted a minimum of 2 in. (5 cm) below the medium surface in shallow pots [5 in. (13 cm)] and down to ½ the depth of the soil in deeper pots [10 in. (25 cm)]. The crown of the tuber, the end with an indentation in which the 'eye' is found, must be oriented to the surface of the medium.

Temperatures
During the growing season 40–79°F (4–26°C). Dormant season 70–100°F (21–38°C).

Dormancy
All of the tuberous *Drosera*, with a few exceptions, require a dormant period in the summer of about 5 months. (*Drosera whittakeri*, is the exception to the rule. It is an alpine plant which grows during the summer and is dormant during the winter.) We have grown *D. peltata* and *D. auriculata* for 15 years in wet soils the year around. They grow, flower, produce seed and die back each year. Our plants grow during the latter part of the winter and into the summer. These 2 species will also grow with a wet and dry season just as well as they do with wet soils the year around. Despite our experience with these 2 species it is best to follow the rule that dormancy is critical for most tuberous *Drosera* species.

Dormancy is presumably initiated by the flowering process. Usually, during flowering, new tubers are formed so that by the end of the flowering period they have developed fully. After flowering, when the plants start to turn yellow and die, allow the soil to dry out slowly by taking the pots out of trays of water if they are maintained this way and/or by withholding water. Once the medium is dry, place the plants out of the sun's direct rays and do not water. Some growers give the plants water once or twice during the dormant period to simulate the rain they get during the summer from infrequent thundershowers in their native environment. Some growers remove the tubers from the soil once they are dormant and place them in plastic bags for storage at room temperature, 68–86°F (20–30°C). It has been reported that this procedure stimulates flowering.

Water & Humidity
During the growing season in their native habitat, rainfall ranges from 15–30 in. (38–76 cm). Obviously *Drosera* require a great deal of water when actively growing. Provide the same environmental conditions by placing the pots in 1–2 in. (2.5–5 cm) of water during the growing season. During the dormant season rainfall is nonexistent except for a few thundershowers; therefore, the medium should be kept dry during the dormant period. When the growing season arrives place them in trays of water again. Also maintain high humidity during their active growing period.

Light
Indirect or filtered sunlight is best. In their native habitat tuberous *Drosera* typically grow among taller plants and so are adapted to semi-shade. The aerial parts of most of the tuberous *Drosera* have a red coloration when they are receiving adequate light. If artificial light is used, start with 1000 foot candles. The photoperiod during the growing season should be about 9½ hours.

Pests
The only known pests are aphids and fungus. See Chapter 8 for treatment.

Feeding
See Chapter 7 for feeding instructions.

Miscellaneous
Unless you obtain the growing plant in a pot, which is next to impossible by mail order, it is best to buy tubers when they are dormant. Before ordering determine when the tubers went into dormancy in order to know how much longer you must provide dormant conditions. The dormant period can be extended in most cases so that you can synchronize the plant's growth cycle with your particular conditions. That is, if you can

provide the correct cultural conditions during the spring and you get tubers during the winter that have already had a sufficient dormant period, they can in some cases be kept dormant for a few more months and then potted and allowed to grow.

Since the tubers of many *Drosera* species are found deep in the ground, they are probably in moist soil even though the surface soil is dry or parched. Wondering if these plants really need a dry period, 2 years ago we planted and kept tubers of 10 species of tuberous *Drosera* in wet soils the year around. These test tubers are completing their second season and their growth and size are excellent. A few more seasons of growth in wet soils will reveal if this method is successful.

Flowering, and therefore dormancy, are apparently initiated by photoperiod. The days are shorter during the growing period than during the dormant season. There may be a biological clock involved because some species start to grow even though the soil is parched. We have stored tubers in a plastic bags at 38°F (3°C) and even under these conditions some species start to grow.

The easier species to grow in this group include *D. menziesii, D. stolonifera, D. auriculata* and *D. peltata*.

PROPAGATION

Sexual Reproduction

Most tuberous *Drosera* produce seed in nature, some of which will germinate readily while some may require 3 or more years to germinate. There is apparently some factor(s) that inhibits germination, perhaps for survival purposes. Some seeds require effects of fire to break their dormancy. *Drosera peltata* and *D. auriculata* are the only two species that produce seed for us under cultivation. Perhaps the other species require cross-pollination to produce seed.

Asexual Reproduction

1. Secondary tuber: The tuberous species, when mature, commonly reproduce in nature by producing secondary tubers on lateral rhizomes; secondary tubers at times have exceeded a dozen in number.

2. Leaf cuttings: Remove the whole leaf including the petiole and place it on damp medium such as sphagnum moss; maintain a high humidity in bright light within a temperature range of 65–75°F (18–24°C). After the plantlets have grown for 5–6 months or longer it is advisable to synchronize them to your growing season so that they can be provided with conditions to induce dormancy. After dormancy has been achieved, the small tubers can be transplanted into pots. We have successfully propagated *D. gigantea* following this procedure.

3. Other methods: Reports of other methods for reproducing tuberous *Drosera* are listed below. Since we have not tried them yet we cannot vouch for them.

One technique involves growing the tuber into a shoot. As soon as the new shoot breaks through the soil surface, carefully dig into the soil and detach the tuber from the shoot and replant the tuber at the same depth as it was when it was attached to the shoot. The shoot will produce another tuber and the replanted tuber will produce a new shoot.

Another method involves cutting the tuber in half through the eye which is located in the indentation at the top or crown of the tuber. The cut surfaces are coated with wax to prevent infection and desiccation before they are planted. Each half should grow into a plant.

Temperate *Drosera* _____

NATURAL HABITAT

Discussed in this section are the *Drosera* species that grow in the temperate climatic regions of the world. A few species listed in this section are also listed with the tropical *Drosera* species because they grow in both climatic regions.

DESCRIPTION OF PLANT

The growth habit of plants in this group varies from prostrate rosettes to erect. (Photo 4-7) Leaf shape ranges from almost round to thread-like. Flowers are various shades of red and white. (Photo 4-8) A few species produce tubers. All the species listed in this section survive temperatures that dip to about 40°F (4°C) during the winter or the plants' dormant period. Some species produce winter buds, called hibernaculum; others simply cease to grow, retaining their leaves during dormancy. The winter bud is a small tight cluster of undeveloped leaves surrounding the growing point. (Photo 4-9) It is formed at the center of the crown or rosette of leaves and usually after formation, the old leaves die back.

SPECIES AND HYBRIDS OF THE TEMPERATE TYPE OF THE GENUS *DROSERA*

D. aliciae *
D. anglica A—*
D. arcturi A
D. auriculata F—C—*
D. binata var. *binata* A—B
D. binata var. *dichotoma* A—B
D. binata var. *multifida* A—B
D. brevifolia E—*
D. burkeana *
D. burmannii D—*
D. × *californica* A
D. capensis *
D. capillaris *
D. cistiflora F—C—*
D. cuneifolia F-*
D. filiformis var. *filiformis* A—*
D. filiformis var. *tracyi* A—*
D. glabripes
D. glanduligera D—*
D. spp. golden sundew
D. hamiltonii
D. hilaris
D. × *hybrida* A
D. intermedia A-*
D. linearis A—*
D. montana *
D. × *Nagamoto* A
D. natalensis *
D. × *obovata* A
D. peltata F—C—*
D. ramellosa F—C—*
D. regia —B
D. rotundifolia A—*

D. spathulata *

D. stenopetala *

D. trinervia

D. villosa

D. whittakeri C

KEY

A= Aboveground parts of the plant die back to a winter bud or a growing point.

B= Aboveground parts remain evergreen at temperatures of about 45°F (7°C) or above and will die back at lower temperatures.

C= Aboveground parts die back leaving a viable tuber or rhizome in the soil.

D= An annual.

E= Can behave as either an annual or perennial.

F= Dormant during the summer.

* = Will self-pollinate.

DESCRIPTION OF COMMERCIALLY AVAILABLE SPECIES

D. aliciae The wedge-shaped leaves form a compact rosette. Flowers are light purple to pink. Evergreen growth habit. Leaves are 2 in. (5 cm) long. Some consider it to be a member of the *D. spathulata* complex.

D. auriculata Form is similar to *D. peltata*. Both a basal rosette and elongated stem are produced. They can be distinguished by sepal characteristics, *D. auriculata* has glabrous sepals with black dots while *D. peltata* has pubescent sepals.

D. binata var. *binata* Erect linear leaves fork to form a "Y". The leaves can reach lengths of 20 in. (51 cm). Flowers are white. Goes dormant in winter when exposed to low temperatures. (Photo 4-10)

D. binata var. *dichotoma* Similar to *D. binata* var. *binata* except the leaves are divided into 4 linear segments. The dichotomy is sometimes irregular with more or fewer divisions occurring in some leaf blades.

D. binata var. *multifida* Similar to *D. binata* var. *dichotoma* except the leaf blade is divided into 6 or more linear sections.(Photo 4-11)

D. brevifolia The wedge-shaped leaf blades gradually taper to a short petiole. The leaf blade length is 0.2–0.7 in. (0.5–1.8 cm) and is usually longer than the petiole. The small plant forms a basal rosette. One to 8 white to rose-pink flowers are borne on a glandular-pubescent scape.

D. burmannii The blunt-ended spathulate leaves tend to have an overall maroon coloration and very long tentacles. The growth form is a basal rosette. Flowers are usually white but may be red.

D. burkeana A rosette with prostrate leaves, petiole up to 0.8 in. (2 cm) long with a roughly triangular-shaped blade that is up to 0.4 in. (1 cm) long and 0.3 in. (0.8 cm) wide. From 2–12 pink or white flowers are borne on each scape.

D. capensis Leaves erect with the blade curving gracefully downward. The leaf blade is linear and about as long as the petiole with the entire leaf being 2.8–5 in. (7–13 cm) long. Numerous pink flowers are borne on each scape. (Photo 4-12)

D. capillaris Leaf blades are longer than broad, and are egg-shaped. Leaf length is 0.4–1.2 in. (1–3 cm). Leaves form a prostrate rosette. This plant is often mistaken for *D. rotundifolia*. The species can be distinguished from each other by the leaf blades. *D. rotundifolia* leaf blades are broader than long while *D. capillaris* blades are longer than broad. One to 12 rose-pink to white flowers are borne per scape.

D. filiformis var. *filiformis* Erect thread-like leaves have no distinction between blade and petiole. Circinate vernation is evident in uncoiling of the leaves whose length is 0.4–12 in. (1–30 cm). One to 25 purple flowers are borne on each scape. Winter buds are formed during dormancy.

D. filiformis var. *tracyi* Differs from *D. filiformis* var. *filiformis* in that it is more robust. Leaves are longer and floral parts are larger. Tentacles are green rather than red.

D. intermedia Elongated, somewhat oblong-shaped blades are borne on the ends of semi-erect petioles. The leaf blade is about 4 times longer than wide and tapers to a long, slender petiole forming a leaf that is about 2 in. (5 cm) long. Leaves usually form a rosette, but when the environment is extremely wet, the leaves develop on an elongated stem. There may be 1–20 white flowers on a single scape. Winter buds are formed during dormancy.

D. hamiltonii The basal rosette consists of leaves 1.5 in. (4 cm) long. The leaves have narrow blades tapering into the petiole. The scape bears from 5–12 bright pink flowers. Growth ceases during dormancy.

D. peltata The leaves forming the basal rosette are round. The long petioled leaves on the erect stem, which may be 10 in. (25 cm) high, are peltate and shield-shaped. Several white flowers are borne on the scape. Plant is dormant during the summer with the aboveground part of the plant dying, leaving a viable underground tuber.

D. rotundifolia Leaves consist of a round to broader than long blade attached to a long narrow petiole. Leaves are about 3.5 in. (9 cm) long. Growth form is prostrate. One to 25 white to pink flowers are borne on a single scape. A winter bud is formed during dormancy.

CULTURAL INFORMATION

Planting Media

Sphagnum peat moss, sphagnum moss (living or dried), sand, mixtures of sand with sphagnum peat moss, mixtures of sphagnum peat moss with vermiculite and/or perlite. *D. linearis* grows in both slightly alkaline and acid soils in nature. An alkaline medium suitable for this species is made from 1 part sand and 1 part vermiculite with or without 1 tablespoon of ground limestone or dolomite stone per quart of medium mixture.

Temperatures

Summer 70–100°F (21–38°C). Winter 38–45°F (3–7°C). Some will survive subfreezing temperatures.

Dormancy

Plants listed in chart 1 with an A after their name (not A-B) must have a dormant period at temperatures of 38–45°F (3–7°C) for 4–5 months. Most of these species will withstand subfreezing temperatures, although temperatures this low are not necessary for dormancy. *D. linearis* is particularly sensitive to changes in temperatures and photoperiod during its dormancy period. Toward late August or early September (in the Northern Hemisphere) light intensity and temperatures should be reduced to prepare *D. linearis* for dormancy which is manifested by the formation of a winter bud. Once initiated it is very important with this species to keep dormancy conditions constant for at least 5 months.

Photoperiod should be from 8–10 hours with a temperature close to or at freezing so that dormancy will not be broken prematurely, resulting in subsequent weak vegetative growth. The other species in the temperate group will survive the winter temperatures listed under the section on temperature but they will also thrive the year around at the temperatures given for the summer season. One advantage of lowering the temperature for these species during the winter is that the temperature change promotes uniform flowering in the spring.

Water & Humidity

All species require high humidity and a wet medium during the growing season. The medium should be drier during dormancy.

Light

Temperate *Drosera* can be exposed to direct or filtered sunlight. Under artificial light start with 1,000 foot candles for a 14–16 hour photoperiod during the growing season and 800 foot candles for an 8–10 hour photoperiod during the dormant season. Species that form winter buds do not need any light during dormancy.

Pests

Aphids, mites, mealy bugs, and *Botrytis.* See Chapter 8 for control measures.

Feeding

See Chapter 7 for feeding directions.

Miscellaneous

D. linearis thrives best if summer temperatures do not exceed 80°F (27°C) with winter temperatures close to or about at freezing temperatures. *D. linearis* does not tolerate competition from other plants. *D. peltata, D. auriculata, D. ramellosa,* and *D. cistiflora* grow during the cool, moist, fall and winter and are dormant the rest of the year. The easier species to grow in this group include *D. aliciae, D. binata* var. *binata, D. binata* var. *dichotoma, D. binata* var. *multifilda, D. burmannii, D. capensis, D. capillaris, D. hamiltonii, D. montana, D.* × *Nagamoto,* and *D. spathulata.*

PROPAGATION

Sexual Reproduction

Some temperate *Drosera* species will self-pollinate and produce viable seed while others will not. Some species such as the *D. binata* complex must be pollinated with pollen of plants from another clone. Some species have never flowered under culture while others have flowered profusely but never set seed. As far as is known none of the *Drosera* hybrids will produce viable seed as the *Sarracenia* hybrids do. Those plants that are self-fertile to our knowledge are identified by an asterisk following their name on pages 92–93. The seeds from plants that form winter buds must be stratified. Experience has shown that stratification is not detrimental to seed from species that do not form winter buds, such as *D. spathulata* and, in fact, results in a more uniform germination rate. Sow seed on the soil surface followed by a sprinkling of fungicide. Keep the humidity high, place seed in bright light and keep them within a temperate range of 70–85°F (21–29°C). Germination is quite variable for different species. Through experience we have learned that some seeds which are supposed to germinate in a few weeks will, at times, take a year or more. We keep all sown seed for at least 2 years before giving up and discarding them.

Asexual Reproduction

The best medium for propagation of most species is live sphagnum followed by nonliving sphagnum moss.

1. Leaf cuttings: To our knowledge all of the temperate species except *D. spathulata, D. aliciae, D. regia, D. arcturi,* and *D. whittakeri* can be propagated by leaf cuttings. Remove the whole leaf, being careful to include the leaf petiole. Place the cutting on damp soil, keep humidity high, and in strong light. Maintain leaves at 70–80°F (21–27°C). An easy way to maintain the leaf cuttings is to put the medium, preferably sphagnum moss, and leaves in a plastic bag. Insert a rod into the soil in the bag then blow up the bag and fasten the top of the bag to the top of the rod. The plastic bag acts as a mini-greenhouse requiring virtually no attention. The rod will support the bag and prevent the sides from falling on the leaf cuttings. We have found that leaves of the *D. binata* complex, *D. capensis*, *D. intermedia*, *D. capillaris*, *D. rotundifolia*, and *D. × Nagamoto* will root when floated in water. This is not a complete list as we have not tried leaves from all temperate species.

2. Root cuttings: Gently probe the medium around the plant until a root is located. Roots can be removed from a plant without uprooting the entire plant. Then remove the medium around it. Cut off about half the length of the root. About half of each root can be removed from a plant without any detrimental effect. If the plant has been growing in a relatively small pot for a year or so, the roots will often be found growing around the edge and bottom. In this situation allow the medium to dry out a little and then invert the pot holding the plant and tap the edge of the pot sharply. The plant with a ball of medium should fall out of the pot. Locate the thickest roots and cut them off. Cut the roots into 1 in. (2.5 cm) pieces, lay them on damp sphagnum moss, keep the humidity high, maintain in strong light at a temperature range of 70–85°F (21–29°C).

Species which are known to be amenable to this technique are *D. binata* var. *binata*, *D. binata* var. *dichotoma*, *D. capensis*, *D. hamiltonii*, *D. spathulata*, and *D. regia*.

Tropical *Drosera*

NATURAL HABITAT

This group of *Drosera* grow in tropical areas of the world. Their habitat is quite diverse, some growing in a wet, humid environment the year around while some live in a Mediterranean-type climate which has a wet season and a dry season.

DESCRIPTION OF PLANT

The growth habit of plants in this group varies from rosettes which tend to be prostrate to erect plants. Leaf shape varies from round to almost linear. Flowers are shades of red and white. A few of the species produce tubers.

SPECIES OF THE TROPICAL TYPE OF THE GENUS *DROSERA*

We have listed only those species for which cultural information is presently available. Thus, our list does not pretend to be complete. Some species are also listed with the temperate *Drosera* because they will also grow under temperate environmental conditions, except they will not survive a frost, and grow much better at higher temperatures.

D. adelae
D. affinis
D. banskii
D. burkeana
D. burmannii—an annual
D. indica—an annual
D. madagascariensis
D. peltata
D. petiolaris
D. pilosa
D. prolifera
D. schizandra
D. spathulata

DESCRIPTION OF COMMERCIALLY AVAILABLE SPECIES

D. adelae Erect with narrow lanceolate leaves, 4–10 in. (10–25 cm) long, crowded on a short stem. Scapes 1–3 with numerous red flowers on each. (Photo 4-13)

D. burkeana A rosette with oval leaves. The petiole is narrow, up to 0.8 in. (2 cm) long, broadening abruptly into the blade which is about 0.4 in. (1 cm) long. Two to 12 white or pink flowers are borne on each scape.

D. burmannii A basal rosette with reddish leaves having unusually long tentacles. The circular blade is about 0.47 in. (12 mm) long and 0.43 in. wide narrowing to a short flat petiole. There are 1–5 scapes per plant with 3–14 white flowers on each.

D. peltata Described in Temperate Sundew section.

D. prolifera A basal rosette that is semi-erect. Petiole is narrow, 2 in. (5 cm) long attached to a kidney-shaped blade 0.6 in. (1.5 cm) long and 0.8 in. (2 cm) wide. The scapes (1–3) bear 2–6 pink to red flowers and tend to trail on the soil surface. There is a vegetive bud at the end of the scape that will develop into a plant.

D. schizandra Large leaves form a rosette from which a short scape bearing 2–6 white flowers emerges. The leaf petiole is very short while the blade can be up to 5 in. (13 cm) long and 2.5 in. (6 cm) wide with or without a notch on the end or apex of the blade.

D. spathulata Leaves whose outline varies from spoon-shape to wedge-shape form a basal rosette. This species is widespread geographically and the shape of the leaf varies in different areas resulting in plants that appear to be distinct species. The group is referred to as the Spathulata Complex. Petioles are up to 1 in. (2.5 cm) long, gradually widening to the blade that can be up to 0.5 in. (1.3 cm) long. One to 15 white or pink flowers are borne on each scape which can number from 1 to 3.

CULTURAL INFORMATION

Planting Media
Sphagnum peat moss, sphagnum moss (living or dead), one part sphagnum peat moss to one part perlite, or one part sand and various mixtures of sphagnum moss and sphagnum peat moss.

Temperatures
Summer: 70–95°F (21–35°C). Winter: 60–70°F (16–21°C). Tropical *Drosera* can be grown year around at the summer temperatures given above, but for most, a lower winter temperature insures more uniform flowering in the spring.

Dormancy
D. peltata dies back during the summer leaving a viable tuber in the soil and resumes active growth during the winter. The other tropical *Drosera*, except the annuals, usually grow very little, if any, during the winter season.

D. burmannii and *D. indica* are annuals. To maintain a supply of plants, their seed must be collected and sown each year. Allowing the seed to fall to the surface of the soil in the pot and regrow in the same soil is satisfactory for a few years, but the soil should be changed every 3 years or sooner if growth is not as vigorous as before and/or if plant pests appear.

Allowing the seed to drop and germinate at the base of the plant will result in a very thick crop of young plants which must be thinned to avoid an environment conducive to fungal infections. It is usually efficacious to collect the seed and sow the amount required for your needs and save the rest.

D. petiolaris should have reduced water during the summer. (Photo 4-14) The soil should be much drier during the summer than winter, but not thoroughly dry. During the winter, its normal growth period, the temperature should be in the summer range and the soil should be wet. The other tropical *Drosera* species usually cease to form new leaves during the winter.

Water & Humidity

All species require high humidity and wet medium during the growing season. The medium should be drier when they are not actively growing.

Light

All of the tropical *Drosera* grow in bright light in their native habitat save for *D. adelae, D. prolifera* and *D. schizandra* which grow in shaded areas. We have grown *D. prolifera* and *D. adelae* in very bright light without any apparent harm, but the leaves are smaller than when grown in subdued light. We have found that *D. schizandra* grows best in weaker light. When under artificial light use 1000 foot candles with all species except for *D. schizandra* which should be at about 750 foot candles. Photoperiod: Growing season about 14 hours, dormant season about 11 hours.

Pests

The only pests we have had are aphids and fungus. See Chapter 8 for treatment.

Feeding

See Chapter 7 for feeding instructions.

Miscellaneous

D. schizandra grows best in living sphagnum moss and with a relatively uniform temperature. It apparently requires extremely high humidity, as it does not grow well in the greenhouse in which we grow our *Nepenthes*. We provide a higher humidity for *D. schizandra* plants by planting them in living sphagnum moss and placing them in sealed plastic bags which are then kept in the *Nepenthes* greenhouse. The result is much better growth. The easier species to grow in this group include *D. adelae, D. burmannii, D. prolifera,* and *D. spathulata.*

PROPAGATION

Sexual Reproduction

To our knowledge *D. burmannii, D. indica, D. burkeana, D. affinis, D. spathulata, D. madagascariensis, D. pilosa, D. peltata,* and *D. banksii* will flower, self-pollinate, and produce viable seed under cultivation. Although our *D. adelae* and *D. prolifera* flower profusely, they have never set seed. Cross-pollination efforts have not been successful. *D. petiolaris* and *D. schizandra* flower occasionally but neither one has produced seed. Sow seed on the surface of the planting medium, maintain a high humidity and bright light with a temperature range of 70–95°F (21–35°C).

Asexual Reproduction

1. Leaf cuttings: All the species except *D. burmannii, D. indica,* and *D. spathulata* will produce new plants from leaf cuttings. Remove the entire leaf including the petiole, place it on damp planting medium, preferably living sphagnum moss, keep the humidity high, the light bright and at a temperature from 70–85°F (21–29°C). Once new plants are fully rooted they can be transplanted.

2. Stolons: *D. prolifera* produces scapes that sometimes bear flowers, while at other times produce plants. To further complicate matters, the same scapes sometimes produce both flowers and plantlets. (Fig. 4-6) When the plantlets produce a root system they can be severed from the mother plant and transplanted. (Photo 4-15) We have found it is best to sever the plantlet from the mother plant about 1 month in advance of transplanting it. The latter technique helps insure against losing the plantlet when transplanting.

3. Root cuttings: *D. adelae, D. prolifera, D. schizandra,* and *D. spathulata* will reproduce from root cuttings. Select fleshy (thicker) roots, cut them into 1–2 in. (2.5–5 cm) lengths and follow the procedure given for leaf cuttings. This procedure may work with other species in this group also. (Fig. 4-7)

4. Decapitation: The aerial part of the plant is cut away from the root system just below the crown. The removed part is treated as a cutting would be and will develop roots in 1–2 months. The roots left in the medium will produce new plants. All species that can be propagated by root cuttings are amenable to this procedure.

5. Stem cuttings: *D. adelae, D. affinis,* and *D. pilosa* can be propagated by stem cuttings. Remove 2–3 in. (5–8 cm) from the top of the plant and place the removed section in sphagnum moss. Keep the cutting under the same conditions as prescribed for leaf cuttings. The remaining portion of the mother plant will continue to grow.

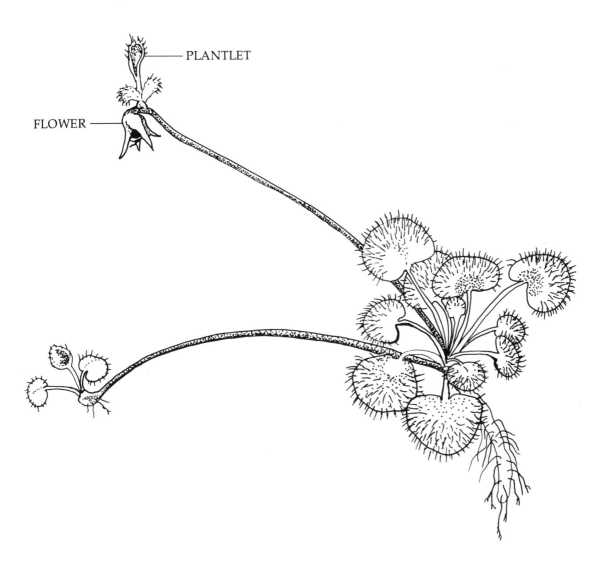

Fig. 4-6 *Drosera prolifera* plant. Leaves form a rosette. Flower scapes sometimes bear flowers or plantlets or both.

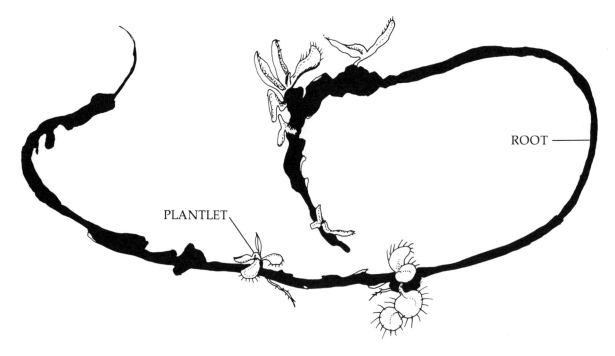

Fig. 4-7 Plantlets of *Drosera adale* produced by means of root cutting.

Drosophyllum

HISTORY

Drosophyllum's ability to capture insects was well known for hundreds of years before any thought was given to its possible carnivorous nature. Darwin investigated *Drosophyllum* for carnivory, but it was A. Quintanilha of Portugal who did the critical study of *Drosophyllum*, verifying that it secreted a digestive enzyme that effected digestion without bacterial assistance. The first part of the name *Drosophyllum* is derived from the Greek *drosos*, meaning dew, and *phyllum* is from the Greek *phylon* for race or tribe.

NATURAL HABITAT

Drosophyllum lusitanicum is the only species in the monotypic genus, *Drosophyllum* of the Droseraceae. It grows in a relatively dry environment in rocky, sandy soil. All the wild plants are found in Spain, Portugal and Morocco. In its native habitat it is subjected yearly to a wet and a dry season. During the summer, which is the dry season, the plants obtain moisture from the dew and/or fog which is prevalent where they grow.

DESCRIPTION OF PLANT

D. lusitanicum is an erect, woody shrub that can grow to be 4.5 ft. (1.4 m) high with a fibrous root system. The long, narrow, tapering, linear leaves are light green and reach lengths of 10 in. (25 cm). Each leaf has a groove along its length on the upper surface. The leaves do not abscise when they die, but rather droop down to the ground forming a "grass skirt" around the base of the stem. Each leaf is clothed with 2 types of glands: the stalked tentacle glands which produce the mucilage for trapping prey and the sessile glands which secrete digestive enzymes upon stimulation and also absorb the products of digestion. Tentacles are most abundant on the under surface and along the edges of the leaves while sessile glands occur on all leaf surfaces. The tentacles are similar to those found on *Byblis* leaves, in that they do not move when capturing prey. Tentacles develop a red coloration when exposed to strong light. While the plant is a perennial in nature, when grown under conditions of constant high soil moisture it grows as a biennial. (Fig. 4-8)

Flowers
The bright yellow flowers which can be 1.5 in. (4 cm) in diameter are borne in panicles. In its native habitat flowering occurs during April and May. Under greenhouse conditions the plants flower during the summer or fall. The flowers, having 5 sepals and 5 petals, open during the day and close at night. The plants are self-fertile and will produce viable seed without any outside pollinating agent. (Photo 4-16)

TRAPPING

Luring is accomplished by the red coloration of the tentacles and the honey-like odor of the mucilage. After landing on the leaf, prey is captured when, because of its struggle to free itself, it becomes mired in the mucilage of the tentacles. The tentacles are not active in prey capture. The sessile glands secrete digestive enzymes and then absorb the products of digestion. (Photo 4-17)

SPECIES OF THE GENUS *DROSOPHYLLUM*

D. lusitanicum

CULTURAL INFORMATION

Planting Media
Sphagnum moss (living and nonliving), sphagnum peat moss, 1 part sphagnum peat moss to 1 part perlite or 1 part sand, 1 part sphagnum peat moss to 3 parts sand or 3 parts perlite. Some growers add powdered limestone or dolomite at a rate of 1 teaspoon (5 ml) per quart (liter) of medium.

Temperatures
Plants will survive a light frost and temperatures up to 100°F (38°C). They grow best at lower temperatures of 40–75°F (4.5–24°C).

Dormancy
In their native habitat *Drosophyllum* plants usually cease to grow during the hot, dry summers. Consequently, when grown in culture the planting medium must be drier during the dormant period.

Water & Humidity
The key to growing this plant as a perennial is to use a well-drained medium which is kept slightly moist. If the medium is constantly wet, the plant will grow as a biennial. When growing plants from seed, medium is kept wet until the seeds germinate and thereafter on the dry side until the seedlings are 4–6 in. (10–15 cm) high.

Light
Drosophyllum plants grow best in strong light and will thrive in full sunlight. If they do not receive enough light they develop elongated internodes, weakening the stem and causing it to fall and grow along the surface of the medium. When this happens the

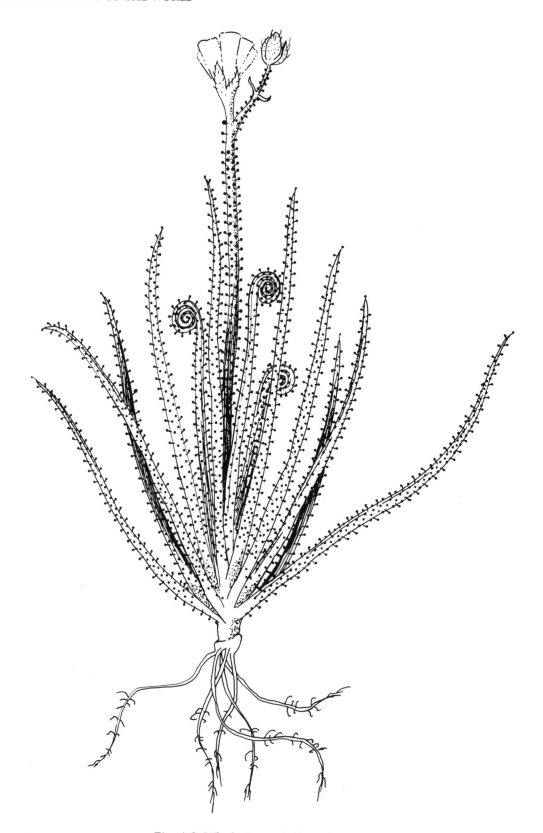

Fig. 4-8 Whole *Drosophyllum* plant.

suppressed buds in the leaf axils will start to grow, producing secondary stems along the primary stem resulting in an unusually shaped plant.

With strong light *Drosophyllum* plants will grow into compact shrub-like structures with very short internodes and red colored tentacles. (Photo 4-18)

If using artificial light provide the plants with at least 1500 foot candles. Photoperiod: summer about 14 hours, winter 10 hours.

Pests

The known pests are mealy bugs, aphids, and fungus. See Chapter 8 for treatment.

Feeding

See Chapter 7 for feeding directions.

Miscellaneous

Once *Drosophyllum* plants have reached heights of 4–6 in. (10–15 cm) they can be watered freely or kept in standing water and will grow well. Under these conditions they will grow as biennials and will produce viable seed the second year. The seed assures a steady supply of plants. A few precocious plants will flower the first year but usually do not produce viable seed. First-year flowers should be removed so that the plants can direct their energy to vegetative growth.

Plants can be grown as perennials by adhering to the following procedure. Use a planting medium of 1 part sphagnum peat moss to 3 parts sand or perlite. Keep the medium wet until the seed germinates. Following establishment maintain the plants in an almost dry medium. The plants will grow continuously for several years in this almost dry environment. We have one plant that has been growing for 8 years. The key for maintaining *Drosophyllum* plants as perennials is to use a well-drained medium and to keep it damp but not wet.

Plants grow much larger when a single plant is grown per pot. The plants produce a chemical that inhibits the growth of nearby plants of the same species.

PROPAGATION

Sexual Reproduction

Flowers self-pollinate to produce viable seed. When the seeds are mature they will be visible in the translucent, cone-shaped seed pod. The seed is enclosed in a hard coat which inhibits germination. If the seeds are not treated, germination can take up to 4 years. To encourage germination scratch the seed coat. When the seed coat is scratched, germination usually takes place within a month.

We have discovered that cutting a very thin slice from the widest end of the seed greatly speeds germination. When done correctly a white color should be visible inside the seed coat. (Fig. 4-9)

There are reports that soaking the seed for about 10 minutes in a strong solution of detergent will hasten germination. Seeds will germinate at temperatures as low as 40°F (4°C), but they take longer at this low temperature, so we recommend maintaining the temperature at 70°F (21°C). Since *Drosophyllum* plants grow most actively during cool, wet winters, the seed should be planted in late summer or early fall so that the plants will be well developed before the summer.

Drosophyllum plants inhibit each other's growth. Therefore, plant only one plant per pot, if large plants are desired. To insure that you will end up with one plant per pot, plant 2–3 seeds in each. Plant seeds about 0.25 in. (0.6 cm) below the medium surface. If the intention is to transplant the extra seedlings, the seed should be planted as far apart as possible. After germination the largest and strongest seedling is left in the pot. These plants are almost impossible to transplant successfully except in the seedling stage. It is important when transplanting the seedlings to move them with as large a ball of medium as possible. Medium should be kept quite damp or wet until the seeds germinate and thereafter kept on the dry side to prevent both damp-off, (that is, a fungus infection,) and a biennial growth pattern. Spraying the medium and seeds with a fungicide will help control damp-off. After the plants reach a height of 4–6 in. (10–15 cm) the danger of damping off is minimal.

Asexual Reproduction
None reported to date.

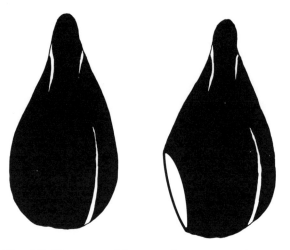

Fig. 4-9 How a seed is cut to hasten germination.

Byblis

HISTORY

The genus was formerly classified as a member of the families Lentibulariaceae and Droseraceae but now is classified in Byblidaceae. *Byblis gigantea* was first discovered by James Drummond. The carnivorous nature of *Byblis* was suggested by Ms. A. Nikon Bruce during the early 1900s. *Byblis gigantea* and *B. liniflora* are the sole species in this genus and are indigenous to Australia and New Guinea. The name *Byblis* is derived from the Greek word "byblis" which refers to a nymph who loved her brother.

NATURAL HABITAT

Byblis gigantea is a perennial that grows in southwestern Australia in sandy soils in areas marked by hot, dry summers and cool, wet winters. In areas where the soil dries out, the plants die back to their rootstock during the dry season with new growth produced after the arrival of rain. In places where the soil is moist all year, the plant does not die back but rather is evergreen.

Byblis liniflora grows in northern Australia and New Guinea usually in sandy soils. Much of the area in which it grows is dominated by monsoonal weather, with a wet season during the hot summer (December-April) and a dry season during the winter in which temperatures range from 60–104°F (16–40°C). In areas where the soil is wet part of the year and then dries out, *B. liniflora* grows as an annual, but in permanently moist situations it is a perennial.

DESCRIPTION OF PLANTS

Byblis gigantea is an erect, shrub-like plant reaching heights of 28 in. (71 cm) having yellow to pale yellow-green leaves and grows from a rhizome. The plant usually has one main, aboveground stem, but older plants may develop more than one main stem and occasionally side branches. The long linear leaves taper to a point at the apex and can reach lengths of 12 in. (30 cm). In cross-section the base of the leaf is triangular with rounded edges but becomes almost circular in cross-section at the tip. Two kinds of glands clothe all the plant's aboveground surfaces. Tentacles are the stalked glands which produce the shiny, sticky mucilage that traps the prey. The sessile glands which produce enzymes to digest the prey are stalkless. (Photo 4-19)

Byblis liniflora is very similar to *B. gigantea* in structure except it is more refined and delicate. Its growth pattern is vertical until it reaches 6–12 in. (15–30 cm) at which height it tends to topple over and grow along the surface of the soil or on other plants. (Fig. 4-10) The plant may reach lengths of 35 in. (89 cm) in this growth habit. The individual leaves may attain lengths of 4 in. (10 cm). The tentacles and sessile glands, again, are the same as in *B. gigantea* but smaller and shorter.

Flowers

Flowers can reach diameters of 2 in. (5 cm) in *Byblis gigantea* and have petal color described as purplish red, lilac, magenta or reddish purple. The flowers are borne singly on scapes that arise from the leaf axils. The flowers open about midday and close in late afternoon; this process is repeated for several days. Flowers have 5 petals, 5 sepals and 5 stamens of unequal length that curve toward the pistil. (Photo 4-20) Flowering occurs in September, through December.

Floral structure is basically the same in *B. liniflora* as in *B. gigantea,* but the flowers are smaller and petal color is pale blue and occasionally white. (Fig. 4-11) Plants which grow as perennials tend to bloom irregularly, whereas those that grow in habitats where soil is moist part of the year and dries out the other part, bloom mainly in the wet season, which in their native Australia is from December to April.

TRAPPING

Prey is lured by the glistening droplets of mucilage on the tip of the tentacles. Insects are captured by becoming mired in the thick sticky mucilage on the leaf surface, where digestion and absorption also take place. The tentacles of *Byblis* do not move. As is the case in some other carnivorous plants, some insect species are, or at least appear to be, immune to these plants' digestive and trapping mechanisms and share in the plants' booty. One of these is the wingless caspid which is able to walk over the mucilage with impunity. This capability is observed but not understood.

SPECIES OF THE GENUS *BYBLIS*

B. gigantea
B. liniflora

CULTURAL REQUIREMENTS

Planting Media

Sphagnum peat moss, sphagnum moss (living or dead), 1 part sphagnum peat moss to 1 part perlite or sand (coarse), or 1 part sphagnum peat moss to 2 parts perlite or sand (coarse). The latter mixture is the preferred medium. *B. liniflora* will grow as a perennial if the planting medium is maintained in a moist condition but not when wet or waterlogged.

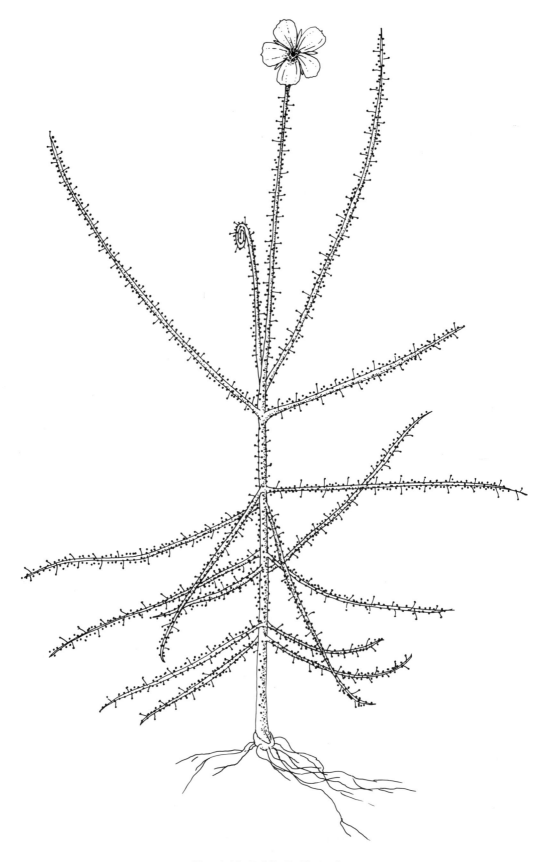

Fig. 4-10 *Byblis liniflora* plant.

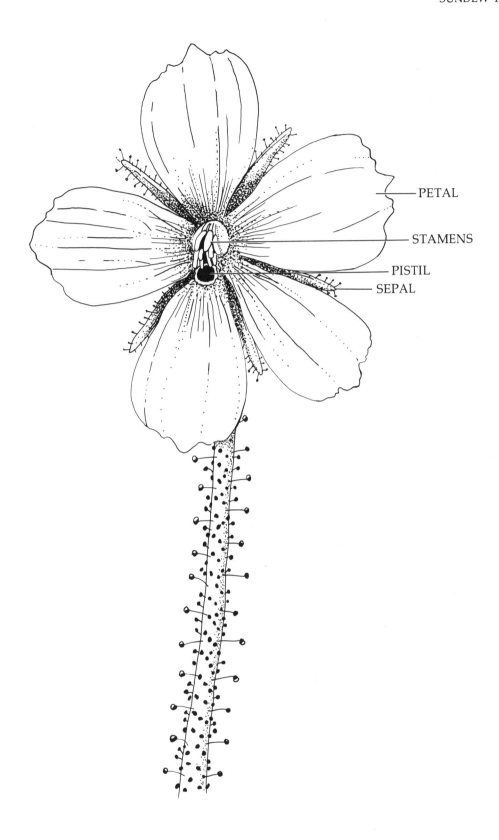

Fig. 4-11 *Byblis liniflora* flower.

Temperatures

B. liniflora: 65–90°F (18–32°C). *B. gigantea:* 40–80°F (4–27°C). Grows best at a temperature of at least 70°F (21°C), but less than 80°F (27°C).

Dormancy

B. liniflora is an annual in its native habitat where soils dry out part of the year. In situations of permanently wet soils it is a perennial. *B. liniflora* will grow as a perennial under culture if grown in a sandy, well-drained planting medium which is kept moist but not soggy.

B. gigantea dies back to its rootstock or base during the dry, hot Australian summer and grows during the cool, wet winter in areas where the soil dries out. In regions where the soil is moist, the plant is evergreen and does not die back to the rootstock.

Under cultivation it will not go dormant if kept moist, but the rate of new growth decreases during the winter. We maintain *B. gigantea* at 40°F (4°C) during the winter. With the arrival of spring and warmer temperatures, the rate of new growth increases, accompanied by profuse flowering until late fall or early winter when growth slows or ceases. The plants remain evergreen during the winter. The second, and subsequent springs, the plants will do one of two things. On the one hand, the new growth starts at the base at which time the top of the plant dies back to the base. Alternatively, the plant puts forth new growth from the top of last year's stem. When top growth occurs the plant must be physically supported for the season with a stake.

Water & Humidity

High humidity and moist soils are needed for *B. liniflora* at all times and for *B. gigantea* during the growing season. Keep the planting medium much drier during the dormant season.

Light

Although *B. liniflora* grows near the equator, it is shaded by other plants. Indirect or shaded sunlight is suitable and if using artificial lighting, start with 1200 foot candles for a 14 hour photoperiod for *B. liniflora.*

Some direct sunlight is good for *B. gigantea* during the season of active growth. If using artificial light, start with 1200 foot candles for a photoperiod of 14–16 hours during the active growing season and 800 foot candles with a photoperiod of about 9 hours during the resting period.

Pests

Aphids and fungus. See Chapter 8 for control.

Feeding

See Chapter 7 for feeding directions.

Miscellaneous

As *B. gigantea* plants grow older they tend to become straggly and rather unsightly. To remedy, cut off the top of the stem leaving 1–2 in. (2.5–5 cm) above the base, just before the season of active growth begins. Use the top for a cutting as outlined in the section on asexual propagation. You will not only gain another plant, but the new growth that develops from the stump left in the pot will produce a compact plant.

B. liniflora usually is not able to support itself vertically, after reaching a height of about 5 in. (13 cm). When a plant attains this height it usually falls to the soil or on other plants. When this happens cut off the upper part of plant and root as a cutting. The original plant will then produce side shoots.

PROPAGATION

Sexual Reproduction

To insure fertilization of the flowers in both *Byblis* species the stamen, which is yellow, must be vibrated gently to induce it to give up its pollen. A toothpick or similar object is a useful device to assist in releasing the pollen. Follow this procedure every afternoon for a few days. The flower will close as darkness falls and reopen the next day. The yellow pollen is easily seen on the surface of the stigma and petals when it is released.

As the seeds develop, the ovary of the flower will swell. In 4–6 weeks the seed pod of *B. liniflora* will become translucent and dehisce (split) to release the seed. *B. gigantea* seed pods do not dehisce upon maturity, but rather dry up retaining their seed.

B. liniflora seed must be stored at least 2 months before planting. They can be dried for a few days at room temperature, placed in a vial or small plastic bag and stored under refrigeration for sowing at a later date.

B. gigantea seeds are much more difficult to germinate than seeds of *B. liniflora*. In their native habitat, fire is apparently necessary to meet their dormancy requirement. Listed below are several methods which have been used successfully for treating seeds to promote germination.

1. Place the seed, which has been soaked for a day in water, on damp planting medium. Scorch both the seeds and the soil surface with a flame from a Bunsen burner or butane torch until steam (condensed water vapor) is visible.

2. Crumple a paper towel or a couple sheets of writing paper and place them on the surface of the damp planting medium on which seeds soaked in water for a day have been sprinkled. Ignite the paper. After burning the paper, carefully and thoroughly water the surface of the planting medium.

3. Pour boiling water over the seeds which have been sprinkled on the surface of the planting medium. Repeat at least 4 times in succession to be certain that the seed and soil have been heated sufficiently.

4. Soak a piece of filter paper or paper towel in a solution of 1 part of Gibberellin (75% Potassium Gibberellate salt) to 1000 parts of distilled water. Sprinkle the seed on the filter paper. The next day remove the seed from the paper and spread on the surface of the planting medium. Some growers prefer to leave the seed on the filter paper until it germinates, at which time the seedlings are transplanted to the planting medium. If the later procedure is followed, the filter paper must be kept damp using plain water.

After treating *B. gigantea* seed, follow the same procedure given for germinating *B. liniflora* seed. The seedlings of both species are very subject to damping off (fungus disease). To control the fungus, dust the seed with a fungicide. Keep humidity high, light bright and temperatures 70–90°F (21–32°C). Germination usually takes place within 2 months.

Byblis plants do not as a rule transplant easily, so if they must be transplanted do so while the plants are young seedlings. When transplanting, remove a ball of soil with the roots.

Asexual Reproduction

B. gigantea

1. Root cuttings: Carefully remove the soil on one side of the plant to locate a thick root. Remove about ⅔ of its length and recover the remaining root with medium. Cut the root section into 1 in. (2.5 cm) lengths. Place the pieces horizontally on the surface of sphagnum moss, preferably living. Keep the humidity high, light bright and the temperature 70–80°F (21–27°C). Several plantlets will usually develop along the length of each section within 6 weeks. After the plantlets have developed their own root system they can be severed from each other. This practice may be repeated yearly. In doing so, be sure to alternate sides of the plant for root removal.

2. Stem cuttings: If the plants are given a dormant period the top 6 in. (15 cm) of the stem is cut off before the stem dies back to the rootstock. If the plants are not given a dormant period, a cutting of similar length is taken just before active growth begins. Place the cutting in sphagnum moss following the same directions as given for *B. liniflora* stem cuttings. The cutting will root in about 3 months. The remainder of the original plant will produce a new stem.

   B. liniflora

1. Stem cutting: *B. liniflora* will grow erect until it reaches 4–10 in. (10–25 cm), when it typically becomes top-heavy and topples to the ground, after which the terminal end of the plant will start to grow vertically again. A stem cutting about 2 in. (5 cm) long can be taken from the top of the plant before it tumbles over. The cutting, which should include the growing tip, is inserted in planting medium so that about ½ of the stem is below soil level. Keep the humidity high, light strong and at temperatures 70–85°F (21–29°C).

   When rooted, the plant will start growing again. This procedure provides both a new plant and a bushier mother plant due to increased side branching.

2. Leaf cuttings: Leaves removed from *B. liniflora* plants are placed on damp planting medium. Under conditions of high humidity and bright light they will produce plantlets.

5

Pinguicula—Butterworts

Pinguicula _____

HISTORY

Leaves of these plants feel greasy, hence the name *Pinguicula* which is derived from Latin, meaning fat and small. W. Marshall observed that insects became mired on the leaves of these plants. Being aware of Darwin's studies of the carnivorous nature of *Drosera*, Marshall communicated his observations to Darwin. Darwin subsequently investigated the matter and proved to his satisfaction that plants in the genus *Pinguicula* are indeed carnivorous plants. The common name for this genus is Butterwort.

NATURAL HABITAT

Pinguicula are distributed worldwide. They grow in Arctic, temperate, and tropical areas of the world in damp or wet, acid or alkaline, soil in a humid environment.

DESCRIPTION OF PLANT

Pinguicula is a herbaceous perennial. The plant consists of a flattened rosette of prostrate leaves and a fibrous root system. Each species has a characteristic leaf shape which is a variation of a basic elongated oval terminating in a blunt point. The edges of the leaves exhibit varying degrees of rolling in and are green to yellow-green to reddish in color. (Fig. 5-1) Most *Pinguicula* are homophyllous, meaning the leaves have the same shape and size throughout the entire growing season. The heterophyllous *Pinguicula* produce leaves after flowering that differ from leaves produced before flowering in size and shape. These are listed in Chart 1. Tentacles and sessile glands cover the leaf surfaces.

Flowers
Flowers are borne singly on scapes in the spring, with some of the tropical species

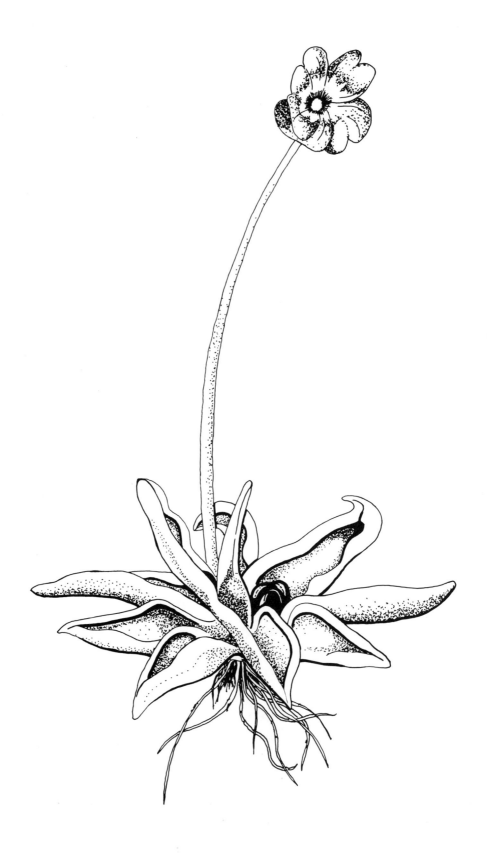

Fig. 5-1 *Pinguicula* plant.

flowering a second time later in the growing season. Plants, depending on the species, may have one or more flower scapes which are usually covered with tentacles.

Flower color ranges from shades of yellow, white, blue, and violet to purple. The zygomorphic flowers are sympetalous with the bottom 3 petals forming the lower lip of the flower and the top 2 petals forming the upper lip. The closed, cylindrical end of the corolla narrows to almost a point forming the spur. On the lower lip of the floor of the entrance to the flower is a raised, pubescent structure called the palate, whose degree of exsertion depends upon the species. (Photo 5-1) The flower has 2 curved stamens lying flat on the corolla with the 2 anthers almost touching each other and covered by part of the pistil. (Fig. 5-2)

TRAPPING

The fungal odor of *Pinguicula* is believed to be a prey attractant. Insects are trapped when they light or crawl on the surface of the leaves which are coated with a sticky mucilage. Only the smallest insects can be captured. Usually the struggling of insects attempting to escape results in their being hopelessly entrapped, as well as being suffocated, by the mucilage. The prey is digested and the digestion products absorbed for use by the plant. *Pinguicula* leaves show little motion during prey capture, as compared to the Sundews. What little motion occurs does not aid in prey capture. The margins of the *Pinguicula* leaves tend to curl up during and after prey capture to form a shallow bowl which contains the digestive fluids and prevents loss of prey. (Photo 5-2) Often the leaves tend to become distended beneath the spot where larger insects have been trapped.

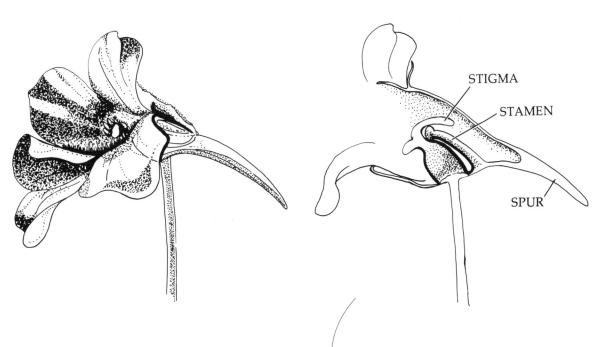

Fig. 5-2 Flower of *Pinguicula*. Longitudinal section reveals the relationship of stigma and stamen.

SPECIES OF THE GENUS *PINGUICULA*

The genus *Pinguicula* can be divided into 2 groups according to their seasonal growth pattern: plants that form winter buds, or temperate climate species; and plants that do not usually form winter buds, tropical or subtropical species. Chart 1.

Chart 1

Temperate *Pinguicula*
(Form winter buds)

P. algida A
P. alpina A,B
P. balcanica A,B,C
P. corsica A
P. grandiflora A,B
P. leptoceras A,B
P. longifolia B,C
P. macroceras A,B
P. nevadensis A
P. ramosa A
P. vallisneriifolia B,C
P. variegata A
P. villosa A
P. vulgaris A,B

KEY
A=acid soil
B=basic soil
C=heterophyllous

Tropical & Subtropical *Pinguicula*

P. acuminata C
P. agnata
P. albida
P. antarctica
P. benedicta
P. caerulea A
P. calyptrata
P. chilensis
P. cladophila
P. colimensis C
P. crenatiloba
P. crystallina
P. cyclosecta C
P. elongata C
P. esseriana
P. ehlersae
P. filifolia
P. gypsicola B,C
P. heterophylla C
P. hirtiflora A
P. imitatrix C
P. involuta
P. ionantha A
P. jackii
P. kondoi C
P. lignicola
P. lilacina
P. lusitanica
P. lutea A
P. macrophylla B,C
P. moranensis B,A,C
P. oblongiloba B,A,C
P. parvifolia C
P. planifolia A
P. primuliflora A
P. pumila A
P. zecheri

DESCRIPTION OF COMMERCIALLY AVAILABLE SPECIES

P. caerulea The yellow-green leaves resemble an elongated oval. They attain lengths of up to 2.4 in. (6 cm). Flower color ranges from violet to blue-violet with dark veins. (Photo 5-3)

P. colimensis Summer leaves are egg-shaped. The winter leaves are similar in outline except thicker. Flower color is pinkish purple. The diameter of the rosette can reach 3 in. (8 cm).

P. gypsicola The distinctively shaped, light green summer leaves are subulate terminating in a rounded point and are about 2.5 in. (6.4 cm) long. In the fall small leaves are produced, forming the winter rosette of spathulate-shaped leaves. Flower color is purple.

P. ionantha The green leaves are oblong with rounded tips and may be up to 3.2 in. (8 cm) long. Flower color ranges from white to violet. *P. ionantha* is distinguished from *P. primuliflora* by their floral characteristics. The petals of the former are longer than broad while the petals of *P. primuliflora* are as broad or broader than long and have a ring of white just above the corolla tube.

P. longifolia The yellow-green leaves are elongated elliptical, taper to the wide petiole and have a wavy margin. Flower color varies from purple to lavender with white areas. (Photo 5-4)

P. moranensis (Former name *P. caudata*) Summer leaves are long egg-shaped. The diameter of the rosette can reach 7 in. (18 cm). Winter leaves are spathula-shaped and succulent. The large flowers range in color from white to pink to purple. (Photo 5-5)

P. planifolia The elliptical shaped leaves are up to 3.2 in. (8 cm) long. They are green to dark maroon in color which varies with the intensity of sunlight. Flower color ranges from blue-violet to purple to white. Petal shape is distinctive in that the petals are much longer than broad and deeply incised.

P. primuliflora The green elliptical leaves reach lengths of up to 3.5 in. (9 cm). Flowers are violet with a ring of white coloration just along the corolla tube, distinguishing it from the violet flowers of *P. ionantha*.

P. pumila The egg-shaped, light green leaves terminate in a point. They are about 0.4 in. (1 cm) long. Flowers are violet to white.

Temperate *Pinguicula*

CULTURAL INFORMATION

The temperate species can be divided into 3 groups, each with similar growth requirements. Chart 2.

Chart 2

Temperate *Pinguicula*

Group 1
  P. corsica
  P. grandiflora
  P. longifolia
  P. vulgaris
  Winter temperatures: 32–34°F (0–1°C)
  Summer temperatures: 46–68°F (8–20°C)
  Growing period: 4–6 months.
  Dormant period: 6–8 months.
Group 2
  P. longifolia ssp. *reichenbachiana*
  P. macroceras ssp. *nortensis*
  P. ramosa
  P. vallisneriifolia
  Winter temperatures: 34–39°F (1–4°C).

Group 2 (cont.)
Summer temperatures: 59–84°F (15–29°C).
Growing period: 7–9 months.
Dormant period: 3–5 months.
Group 3
P. algida
P. alpina
P. balcanica
P. leptoceras
P. macroceras
P. nevadensis
P. variegata
P. villosa
Winter temperatures: 26–34°F (-3–1°C).
Summer temperatures: 45–65°F (7–18°C).
Growing season: 3–4 months.
Dormant season: 8–9 months.

Planting Media

The temperate *Pinguicula* are divided into 3 groups, those that grow in acid soil, basic soil, or in either. Their soil preference is indicated on Chart 1.

Acid growing media: Sphagnum peat moss; sphagnum (living or dried); 1 part sphagnum peat moss to 1 part perlite to 1 part sand (silica); 1 part sphagnum peat moss to 1 part perlite or silica sand; 1 part chopped sphagnum to 1 part sphagnum peat moss.

Basic or alkaline growing media: Equal parts of sphagnum peat moss, perlite or vermiculite and ground dolomite or limestone (some growers prefer to use less limestone). Various recipes call for a minimum of 1 tablespoon (15 ml) per quart (liter), of growing medium up to ½ of the medium mixture; 1 part perlite to 1 part vermiculite; or 100 percent perlite.

Temperatures

The temperature range required by each group is given in Chart 2. Generally, during the growing season it is best to maintain the temperature around the middle of the range. Night-time temperatures should be several degrees lower than the day temperature. It is vital that a constant temperature be maintained during dormancy, as changing the temperature results in the death of winter buds. In warm parts of the world refrigeration is required during active growth for some of the temperate species of *Pinguicula*.

Dormancy

The greatest loss of plants in temperate *Pinguicula* occurs while they are in dormancy. To reduce and/or eliminate loss, winter buds should be sprayed or soaked (about 15 minutes) in a full strength solution of a fungicide such as Benlate. (Photo 5-6). The treated buds should then be loosely wrapped in damp living sphagnum moss and placed in sealed plastic bags for storage.

Group 2 plants can be stored in a refrigerator (not freezer), preferably near or on the bottom shelf where it is cooler. If the winter temperatures in your area are in the 34–39°F (1–4°C) range, plants can be stored outside. If the outside temperature varies very much from these values, other ways for maintaining low temperatures should be utilized.

Some of the species in the temperate group spend more time in dormancy than in active growth and require low temperatures during active growth. To provide dormancy for those *Pinguicula* species requiring freezing or near freezing temperatures (group 1 and 3) we use two methods.

The first method involves growing the plants in our cool greenhouse; the winter buds are planted in late February or early March. The plants will grow and flower before the heat of late spring and early summer. After flowering, the plants start going dormant. The progress of dormancy in both flowering and non-flowering plants can be ascertained by checking for development of the winter bud in the crown area. When the winter bud starts to form we remove the plants from the greenhouse benches and place them on the floor in the coolest part of the greenhouse until winter bud formation is complete.

Attempting to keep the plants growing after winter bud formation has started is to court disaster. Once the winter buds have formed treat them with a fungicide as outlined previously and place them in sealed plastic bags. We put the plastic bags in the meat storage tray of our refrigerator until the next growing season.

The second method of providing proper conditions for species requiring freezing temperatures during dormancy is simplified by our new refrigerator. It has a meat tray, the temperature of which can be adjusted to be at or below the freezing point by controlling the opening to a portal which connects the meat tray area to the freezer. Once the portal is adjusted for the correct temperature, the winter buds, which are in moss in a sealed plastic bag, are placed in a styrofoam box or a small thermos bottle and then kept in the meat tray. The reason for putting the buds in the plastic box or thermos bottle is to keep the temperature of the buds constant when the meat tray is opened and items are removed or warm ones added. The styrofoam box should not be sealed too tightly and the thermos too should not be completely tightened because the buds are alive and need oxygen for cellular respiration.

Water & Humidity

This group of plants is particularly sensitive to humidity which should be high, over 75%, for best growth. Medium should be wet during the growing season and much drier during dormancy.

Light

As a group, temperate *Pinguicula* grow best in indirect or shaded sunlight. In their native habitat they are usually shaded by taller growing plants. If using artificial illumination, start with about 900 foot candles and a 14–18 hour photoperiod during active growth. While dormant they do not need any light.

PROPAGATION

Sexual Reproduction

The flowers are designed to foster cross-pollination between plants. Thus, it is wise to grow 2 plants of each species. The features of the flower are shown in Fig 5-2. Pollen must be transferred from pistil to stigma a few days after the flowers open. The stigma is an elongated flap-like structure that covers the anthers, with its pollen receptive surface on the side away from the anthers. With care, the flap or stigma can be bent to the front, exposing the anthers which may be examined for pollen development. A small brush, or better yet a toothpick, is used to transfer the pollen. The flowers of some species are quite small so it is sometimes easier to tear open the corolla or to remove most of it in order to expose the stigma. The corolla is the tubelike part of the flower that is made up of the fused or joined petals. If pollination has been successful the ovary will start to swell in a week or two. The mature seed pods will split open to release the seed about 4 weeks after pollination.

Seed to be stored should be dried at room temperature for a few days and then placed in sealed vials or plastic bags and kept under refrigeration. The seeds of the temperate species of *Pinguicula* require stratification before they will germinate. For best results, the period of stratification for each of the species should be at least equal to the minimum period of plant dormancy.

Asexual Reproduction

1. Brood bodies: Species in groups 1 and 2 except *P. vallisneriifolia* produce small brood bodies, which are called gemmae. (Fig. 5-3) They are formed in the leaf axils of the outer leaves toward the end of the growing season. Unless they are removed before the mother plant grows in the spring, they will probably be smothered by the leaves of the adult plant. The brood bodies may be left with the mother plant until spring, at which time they are removed and placed, one each, in a small depression in the planting medium so that the top of the brood body is level with the surface.

2. Runners: *P. vallisneriifolia* produces plantlets at the ends of runners. When the plantlets have rooted they can be severed from the mother plant. Transplanting is most successful when done during the spring before active growth commences.

3. Leaf cuttings: Remove the whole leaf. Dust with fungicide and insert the leaf in sphagnum moss so that the bottom ⅓ is below the moss. Keep the humidity high, light bright and temperature in the summer range for the particular species. We know this procedure is effective for *P. macroceras*, *P. villosa*, and *P. vulgaris*.

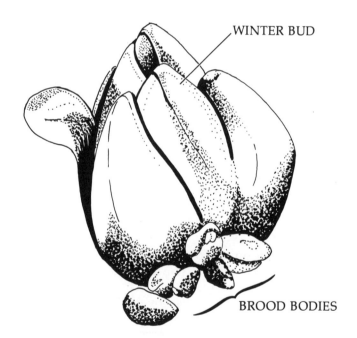

WINTER BUD

BROOD BODIES

Fig. 5-3 Winter bud of *Pinguicula* with smaller brood bodies which should be removed and planted separately. They grow into new plants.

Subtropical and Tropical **Pinguicula** _____

About ⅓ of these species have been successfully cultivated to date. Those for which there is cultural data available have been divided into groups, by the similarity of their cultural requirements.

CULTURAL INFORMATION

The Southern United States Species
P. caerulea
P. ionantha
P. lutea
P. planifolia
P. primuliflora
P. pumila

Planting Media
These plants grow best in acid planting media. The acid media listed for the temperate *Pinguicula* species are suitable for these also.

Temperatures
While summer temperatures in their native habitats may reach and exceed 95°F (35°C), ground or soil temperatures are usually lower. Summer temperatures 70–90°F (21–32°C), winter temperatures 35–50°F (2–10°C). Some species are subjected to light frost in their native habitats.

Dormancy
Growth stops during the coldest part of the year but the plants remain green. They should be kept drier during the dormant season than during the period of active growth. Treatment with a fungicide will ward off decay. It has been reported that some of these *Pinguicula* species go dormant during the summer when there is a prolonged drought.

Water & Humidity
These plants enjoy high humidity and wet soils during the growing season, but the medium should be drier during the dormant period.

Light
Indirect or shaded sunlight is generally suitable. Under artificial lighting use 900 foot candles. Photoperiod for the summer 14 hours, for the winter 10 hours.

Miscellaneous
Many growers have trouble keeping their subtropical and tropical *Pinguicula* spp. growing from season to season due to rotting. We have found that placing ½ in. (1.3 cm) of washed coarse sand or small pebbles on top of the planting medium in a pot eliminates plant rot or decay. The plants' roots must extend into the media below the pebble or sand layer. The sand or pebbles are positioned around the crown of the plant. This allows the crown area to remain relatively dry while the roots are in wet or damp soil.

PROPAGATION

Sexual Reproduction
Flowers must be pollinated by an external agent such as insects or artificially in

order to set seed. Follow the procedure given for temperate species. Seed can be sown immediately and will germinate. We have found stratifying the seed for about 2 months results in a more uniform and a greater percentage of germination.

Asexual Reproduction

Leaf cuttings: Follow the same procedure as given for the temperate *Pinguicula* spp. except that the temperatures should be higher, 70–85°F (21–29°C). The more succulent the leaves the greater the success rate.

Species such as *P. pumila, P. primuliflora,* and *P. planifolia* will develop small plantlets on their leaves while growing under conditions of high humidity, usually in late summer or early fall. (Photo 5-7) These plantlets, if continually removed, can be used to start new plants.

CULTURAL INFORMATION

The Mexican Species
P. colimensis
P. cyclosecta
P. gypsicola
P. macrophylla*
P. moranensis—formerly called P. caudata & P. mexicana
P. oblongiloba*

*Produce winter buds.

Non-Mexican Species
P. hirtiflora
P. lilacina
P. lusitanica*
P. parvifolia*

*Produce winter buds.

The Mexican *Pinguicula* species grow at high elevations where summers are warm and winters cool and dry. The non-Mexican species grow in Mediterranean areas as well as in other parts of the world with a similar climate. Both of these groups require similar cultural conditions and are the easiest of the *Pinguicula* species to grow.

Planting Media
The Mexican *Pinguicula* spp. grow on calcareous or alkaline soils in their native habitat, but they will grow in acid soils also. Both acid and alkaline planting media are used successfully in growing these plants. Any of the planting media listed for the temperate *Pinguicula* spp. can be used for the Mexican *Pinguicula* spp. The non-Mexican *Pinguicula* spp. require an acid medium. Any of acid media listed for the temperate *Pinguiculas* can be used with these species.

Temperatures
Summer 60–85°F (16–29°C). Winter 40–55°F (4–13°C).

Dormancy
The Mexican *Pinguicula* spp. produce thicker and smaller leaves for the winter or dormant season. Species such as *P. macrophylla* and *P. oblongiloba* are described as forming winter buds. Others of the Mexican *Pinguicula* spp. produce small, tight winter leaves. Thus, it is a matter of semantics as to whether they are winter buds or just small winter leaves.

Light

Indirect or shaded sunlight. If artificial light is used, start with about 1000 foot candles and a summer photoperiod of about 13 hours; 800 foot candles for the winter or dormant season with a photoperiod of 11 hours is suitable.

Water & Humidity

Like most *Pinguicula* spp. this group enjoys wet soils and very high humidity during the growing season, with drier soils during dormancy.

Miscellaneous

P. moranesis and *P. collimensis* tend to grow up and out of their planting medium, exposing their root system. At least once a year the leaves should be lifted to view the base of the crown to see if the plant has grown out of the soil. If roots are visible, the plant should be repotted so that all the roots are in the medium or alternatively position medium around the exposed roots.

Some growers prefer to plant Mexican *Pinguicula* in pots which have an inch of sphagnum moss over a bottom layer of perlite. The plant is positioned so the base of the leaves is in the moss with the roots extending into the perlite. A suspension of dolomite (available from health food stores) made by mixing ½ teaspoon (2.5 ml) per quart (liter) of water is used to water the leaves and soil once every 2 months. These plants should be fertilized as per directions in Chapter 7.

PROPAGATION

Sexual Reproduction

Flowers must be pollinated by an external agent such as insects or artificially in order for viable seed to be set. Seeds of both of these groups will germinate without any special treatment. Sow seed on the appropriate medium, keep the humidity high, the light bright and within a temperature range of 60–86°F (16–30°C). Seed will germinate within 2–4 weeks.

Asexual Reproduction

1. Leaf cuttings: Leaf cuttings should be handled in the same manner as outlined for the southern United States species. The thicker, more succulent leaves produce the best results.

2. Runners: *P. oblongiloba* and *P. macrophylla* produce new plants at the end of runners. When plantlets have developed a root system the plants can be severed from the mother plant.

General Information for all *Pinguicula* Species

Pests

Snails, slugs, aphids and fungus diseases. See Chapter 8 for treatment.

Feeding

See Chapter 7 for feeding directions.

Miscellaneous

Pinguicula should be transplanted before active growth starts to reduce losses. Plants can be successfully moved at other times if they are moved with a ball of soil. Some growers claim that those *Pinguicula* spp. requiring alkaline or sweet soils will benefit from 2–3 waterings during the growing season with a solution of hydrated lime, calcium hydroxide. The usual concentration is 1 tablespoon (15 ml) of hydrated lime per quart (liter) of water. Avoid getting liquid on the leaves when watering the plants.

The *Pinguicula* species in order of increasing difficulty to cultivate are Mexican, non-Mexican, southern U.S., and temperate. With the temperate species, the longer the dormant period the more difficult it is to grow the plants.

6

Utricularia—Bladderworts

These plants are dealt with together because three of the four genera are members of the family Lentibulariaceae (*Genlisea, Polypompholyx,* and *Utricularia*) and two of the four genera are primarily aquatic (*Aldrovanda* and *Utricularia*). They are lesser known carnivorous plants although they are just as fascinating to cultivate.

Utricularia

HISTORY

There are almost 300 species of *Utricularia* distributed throughout the world from the tropics to the Arctic. Without a doubt, this is the most widespread genus of carnivorous plants.

The elucidation of the carnivorous habit of this genus began to unfold when Cohn, in 1857, discovered that they captured Perch fry. Both Cohn and Darwin thought that the prey pushed the trap-door open, entered, and when the door closed found themselves entrapped. It was Mary Treat, who in 1876, discovered that the prey did not swim into the trap, but rather were sucked in when the trap was set off and thereby captured.

Early observers, such as Cohn, Darwin, and Goebel, were aware that the prey disintegrated in the bladders. It was difficult to establish, however, if this was the result of decay or the action of digestive enzymes because of the small size of the bladders. Darwin's few experiments on enzymatic digestion produced negative results so he concluded that they did not. Luetzelburg in 1910 was the first to obtain evidence of digestive activity by enzymes in *Utricularia.* The extent of the role of bacterial action has not been established.

Both the United States Fish Commission and the Commissioner of Fisheries for the State of New York, U.S.A., published bulletins in the late 1800s on *Utricularia* under the title of Piscivorous (fish eating) Plants.

Utricularia is derived from the Latin word "utriculus" meaning little bag or sac alluding to the traps of the plant. The common name Bladderwort originated from the bladder-shaped traps of *Utricularia.*

NATURAL HABITAT

This is a very diverse genus of plants. Some aquatic species grow free, floating in water, while others float in water but are attached to the soil below. (Fig. 6-1) They grow in locations such as ponds and margins of lakes. The terrestial species grow in wet, acid soils while the epiphytic species grow on the surface of moss-covered tree trunks, branches or stones. (Fig. 6-2) Some of the aquatic species tend to become terrestrial while some terrestrials become aquatic and some epiphites tend to become terrestial. Some species are annuals while others are perennials. Those that grow in cold regions over winter by forming winter buds while some overcome hot, dry summers by forming tubers, often called corms, or by producing seed that germinates with the arrival of rain. While these plants are of world-wide distribution, none have been found on oceanic islands.

DESCRIPTION OF PLANT

Most of *Utricularia* spp. have long stems or stolons with varying degrees of branching. Some species exceed lengths of 10 ft. (3 m). These thread-like, rootless plants have leaves that vary in size from insignificant to over 10 in. (25 cm) long. There is great variety in leaf sizes and shapes within the genus. There is a species, *U. pubescens* which has mucilage on the upper surfaces of its leaves. It is not yet known whether prey captured by the mucilage is digested. Perhaps this plant has developed 2 methods of capturing and digesting prey.

The leaves of the terrestrial and epiphytic species grow upright. The distinction between stems, branches, and leaves is not clear. Modified stems called rhizoids anchor some species in the growing medium. (Photo 6-1)

The distinguishing feature of this genus is their bladders or traps, which range from extremely small to lengths of up to ¼ in. (6 mm) and are all basically oval-shaped. The shape of the bladder is species specific.

It was once believed that the bladders functioned like pontoons to support the plant and some even thought they extracted air from the water and stored it for the plant's use. But these beliefs were dispelled when it was established that the bladders trapped such prey as tiny animals, insects and baby fish (fry). The bladders grow on leaves of the aquatic species whereas bladders arise from any plant part of non-aquatic species. An unusual characteristic of these plants is that any vegetative part is capable of developing into any other vegetative part.

The racemose inflorescence bears personate flowers with elongated spurs and a bilabiate corolla and calyx. (Photo 6-2) The throat of the corolla is usually blocked by a pubescent palate whose degree of exsertion is specific to the species. There are 2 curved stamens which may or may not be covered by the 2-lipped stigma. (Fig. 6-3) Flower color varies by species and includes shades of yellow, white, purple, blue and red. In some epiphytic species the corolla diameter can exceed 2 in. (5 cm) and strongly resembles orchid flowers, while in most species the corolla diameter ranges from 0.08–1 in. (0.2–2.5 cm). (Photos 6-3, 6-4)

Both cleistogamous (a flower that does not open and is self pollinated) flowers and chasmogamous (flowers which are pollinated when open) flowers can occur on the same plant of some species. Evidence indicates that the environmental conditions determine which kind of flower or if both will occur on a plant.

Annuals which survive the dry season by forming seeds are sensitive to water level fluctuations. It has been observed that if the water level remains above a critical level the plants will not flower at their usual time and contrariwise if the water level drops

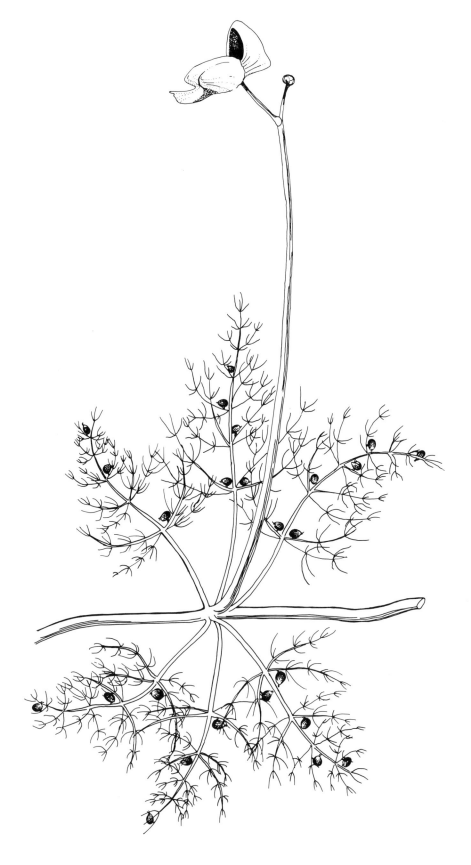

Fig. 6-1 Aquatic *Utricularia* with flower.

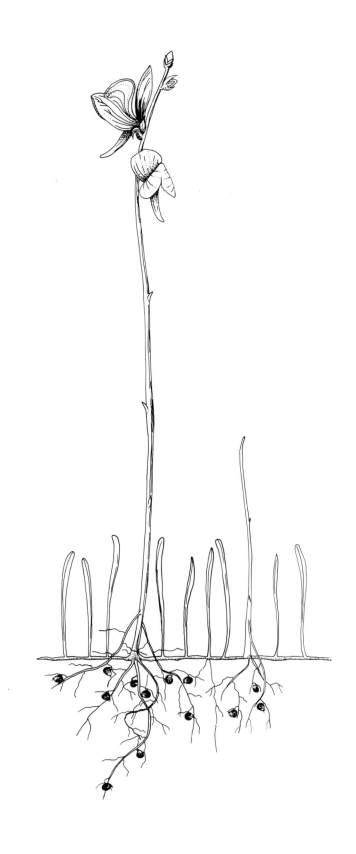

Fig. 6-2 Terrestrial *Utricularia* with scape.

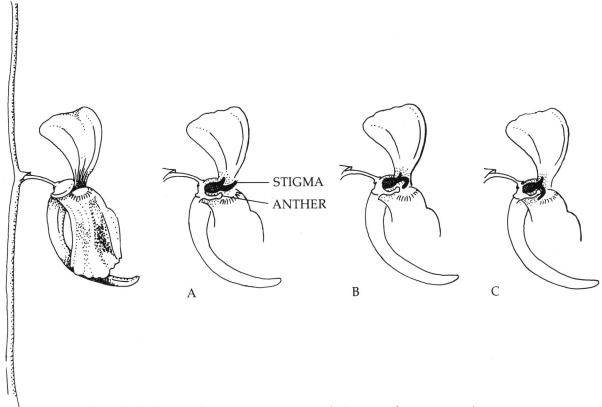

Fig. 6-3 *Utricularia* flower. Arrangement of stigma and stamens varies
with species. In some species the stigma does not cover the anthers and in
other the anthers are partially or completely covered by the stigma.

below the critical level, a plant will flower regardless of how short a time plants have
been growing.

Some species such as *U. inflata* produce tubers on the terminal ends of branches
during periods of low moisture and/or temperatures. These tubers will germinate
upon the arrival of suitable growing conditions.

TRAPPING

Closure of the *Utricularia* trap is faster than that of *Dionaea*. The door in the front of
the bladder is attached to the top of the opening and swings open inward. The door is
very elastic and when closed it rests on the edge of the door opening. There are
projecting hair-like structures near the top of the door. (Fig. 6-4) These projections
funnel the prey into the vicinity of the trap door.

The trap in all species is set by removing most of the water in the bladder. Water is
removed by internal glands which excrete it. The removal of water inside the bladder
results in lower pressure on the inside of the trap than on the outside. Consequently,
the walls cave in giving the trap sides a concave shape. In this state, the door is forced
tightly against the opening and no water enters the trap. If something touches or
brushes against one or more of the trigger hairs on the door, the trap is set off. The door
springs open, water gushes in carrying with it the prey. (Fig. 6-5) The force of the gush
of water is often sufficient to jerk the whole plant. Apparently when the trap is set an
extremely unstable equilibrium in pressure is set up, keeping the door closed.
Therefore, only a very small force is required to set off the trap. Trapping usually occurs
within 1/50 of a second. Traps usually reset themselves within 15–45 minutes.

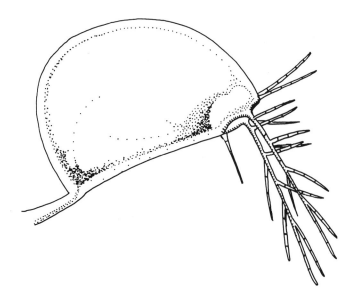

Fig. 6-4 *Utricularia* trap. Hair-like projections funnel prey into the vicinity of the trap door.

While these plants normally capture very small animals, a trap can capture larger or longer creatures by sucking them in a little at a time. That is, after the trap is sprung part of the animal is sucked in, the elastic door closes around it, creating a water tight seal so that the trap can reset itself and again spring to suck in another part of the prey. Movement of the plant parts comprising the trap in the genera *Dionaea* and *Aldrovanda* is, in part, a growth phenomenon, whereas in *Utricularia* spp. it is the result of mechanical action.

Here, as in the case of some other carnivorous plants, digestion results from the action of enzymes secreted by the plant together with bacterial activity. There are organisms that live and thrive in the *Utricularia* spp. trap, feeding on the captured prey without themselves being digested. As wastes accumulate in the bladder, bladder color turns from greenish to dark purple to black and eventually the trap drops off.

Many instructive hours can be spent observing and studying the mechanism of trapping and the structure of the *Utricularia* trap. To observe trapping of prey and gross structure of the trap a magnification of 2–30 times is sufficient. Binocular or dissecting microscopes are particularly efficacious but a simple magnifying glass will reveal a great deal. Higher magnifications are required for examination of glands, details of the opening and other intricate parts of the trap.

Specimens to be examined are placed in a transparent container such as a petri dish or finger bowl. A pair of tweezers with fine points and a dissecting needle or two make manuevering the specimen into a favorable position for observation easier. Conventional dissecting needles are too large to open the door to the trap. They can be modified by grinding them into a smaller sharper point or by substituting a fine sewing needle in the handle.

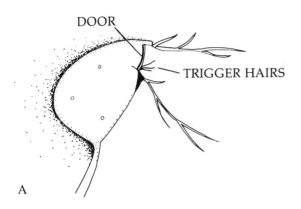

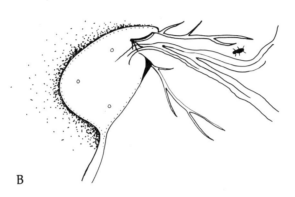

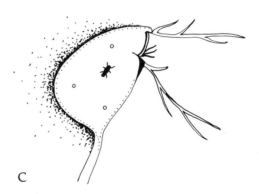

Fig. 6-5 *Utricularia* trapping mechanism. The trap is set by removal of water from the bladder which results in lower pressure within the trap. A longitudinal section reveals the door is forced tightly against the opening. The trap is set-off when the trigger hairs on the door are touched. The door springs open and water rushes in, carrying with it prey in the vicinity. The door then closes entrapping the prey.

SPECIES OF THE GENUS *UTRICULARIA* IN CULTIVATION

Of the almost 300 species of *Utricularia* fewer than one-third have been cultivated. To date this large group of very interesting plants has generally been ignored by carnivorous plant enthusiasts.

The *Utricularia* species for which cultural information is available are divided into 4 groups, with plants within each group having similar cultural requirements. They are tropical, temperate, North American, and tuberous groups. It should be noted that the North American group includes all species that grow in North America, but does not mean that these species do not grow anywhere else, as many of them grow on other continents.

Group 1: Tropical *Utricularia* Species

Terrestrial
U. amethystina
U. calycifida
U. dusenii
U. inflexa
U. jamesoniana
U. leptoplectra
U. lloydii
U. livida
U. praelonga
U. prehensilis
U. pubescens
U. pusilla
U. sandersoni
U. scandens
U. simulans
U. spiralis
U. subulata
U. tricolor
U. uliginosa

Aquatic
U. foliosa
U. hydrocarpa
U. obtusa
U. stellaris

Epiphytic
U. alpina
U. endresii
U. humboldtii
U. jamesoniana
U. longifolia
U. nelumbifolia
U. praetermissa
U. reniformis
U. unifolia

Summer temperatures: 65–95°F (18–35°C)
Winter temperatures: 50–68°F (10–20°C)

Group 2: Temperate *Utricularia* Species

Terrestrial
U. caerulea
U. capensis
U. dichotoma
U. lateriflora
U. monanthos
U. nova-zealandiae
U. racemosa
U. violacea

Aquatic
U. aurea
U. hookeri

Summer temperatures: 65–82°F (18–28°C)
Winter temperatures: 45–68°F (7–20°C)

Group 3: North American *Utricularia* Species

Terrestrial
U. amethystina 2, also known as
  U. standleyae
U. cornuta 1

Aquatic

U. biflora 2

Group 3: North American *Utricularia* Species (cont.)

Terrestrial   Aquatic

U. juncea 1   *U. fibrosa* 1,W
U. resupinata 1,W   *U. floridana* 2
U. simulans 2, also known as   *U. foliosa* 2
    U. fimbriata   *U. geminiscapa* 1,W
U. subulata 1   *U. gibba* 1,W
                                 U. inflata 1,W
                                 U. intermedia 1,W
                                 U. macrorhiza 1,W, also known as
                                     U. vulgaris and *U. australis*
                                 U. minor 1,W
                                 U. ochroleuca 1,W
                                 U. olivacea 2
                                 U. purpurea 1,W
                                 U. radiata 1,W

KEY

1= Will survive freezing temperatures, but grow well and form winter buds with winter temperatures of 34–45°F (1–7°C). Summer temperature range 55–85°F (13–29°C)
2= Summer temperature range 60–90°F (16–32°C). Winter temperature range 40–55°F (4–13°C).
W= Form winter buds.

Group 4: Tuberous *Utricularia* Species

U. menziesii

This species grows in southwestern Australia during the cool winters and goes dormant during the dry, hot summers with just a viable tuber remaining in the soil. Summer temperatures: 70–100°F (21–38°C). Winter temperatures: 40–79°F (4–26°C).

DESCRIPTION OF COMMERCIALLY AVAILABLE SPECIES

Terrestrial Species

Many terrestrial species of *Utricularia* have small, narrow leaves that are similar to minute blades of grass. It is much easier to identify these species by flower color and scape characteristics than by leaf characteristics. Some of the species often grow in shallow water, but they are firmly anchored to the soil.

U. amethystina (Also known as *U. standleyae*) The scape arises from a whorl of small blade like leaves. There are 2 smaller bracts between the large bract and scape. Flower color is variable, shades of white, yellow and purple.

U. capensis Leaves linear to spathulate up to 0.6 in. (1.5 cm) in length. One to 6 flowers that are all yellow or white or light blue with a yellow splotch on the palate.

U. cornuta There are 1–6 yellow flowers on a yellowish green scape that can reach a length of 13 in. (33 cm). The flowers have an unusually long vertical spur.Bracts alternate on the scape and a pair of smaller bracts occur inside the large one.

U. dichotoma Leaves narrow to oval-shaped up to 1 in. (2.5 cm) long. Bracts are spurred, opposite or in sets of 3. There may be from one to several light blue to purple flowers that may occur singly or in pairs of 1 or 2 or in whorls of 3.

U. lateriflora Spathulate leaves up to 0.2 in. (5 mm) long at base of scape. Two to 8 violet to purple flowers with a yellowish to whitish palate on each scape.

U. juncea Plant is very similar to *U. cornuta* except the scape is often purplish green and shorter, reaching lengths of 9 in. (23 cm). The yellow flowers number from 2–12, are smaller than those of *U. cornuta,* and can be chasmogamous or cleistogamous.

U. nova-zealandiae Leaves fan-shaped up to 0.6 in. (1.5 cm) long. Flowers purple to violet with vertical yellow lines on the palate.

U. menziesii During dormancy, the dry season, the above-ground parts of the plant die back to an underground corm-like tuber whose shape and size is that of a rice grain. The single flowers are red with an unusually long, yellow, ridged palate. Bracts are opposite or in sets of 3. (Photo 6-6)

U. prehensilis Leaves are linear to narrow oval in outline and up to 5 in. (13 cm) long. One to 8 yellow flowers are borne on a scape that usually twines.

U. praelonga Leaves have a variety of shapes from short and wide to long and narrow or ribbon-shaped reaching lengths of 8 in. (20 cm).

U. pubescens Leaves are round, peltate, horizontal and the upper surface is covered with mucilage producing glands. Diameter of the leaf blade is up to 0.2 in. (5 mm) with a vertical petiole that can reach a length of 0.4 in. (1 cm). From 1–10 white to light blue flowers are borne on each scape.

U. racemosa Leaves are circular to kidney-shaped. Numerous whitish blue flowers are borne on a scape that often branches.

U. resupinata A single, purple flower is borne on a scape. Bracts occur in pairs opposite each other and are fused forming a tube that encircles the scape.

U. sandersoni The fan-shaped leaves are up to 0.8 in. (2 cm) long. One to 6 whitish to light blue flowers with violet streaks are produced in abundance the year around.

U. simulans (Also known as *U. fimbriata*) One to 8 yellow or yellowish white flowers are borne on each scape. The sepal and bract margins are feathered (fimbriate).

U. spiralis There are several varieties in this species. Leaves tend to be linear to somewhat oval in shape and are up to 2.4 in. (6 cm) long. Flowers 1–15, usually violet with a bluish green, yellow, or white spot on the throat. Scape usually twines.

U. subulata Two to 8 yellow to purple flowers with yellow-orange palates are borne on a zigzag scape. The bracts alternate on the scape. May have cleistogamous and/or chasmogamous flowers.

U. violacea Leaves at base of scape are linear with filaments bearing traps. Bracts are oblong, spurred and opposite on the scape. Flowers are violet.

Aquatic Species

U. biflora Stems thread-like, usually forming mats. Hair-like leaves bear traps. The base of the bracts clasp the scape which bears 1–2 yellow flowers.

U. floridana Thread-like leaves. Two to 8 yellow flowers are borne on a zigzag scape.

U. geminiscapa May have both chasmogamous and cleistogamous flowers. Plant is similar to *U. macrorhiza,* but smaller. Forms a winter bud. Leaves are hair-like. Flowers yellow.

U. gibba The hair-like leaves are alternate on the thread-like stems that often form tangled mats. One to 3 yellow flowers are borne on a scape that originates at the point from which several branches or stems radiate. Sometimes the branches creep along the bottom of shallow bodies of water. The rounded bracts partially clasp the scape. May form a winter bud.

U. inflata Has 4–17 yellow flowers on a reddish scape that is kept afloat by a whorl of 4–11 inflated structures attached to the middle of the scape. Each structure or float is widest at its mid-point and tapers to its point of attachment to the scape. (Photo 6-5) The float also tapers from its midpoint to the free end which is finely dissected and bears traps. Floats may reach lengths of 5.5 in. (14 cm). Bracts are oblong, pointed and longer than wide. Produces tubers when the environment dries out and during the winter. Winter buds may be formed.

U. intermedia An aquatic which at times is anchored to the soil below the water surface. Traps and leaves are borne on separate shoots. Has up to 6 yellow flowers. The middle of the bract is attached to the scape resulting in the formation of a lobe at the bottom. Forms a winter bud.

U. macrorhiza (Also known as *U. vulgaris, U. austrais* and *U. macrorhiza* ssp. *vulgaris*). One of the larger bladderworts often exceeding 13 ft. (4 m) in length with the stem occasionally branching. Leaf margins have tiny bristles. Bracts occur singly on the scape. It has 6–25 yellow flowers which have brown or red streaks on the palate. Forms a winter bud.

U. minor Thread-like stems usually form a jumbled mass. Has the same type of bracts as those of *U. intermedia* except they tend to be purplish. Tips of the leaves are serrated. Bears 2–9 yellow flowers. Forms a winter bud.

U. purpurea Has 2–8 pinkish purple or white flowers that have 2 pouch-like lobes on their lower lip. Bracts are attached above their base to the scape. Whorls of branching stems which bear the traps grow from the central stem, giving the appearance of many wheels with spokes on a single axis.

U. olivacea An extremely small plant. A single, white flower is found on each scape that is usually less than 1 in. (2.5 cm) high. A pair of leaves are located at the base of the scape with bracts alternating on it.

Epiphytic Species

U. alpina Leaves long, narrow, and terminate in an attenuate tip. Up to 6 white flowers with yellow palates. White, oval-shaped, subterranean tubers are formed that can reach 2 in. (5 cm) in length and which turn green when exposed to light.

U. endresii Leaves are up to 8.5 in. (22 cm) long and are similar to the leaves of *U. alpina* except they are narrower. Flowers are pale blue with yellow palates and number up to 6. The oval-shaped subterranean tubers are up to 0.5 in. (1.3 cm) long.

U. longifolia Leaves similar to those of *U. alpina*. Produces no tubers and has up to 10 mauve flowers with yellow palates or violet flowers with an orange palate.

U. reniformis Kidney-shaped leaf blade has a diameter of about 3 in. (7.5 cm) on a slender petiole that can reach 6.5 in. (17 cm) in length. Flowers are light violet with two, vertical yellow stripes on the palate. The tubers are almost spherical.

CULTURAL INFORMATION

Planting Media
Should be acid with a pH between 4 and 6.5.

Terrestrial species: Sphagnum moss living or dried, long fiber or milled, sphagnum peat moss, various mixtures of peat moss with sand or vermiculite or perlite. Living sphagnum moss should not be used with the smaller species as it will quickly overgrow the plants.

Aquatic species: Grow them in any container such as gallon jars, mayonnaise bottles, aquariums, terrariums, plastic washtubs, or outdoors in pools, natural or artificial. If grown in containers, 2–3 in. (5–7.6 cm) of soil should be placed on the bottom.

Any planting medium may be used. If it is not acidic, the water can be acidified as per directions in Chapter 7.

If sphagnum peat moss is used, soak it for about 1 week, then remove any material that has not settled to the bottom with a strainer.

To condition the water for the plants, add a handful of sphagnum moss, living or dried, to the water if the medium is not sphagnum peat moss.

Water depth should be at least 6 in. (15 cm). Many aquatic and terrestrial spp. will grow in very wet watery soils, often referred to as slurries. A slurry is made by mixing 1 part sphagnum moss living or dried or sphagnum peat moss to 1 part water. The slurry is then put in a drainless container and planted.

Epiphytic species: Any of the planting media listed for the terrestrial species are used for epiphytes when they are grown in pots. Epiphytic *Uticularia* spp. can be grown in the same manner as the terrestrial species. If grown in hanging baskets or on boards, such as used for Staghorn Ferns, living or dried long fiber sphagnum moss is best.

Temperatures
As indicated in the table delineating each group of plants.

Dormancy
The plants in Group 3 which form winter buds, called turions, are identified by the letter W after their name. The winter bud is usually a spherically-shaped body which may reach a diameter of ½ in. (1.3 cm) in some species. (Fig. 6-6) These turions tend to sink to the bottom of the water during the winter where they remain until spring.

U. menziesii which is native to southwest Australia, grows during the cool moist winter and survives the hot dry summer as a dormant tuber.

Some of the species in Groups 1, 2, and 3 may stop growing during the winter but remain an evergreen.

Water & Humidity

Terrestrial species: These species are maintained very wet or waterlogged during the summer and drier during the winter. *Uticularia menzesii*—keep medium wet during the growing season (winter) and dry during the dormant season (summer).

Aquatic species: Grow the species in acid water, pH 5–6.5. If the water becomes alkaline, algae growth can become troublesome. Kits used to measure water pH are available from stores handling tropical fish supplies. The same acids and procedures listed under *Aldrovanda* are suitable for use in acidifying water for *Utricularia*.

One grower has found that dissolving 1/10 of a gram of copper sulfate crystals in 18 fluid ounces (540 ml) of water and then adding 1 fluid ounce (30 ml) of this solution for each gallon (4 liters) of water in the *Utricularia* growing container kills unwanted algae. He warns, however, that the weighing and dilution of the copper sulfate crystals accurately is of the utmost importance to avoid poisoning the plants.

Epiphytic species: Thrive best when kept damp and in a highly humid environment.

Light
The North American species will thrive in strong light or full sunlight. The other species prefer indirect sunlight.

Artificial Light: Group 3 species 500–1500 foot candles during summer. Winter 100–300 foot candles for those not forming winter buds. For turion-forming species no light is needed during the winter.

Group 1, 2, and 4 species 500–900 foot candles during the growing season. Group 1 and 2, 300–700 foot candles during the dormant or winter season. Group 4 needs no light during the dormant (summer) season.

Photoperiod: Group 3 species Summer: 12–18 hours, winter: 8–10 hours for the evergreen species. Those forming winter buds need no light during the winter.

Group 1 and 2 species Summer: 14–16 hours, winter: 12 hours. These species can be grown year around with the same photoperiod. Our experience indicates that flowering is more regular when the photoperiod is varied and the plants are kept drier during the winter.

Group 4 species: 8–10 hours during the growing season (winter), none during the dormant (summer) season.

Pests
Aphids and fungus are the only reported pests. See Chapter 8 for control measures.

Feeding
Chapter 7 for directions.

Miscellaneous
Terrestrial and epiphytic species are the easiest to grow. While many of these species will flower in cultivation, none can match the profusion produced by *U. sandersoni.* Once established it flowers continuously year in and year out.

PROPAGATION

Sexual Reproduction

Some species have cleistogamous flowers, which do not open completely and will self-pollinate to produce viable seeds. The other type of flower which opens completely is called chasmogamous. Both kinds of flowers can occur on the same plants of some species. In some species the stigma bends over and covers the anthers, in others it is erect while in others the stigma bends over on itself, but does not cover the anthers. The anthers are positioned one to the right and one to the left of the stigma. (Fig. 6-3) The flower structure is designed to encourage pollen transfer by pollinating agents. To see the stigma and anthers, grasp the lower lip and the upper lip and gently pull them apart. The flower will open as if it were hinged and the floral parts are exposed so that one may pollinate them to produce seed or hybridize them. To our knowledge no one has attempted to hybridize this group of plants. As mentioned before, the flowers of these plants are designed to require a pollinating agent. Yet under some conditions some plants produce seed without an apparent pollinator. Perhaps movements of the flower induced by winds may dislodge pollen grains which tumble onto the stigma.

If the flowers are pollinated the ovaries will swell and in 4–8 weeks the seeds are mature which is evidenced by the almost translucent seed pod.

Seed from the species that form winter buds must be stratified to germinate. Seed not planted is stored in vials or bottles under refrigeration. Seed of terrestrial species is sown on the medium while seed of aquatic species is sown on the water surface. Seed germination is quite variable and may take up to 2 months.

Asexual Reproduction

Terrestrial species: Take a portion of soil with plants and divide it into 2 or more parts. Plant each part in a pot. They will multiply rapidly by vegetative reproduction.

Aquatic species: Cut the plant into pieces about 2–4 in. (5–10 cm) long and replace in water. Each section will develop into a separate plant.

Epiphytic species: Divide the mother plant into several smaller portions and repot.

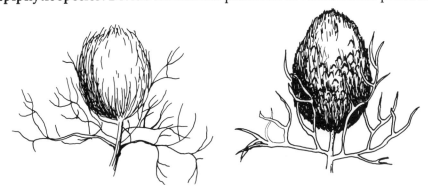

Fig. 6-6 Some *Uticularia* species form resting structures called winter buds or turions. Turion tend to be spherically-shaped.

Fig. 6-7 *Polypompholyx multifida* plants including flowers, basal rosette of leaves and traps.

Polypompholyx

The two species comprising this genus grow in Australia. Both are very similar to the terrestrial species of the *Utricularia* genus differing only in sepal number and trap structure. *Polypompholyx* has a 4-part calyx whereas that of *Utricularia* is 2-part. (Fig. 6-7) Both species of *Polypompholyx* are annuals and are terrestrial plants.

Polypompholyx multifida, commonly known as Pink Petticoat, is found in West Australia. Narrow, oblong, green leaves seldom exceeding 2 in. (5 cm) form a rosette encircling the base of the scape. The scape can be up to 12 in. (30 cm) long and bears from one to several flowers on short pedicels. The flowers are various shades of pink with a yellow palate. There is a white flowered variant. The lower lip is 3-lobed and much larger than the upper. Flowers are usually less than 1¼ in. (3 cm) wide. (Photo 6-7)

Polypompholyx tenella, commonly known as Pink Fans, grows in West Australia, Victoria and South Australia. Flowers and leaves are similar to those of *P. multifida* except they are smaller. Scapes seldom exceed 3 in. (8 cm), leaves are not more than 0.5 in. (1.3 cm) and flower diameter is less than ⅓ inch (0.8 cm). There are 1–2 pink flowers with yellow palates per scape.

Both species are annuals and will not self-pollinate. If they are grown in an area devoid of insects, the plants must be pollinated by hand to insure seed production. The flowers can be opened to reveal the sexual organs in the same manner as the genus *Utricularia* flowers. Pollen can then be transferred with a toothpick or brush from anther to stigma.

The trap in *Utricularia* spp. is attached to the stem at the end of the trap that is opposite from the trap entrance, whereas in *Polypompholyx* the entrance to the trap is on the same side of the trap as its attachment (called a footstalk) to the stem. The footstalk near the bladder is swollen, forming 2 ridges. The covering, called the beak or rostrum, is continuous with the top of the trap and divides to rest on each side of the footstalk. The rostrum touches the top of the ridge, blocking entrance to the lobby of the door from the front, but it forms two lateral wings anteriorly one over each side of the footstalk, resulting in funnel-shaped vestibules to the lobby. There are pointed hairs in

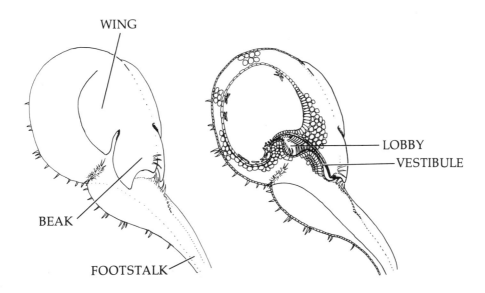

Fig. 6-8 *Polypompholyx* trap and longitudinal section through trap.

the area of both vestibules and in the lobby that direct prey to the door of the trap.(Fig. 6-8) The overall structure of the trap is similar to a hand held palm-upwards with the fingers bent toward the wrist. The wrist is analagous to the footstalk of *Polypompholyx* while the openings between the palm and index finger and pinkie are similar to the funnel-shaped vestibules leading to the lobby and the trap door. Like *Utricularia* spp., the prey is sucked in when the trigger hairs are stimulated. Because of the close similarity of *Polypompholyx* to *Utricularia*, they are assumed to be carnivorous also.

Any of the planting media recommended for terrestrial *Utricularia* spp., except living sphagnum moss, can be used for these plants. Living sphagnum moss should not be used because it will quickly overgrow the plants. A temperature in the 70–100°F (21–38°C) range is suitable. Indirect sunlight is adequate. If artificial light is used start with 1000 foot candles and a photoperiod of 12–14 hours.

Aphids and fungus will attack these plants. See Chapter 8 for control of these pests.

Plants can be fed the same material as the terrestrial *Utricularia* spp.

Genlisea

HISTORY

Auguste de Saint-Hilaire discovered the plants upon which the genus *Genlisea* is based in Brazil in 1833. Warming published the first thorough description of these plants in 1874.

NATIVE HABITAT

Genlisea species grow in tropical Africa, Madagascar, and South America in damp to wet soils. They are closely related to *Utricularia,* but the traps are distinctive. (Fig. 6-9)

DESCRIPTION OF PLANT

Rootless, herbaceous perennials or annuals having 2 kinds of leaves that arise from the slender rhizome. The linear or oblong foliage leaves which grow upward can exceed 2.5 in. (6 cm) in length. The second type of leaf, the trap leaves, are 1–6 in. (2.5–15 cm) in length. Scapes which can reach lengths of 16 in. (41 cm) bear several flowers which may be shades of blue, purple, violet, white or yellow. The flowers are very similar to those of *Utricularia* in structure, which have a 2-parted calyx whereas *Genlisea* has a 5-parted calyx.

TRAPPING

The trap consists of a footstalk which attaches the bulb or bladder to the rhizome. From the bulb a hollow tube connects the bulb cavity with the cavities of 2 spiral or twisted cylindrical arms, terminating in an opening, the mouth. One of the arms twists clockwise and the other counterclockwise. This whole structure, called the trapping leaf, usually hangs downward in the water. (Fig. 6-10) The spiral arms can be likened to a long, narrow piece of paper folded in half along its longest axis and then twisted. The result is that the lower edge of the paper is shorter than the top edge. The space between the edges of the paper at each twist forms the trap entrances. In the arms the 2 layers of tissue are bound together periodically with special cells resulting in numerous separated entrances. Once the prey enters the trap, pointed hairs direct it toward the tube which leads to the bulb where digestion takes place or is completed and subsequent absorption occurs. Some botanists believe that the glands between the row of pointed hairs in the arms and tube secrete digestive enzymes and/or mucilage. In the

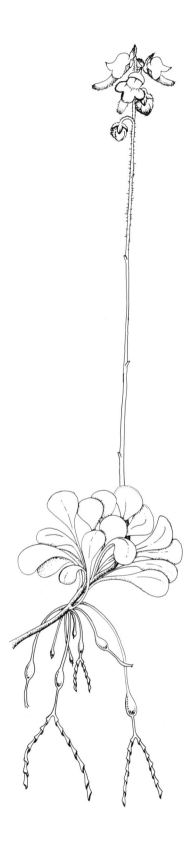

Fig. 6-9 *Genlisia* plant including inflorescence, rhizome with rosette of foliage leaves and trap leaves.

bulb, digestive enzymes are secreted and absorption takes place. It is thought by some that the bulb and tube excrete water from the interior and, as a result, there is a constant flow of water into the arms and tube to the bulb bringing in small prey such as copepods and nematodes. The outer surfaces of the trapping leaves have mucilage-producing glands.

SPECIES OF THE GENUS *GENLISEA*

G. *africana*
G. *angolensis*
G. *aurea*
G. *filiformis*
G. *glabra*
G. *glandulosissima*
G. *guianensis*
G. *hispidula*
G. *margaretae*
G. *pygmaea*
G. *repens*
G. *roraimensis*
G. *sanariapoana*
G. *violacea*

DESCRIPTION OF COMMERCIALLY AVAILABLE SPECIES

Genlisea filiformis The small vegetative leaves are spatulate in shape and form a rosette. The tall flower stalk bears 2–4 yellow to yellow-green flowers.

CULTURAL INFORMATION

Growing Media
Any of the growing media listed for terrestrial *Utricularia* is suitable.

Temperatures
Summer: 75–95°F (24–35°C) Winter: 65–75°F (18–24°C)

Dormancy
None

Light
Indirect sunlight. Artificial light, illuminate with 1000 foot candles in summer with a photoperiod of 14–16 hours and 850 foot candles with a 12 hour photoperiod in the winter.

Pests
None known.

Feeding
The same as for *Utricularia*. See Chapter 7.

Reproduction
Not known. These plants have only been in cultivation a short period of time. Should grow from seed and plant division.

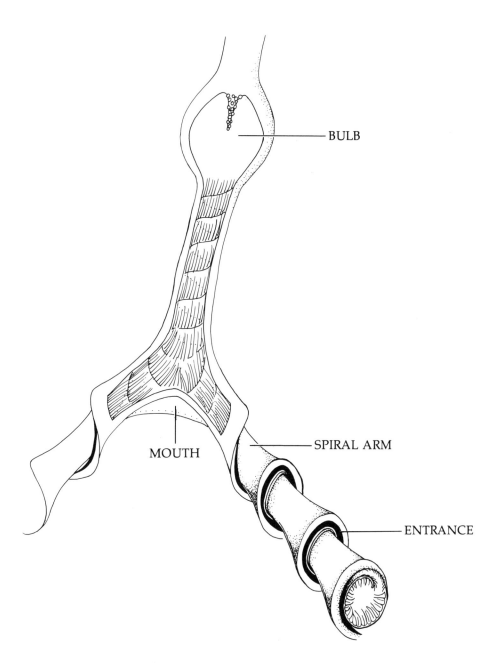

Fig. 6-10 Trapping leaf of *Genlisia*. The footstalk is attached to the rhizome and the bladder or bulb. The bulb is attached to the 2 spiral arms by means of a hollow tube lined with hairs. Insects enter the trap through the spaces in the spiral arms.

Aldrovanda

HISTORY

Aldrovanda vesiculosa was first observed in India in the 16th century. It was listed as *Lenticula palustris Indica* in L. Plukenet's, *Almagestum Botanicum* of 1696. The Italian physician, Dr. C. Amadei, sent some specimens collected from the Dulioli Swamp near Bologna, Italy, to the botanist G. Monti. Monti subsequently named the plant *Aldrovandia* in honor of the naturalist, Ulisse Aldrovandi, in 1747. The name was altered, probably as a clerical error, to *Aldrovanda* which is now accepted as the correct name for the genus. Augé de Lassus in 1861, discovering that the traps closed, thought they were air storage organs to give the plant buoyancy in water. Darwin's experiments with *Aldrovanda* indicated that absorption of prey took place in the traps and, realizing the similarity of this plant to *Dionaea*, assumed *Aldrovanda* secreted enzymes which digested the prey. Fermi and Buscaglione in 1899 confirmed that *Aldrovanda* did indeed digest its prey with enzymes produced by the plant. Common names for *Aldrovanda* are the Waterwheel Plant and Waterbug Trap.

NATURAL HABITAT

The aquatic plants grow just below the surface of fresh water in acid swamps, ditches and other quiet bodies of water in tropical and temperate regions. Its range includes Europe, Africa, Southeastern Asia to Japan and to Australia.

DESCRIPTION OF PLANT

Aldrovanda is a monotypic genus in the Droseraceae. The plant consists of a rootless stem whose length can exceed 8 in. (20 cm), and which tends to branch profusely, terminating in a spherical shoot tip with an abundance of protruding bristles. (Photo 6-8) Along the main stem and branches are numerous whorls of leaves arranged like the spokes on a wheel. Each whorl usually consists of 8 leaves about 0.5 in. (1.3 cm) long. Each leaf terminates in a trap which is usually flanked by 6 long bristles that extend beyond the trap. The plant grows by elongation of the stem and branches. (Fig. 6-11)

Flowers
In the spring small, white flowers are borne out of the water on short peduncles which arise from the leaf axils. The flowers consist of 5 petals which are longer than the 5 sepals, 5 stamens and 1 pistil with 5 styles radiating from the top of the ovary each of which terminates in a branching stigma. Up to 20, oval-shaped seeds are produced by the ovary.

TRAPPING

The traps are semi-circular in shape with about 40 trigger hairs on the inner surfaces, 20 on each lobe of the trap. Mucilage, digestive and absorptive glands are all located on the inner lobes. The 2 lobes are joined along the midrib in much the same manner as *Dionaea* (Venus Fly Trap) lobes. Trap closure is effected by stimulating the trigger hairs. Depending upon the age of the trap and cultural conditions, 1 or more stimulations are required. High temperatures, chemicals and electricity will initiate trap closure. Surrounding the outer edge of the leaves is a row of very closely arranged epidermal hairs sometimes called spikes. These are organized differently than the marginal spikes of the *Dionaea*. In the latter the hairs lie in the same plane as the lobes and point away from the midrib area. In *Aldrovanda* the hairs point down into the trap. When the trap closes, the spikes intermesh as they do in *Dionaea*. This mechanism is

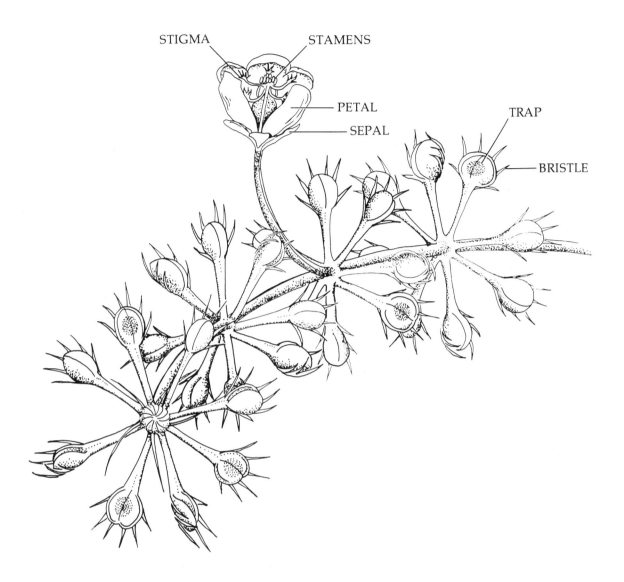

Fig. 6-11 *Aldrovanda* plant consisting of a rootless stem with whorls of leaves arranged like spokes on a wheel and flowers.

external with *Dionaea*, but is internal in the *Aldrovanda* trap. The intermeshed spikes serve as a sieve or strainer to keep the prey in the trap as it closes and water is forced out. An individual trap can close within 1/50 of a second and with such force as to visibly jerk the whole plant. As in *Dionaea*, the trap of *Aldrovanda* becomes narrower with adequate prey. (Fig. 6-12) It takes live, struggling prey to induce the trap to enter the narrowing phase. If digestible prey has been captured the trap will remain closed for about 1 week, if not, it will reopen in a few hours. Each trap can capture several meals before it is exhausted, but if too large a meal is captured, the trap will die. Since growth processes are involved in the working of the traps, increasing age leads to a decrease in functional ability.

SPECIES OF THE GENUS *ALDROVANDA*

Aldrovanda vesiculosa

CULTURAL INFORMATION

Planting Media

The plants require an acid water pH 6–6.9. Place at least 2 inches of garden, swamp or woodland soil or sphagnum peat moss in the bottom of the container which must be deep enough to provide the plant with a water depth of 6–12 in. (15–30 cm). If sphagnum peat moss is used, the moss will float for about a week until it becomes thoroughly wet and settles to the bottom of the container. (Strain the floating debris from the surface after the moss has sunk.)

After the water has cleared, check the acidity or pH with a pH meter or test paper. Kits for measuring pH are available from tropical fish stores. You do not need the whole kit, just the chemical bromthymol blue which is used as follows. Add 3 drops of bromthymol blue to 2 tablespoons (30 ml) of water. If the color of the water changes to yellow it is too acid, if the water turns blue the water is sweet or alkaline and if it turns green, it is just right. If the water is too acid, add a very small quantity of a base such calcium oxide, calcium hydroxide, baking soda or sodium biphosphate. Wait a few hours and then check the pH again. Continue adding the base and checking the results until the desired pH is achieved. If pH is too high, that is, it is alkaline, add acid in the form of dilute sulfuric acid, citric acid, tannic acid, or acetic acid (vinegar) in small quantities until the correct pH is achieved. Some growers lower the pH by adding chopped straw, grasses, sedges, cattails, and pine or fir or spruce needles. A general rule is to add ¼ cup (60 ml) of such plant material per gallon of water. In a few days the water will turn yellowish brown.

Another technique is to soak sphagnum peat moss in water for a few days. Drain off the water and add it to the *Aldrovanda* water.

Irises (*Iris*), rushes (*Juncus*), reeds (*Phragmites*), arrowhead (*Sagittaria*), and cattails (*Typha*) grown in the same container condition the water for improved growth and flowering of *Aldrovanda*. Water color should be yellowish like beer or urine. If the water turns black, change it at once and review cultural conditions to prevent reoccurrence. The water should not all be replaced at one time in order to maintain a proper pH. Replace some each day or so with fresh water until the water has regained a yellowish color.

Temperatures

Aldrovanda plants grow in the tropic and temperate regions of the world. In some temperate regions the plants are subjected to freezing temperatures. Under our growing conditions the plants produce winter buds at temperatures below 50°F (10°C). We over-winter our plants at a temperature of 35°F (2°C). We maintain summer temperatures (growing season) in the 70–86°F (21–30°C) range.

Dormancy

In temperate regions *Aldrovanda* plants go into dormancy and form winter buds which settle to the bottom of the water until conditions are suitable for growth. In tropical areas the plants are evergreen and grow the year around. Therefore, they do not form winter buds.

Light

Aldrovanda is accustomed to and requires strong light for vigorous growth. The plants can utilize several hours of direct sunlight as long as the water temperature does not exceed about 86°F (30°C). Growth is poor above this temperature. If the plants are

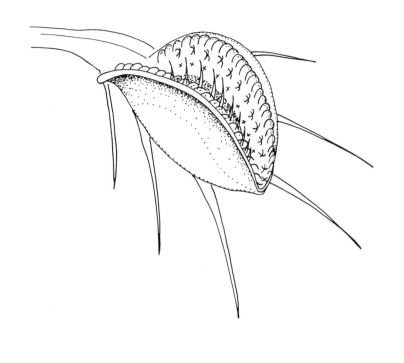

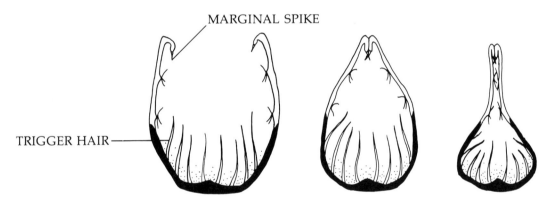

MARGINAL SPIKE

TRIGGER HAIR

Fig. 6-12 *Aldrovanda* trap with inward pointing spokes which intermesh upon closure. Sequence of closure is from left to right. Final closure, the narrowing phase is induced by struggling prey.

growing in a container with transparent walls and placed in direct sunlight, the sides of the container should be covered with white opaque materials to prevent sunlight from overheating the water.

Direct sunlight tends to encourage algae growth, particularly if the water is not sufficiently acid. Algae growth inhibits *Aldrovanda* growth.

A grower reports that a product called Acurel E, available from Lilyponds Water Gardens, Lilyponds, MD 21717 U.S.A., will kill the algae without harming *Aldrovanda*. Four drops per gallon of water is sufficient. He advises that the water may turn purple but will soon clear.

Artificial light—1500 foot candles during growing season. Very little light is needed during dormancy. Photoperiod 14–16 hours during the growing period and 6–10 hours during dormancy.

Pests

None reported to date.

Feeding

Adding fertilizer to the water for these plants is usually not advised as the fertilizer induces algae growth. Add very small water animals such as *daphnia*, water spiders, and microworms to feed the plants. See Chapter 7 for directions.

Miscellaneous

A few snails added to the water in a glass container will keep the glass walls clean. Some growers use aerators to bubble air through the water.

When the plants have elongated and branched out so that the surface of the water is occupied, further growth will be inhibited. In this case transfer the plant to a larger container or divide it and place parts of it in other containers.

If the cultural environment is excellent the terminal bud will be spherical and plump.

PROPAGATION

Sexual Reproduction

Aldrovanda plants require a pH of about 6, a temperature at about 77°F (25°C) and several hours of direct sunlight per day to flower and set seed.

We have hand pollinated the flowers and viable seed was produced. Their ability to self-pollinate in culture is unknown. Since it is rare for these plants to flower for us, we decided not to take any chances and hand-pollinated them. Based on our experience, light and dormancy seem to be the critical factors in promoting flowering once the correct environment has been established as indicated by vigorous growth and large plump terminal buds. The plants that have flowered for us are those grown in sufficient light and which have had a dormant period of near freezing temperatures.

Asexual Reproduction
Stem cuttings:

Cut the stems and/or branches in pieces 2–3 in. (5–8 cm) long in the spring and replace in the water. Each section will develop into a plant.

SECTION II

7

Cultivation

Starting a Collection

The best way to start a successful collection of carnivorous plants is to grow those plants which are easy to cultivate. Plants which are native to your immediate area usually will be relatively easy for you to grow successfully. Often the environment is suitable so that plants can be grown outdoors in the same soil as your garden.

In portions of the southeast coastal states of the United States *Sarracenia* species, some *Pinguicula, Drosera* and *Utricularia* can be grown outdoors in pots. Further south in southern Florida *Nepenthes* species can be grown outdoors.

In southwestern Australia local carnivorous plants can be grown outdoors in pots or in beds. The same is true for many other parts of the world enjoying similar climatic conditions.

Residential areas near natural growing sites may not have the proper humidity in which to grow carnivorous plants but they share the same temperature, daylight periods and seasonal changes. The humidity can be provided by a greenhouse or terrarium-type structure. The important controlling environmental factors, light, temperature and seasonal changes, are provided by nature and are the parameters to which the carnivorous plants in the area are adapted.

Another way to start a successful carnivorous plant collection is to grow species that are easy to cultivate. By "easy" we mean those plants that do not have definite dormancy requirements and can survive in a typical home the year around if placed near a bright window or illuminated with artificial light and grown in a container that will insure a high humidity.

Once some experience is gained with these species, then one can move on to the more demanding ones.

Some of the easier carnivorous plants to grow include the lowland *Nepenthes* spp.; *Cephalotus;* all of the tropical *Utricularia* spp.; terrestrial *Utricularia* spp., *Drosera* spp. such as: *D. capensis, D. spathulata, D. capillaris, D. adelae, D. binata,* complex, and *D. pygmaea;* and Mexican *Pinguicula* spp.

Temperature and Dormancy

TEMPERATURE

The best temperature for growing carnivorous plants is that of the plants' native habitat. If a mixture of plants from different regions of the world are grown together it will be difficult, if not impossible, to reproduce their diverse native temperatures completely. Experience indicates that temperatures for many species can be varied considerably without detrimental results.

There are different temperature areas within every greenhouse or outdoor growing area. Temperatures at the soil level on a bench will be higher than at ground level in the greenhouse. So those plants which require cooler temperatures can be placed on the ground while the others can be grown on benches. Temperatures on the ground vary also, with those areas near the side of the greenhouse exposed to direct sunlight being higher than the shaded areas. The temperature in various parts of the outdoor growing area vary depending upon the degree of shading and protection from winds.

For best results ascertain the optimum temperature for the species to be grown. If average temperature charts are consulted, be sure to consider the elevation of the plant's natural habitat.

If plants grow in the tropics a picture of a hot, steaming jungle may come to mind, but that is not always the case. Figures 7-1 and 7-2 give average world temperatures respectively for January and July. For example, the average temperature for Malaysia is 80°F (26.5°C). What the charts do not reveal and which must be considered is the elevation of the area; that is, how high is it above sea level. *Nepenthes* species; for example, grow at various elevations. Examine the temperature data for Mt. Kinablua in Malaysia. The maximum and minimum temperatures for the various elevations above sea level are as follows: from 0–1000 ft. (305 m), 75–85°F (24–29°C); at 3000 ft. (914 m), 70–75°F (21–24°C); at 6000 ft. (1829 m); 59–72°F (15–22°C); and at 9000 ft. (2743 m) 55–68°F (13–20°C). *Nepenthes* species grow at all of these elevations on this mountain. Thus it is evident that not all *Nepenthes* species require high temperatures to grow.

DORMANCY

Failure to understand and provide for dormancy is a major cause of plant loss. The onset of dormancy is indicated in various ways such as:
1. The formation of winter buds, known as hibernaculum. These tend to be somewhat spherically-shaped and are formed by tight overlapping undeveloped leaves. Associated with their formation is the dying back of the above-ground parts of the plant.
2. The plant stops growing; that is, after producing crops of new leaves upon the onset of the growing season, there is a cessation of new leaf formation.
3. The dying back of the above-ground parts of the plant, leaving an underground rhizome, root, tuber, or bulb.

Dormancy in plants is a time of rest when there is no active growth and just enough biological activity to keep the plants alive. This rest period can occur in the summer, as it does for many Australian species of *Drosera,* or winter as is the case with some North American *Drosera* species. Some plants such as *Aldrovanda* will go into dormancy if conditions are correct. If not they will continue to grow, but often at a slower rate, while other plants need the dormant period or they will not survive. Frequently, plants which do not go into a dormancy cycle, partially or completely, do not exhibit regularity in flowering pattern.

Trying to force plants to continue to grow when they should be entering dormancy, or forcing plants to grow that have not been dormant long enough, will result in feeble growth, easily attacked by fungi or disease resulting in the death of the plant.

AVERAGE JANUARY TEMPERATURE (F°)

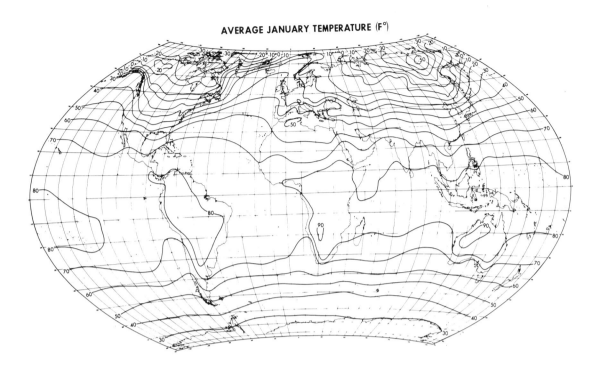

Fig. 7-1

AVERAGE JULY TEMPERATURE (F°)

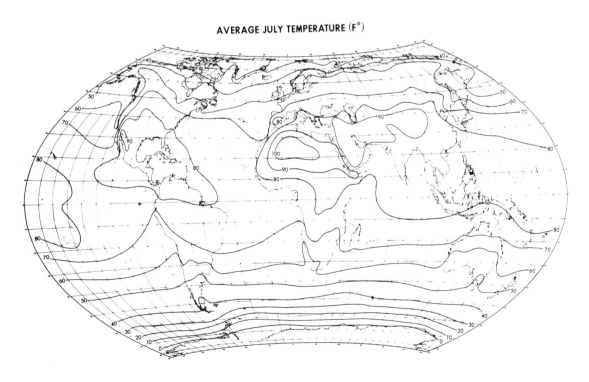

Fig. 7-2

Sometimes, the plant will not grow at all, but simply decay.

There are two basic types of dormancy: winter and summer. Let us examine the winter dormancy pattern first. With the arrival of fall and winter, the photoperiod, temperature, and intensity of sunlight decrease. To provide a winter dormant environment in cultivation, the temperature, photoperiod and intensity of light should be reduced. If your plants are growing in an outdoor bog or greenhouse in the temperate climate, Mother Nature will automatically take care of dormancy, providing the plants can withstand the lowest temperatures that may be reached in your area. In an outside greenhouse open the ventilator windows and doors so that the inside temperature will approximate the outside temperature. When it starts to freeze, the windows and doors should be closed if some of the plants cannot take freezing temperatures. If the plants can tolerate freezing temperatures then the windows and doors can be left open unless the temperature plunges. Because a plant can withstand freezing temperatures does not necessarily mean it can survive at any temperature below freezing. We keep all of our plants except *Nepenthes,* some tropical *Drosera* and some tropical *Utricularia* in a greenhouse which is kept at about 39°F (4°C) during the winter. If you are not around during the day to open and close the windows to control temperatures you will need an automatic window opener which operates thermostatically to open or close the ventilator windows.

Temperatures in a greenhouse with clear glass can reach 90° F (32°C) when the sun is shining even though the outside temperature is well below freezing. This elevated temperature during the winter can cause problems by either preventing plants from going into full dormancy or breaking dormancy too early.

A solution to the problem is to spray white latex paint or shading compound on the outside of the greenhouse glass to reduce the amount of sunlight entering. Paint will last for weeks, but rain and/or snow will wash it off eventually. Shading materials are also beneficial in the summer. They reduce temperatures, reduce evaporation, and hence the frequency of watering and concomitant mineral build-up in the soil. There will be more than adequate light for healthy and vigorous plant growth if used judiciously. Apply the shading material in small quantities because it is much easier to apply more later if needed, than to have to take some off. We apply a layer early in the spring. The white paint is diluted about 10 times, that is 1 quart of paint is mixed with 9 quarts of water. As the temperature warms, we apply more so that by the hottest part of the summer we have a very thick layer. During the early fall we check to see how it is lasting. If thin, we apply more. The material does not adhere well at temperatures below 50°F (10°C). The rain and snow of winter will remove some of the shading material so that as the winter progresses more light is allowed to enter the greenhouse, keeping the temperature higher and resulting in a saving of fuel costs. Around April or May we start to build up the thickness of shading material again in anticipation of the heat of summer.

There are also various fabrics which can be purchased to be placed over the outside glass of the greenhouse to control the amount of sunlight entering.

For growers without an outdoor greenhouse, living in temperate or cold regions, cool cellars, garages, and enclosed porches can be adapted to provide a satisfactory environment for dormant plants.

Growers living in the warmer parts of the world may have to utilize some form of refrigeration. If you use refrigeration, the plants should be uprooted and the tops cut off to save space. The roots or tubers should be sprayed or soaked in a regular-strength fungicide solution for about 5 minutes. We have found that living sphagnum moss is the best medium to store plants in. Wrap damp moss around each plant, so as to avoid having the plants in direct contact with each other. They should then be placed in sealed plastic bags and placed under refrigeration at 35–45°F (1.7–7°C).

If you are growing the plants under lights, the photoperiod can be easily reduced, using a timer. Shortening the day length should be done gradually. The intensity of the light can be reduced by either moving the lights farther away from the plants or by removing a bulb or two from the fixture. The latter practice is more desirable because less heat is produced by the remaining bulbs or tubes helping induce a lower temperature which is conducive to dormancy, as well as saving energy and money.

Keep the dormant plants drier than during the growing season to reduce disease problems and loss of plants.

Now to turn to summer dormancy. Some carnivorous plants, particularly a few *Utricularia* and the tuberous *Drosera*, most of which are from southwestern Australia, enter dormancy during the hot, dry summer. The plants' above-ground parts die back, leaving a tuber or rhizome in the ground to produce a new plant with the arrival of winter and the wet season. It is easy to provide this dormancy period during the summer by withholding water. The problem then is to provide the relatively cool temperatures, from 50–70°F (10–21°C) with plenty of light during the winter for their growth.

Light

Light is one of the most crucial factors in the growth of carnivorous plants. It is vital to the food-manufacturing process and is a timing mechanism for dormancy and/or flowering in most species. Carnivorous plants grow best in natural sunlight because of its spectral balance. Insufficient illumination will result in plants becoming taller or longer than normal, with the result that they are spindly, and weak with oversized leaves which may be malformed. Some plants such as *Sarracenia* will not form open pitchers when grown under inadequate light. An indication of sufficient light is the development of red coloration in the leaves of many of species. Caution! Don't overdo the light, as a light source too intense can retard growth and cause death, particularly of young plants and seedlings.

Outdoor growing areas, an outdoor greenhouse or windows with good exposure to sunlight will provide the necessary light.

A confined growing area in direct sunlight must have adequate ventilation in order to prevent excessive temperature build-up. Direct sunlight on a terrarium with the cover partially or completely off presents no problems in the winter when the sun is low in the sky, but in the summer when the sun is high in the sky, temperatures within the container can quickly become too high, particularly in the warmer regions of the world.

While natural light is ideal for growing carnivorous plants, they can be successfully grown utilizing artificial light, either fluorescent or incandescent. The disadvantages of the latter are twofold: they produce tremendous quantities of heat which can cause over-heating in a confined area and their spectral balance is not the most conducive for plant growth. Fluorescent lights, on the other hand, have a much better spectral balance, produce much less heat and are more efficient producers of light. Cool-white and warm-white tubes are used successfully to grow carnivorous plants. There are fluorescent tubes whose spectral balance more closely approximates that of the sun, some of which are Gro-Lux, Naturescent, Vita-Lite, Plant-Lite and Agro-Lite. The Wonderlite is an incandescent light bulb which can be used in any conventional light socket and has good spectral balance. If the growing area is large enough the use of Lucalox or multivapor lamps, normally used for street lighting, should be considered. Some growers use a combination of incandescent lamps together with cool-white or warm-white fluorescent tubes to obtain a better spectral balance.

For those serious about growing carnivorous plants, the recommended minimum light source is a 2-tube, 40-watt fluorescent assembly with a metallic reflector. A 4-tube, 40-watt fixture is, however, preferable.

Light intensity is commonly measured in units called foot candles. A foot candle is a measure of the amount of light in the visible spectrum incident to a surface. In addition to visible light, there are portions of the spectrum in the invisible range which are important to plant growth that are not recorded by a foot-candle meter. In spite of this deficiency, the foot-candle unit is still a useful and convenient measurement.

With artifical lights, the distance of the light fixtures from the plants is very important. The influence of distance is illustrated by Chart 1, which was compiled by the United States Department of Agriculture.

Chart 1

Illumination in foot-candles at various distances from 2- and 4-tube, 40-watt standard cool, white fluorescent lamps mounted approximately 2 inches from a white painted reflector

Distance from lamps (inches)	Two lamps[1] Used[2] Ft.-c	Four lamps[1] Used[2] Ft.-c	Four lamps[1] New Ft.-c
1	1,100	1,600	1,800
2	860	1,400	1,600
3	680	1,300	1,400
4	570	1,100	1,300
5	500	940	1,150
6	420	820	1,000
7	360	720	900
8	330	660	830
9	300	600	780
10	280	560	720
11	260	510	660
12	240	480	600
18	130	320	420
24	100	190	260

1 Center-to-center distance between the lamps is 2 inches.
2 These lamps had been used for approximately 200 hours.

This data reveals that doubling the distance of the light from 1 in. (2.5 cm) to 2 in. (5 cm) results in a 22% decrease in illumination when using a 2-tube fixture, while a 4-tube fixture results in a 12% decrease. If a 2-tube fixture is 6 in. (15 cm) above the plants and then raised to 12 in. (30 cm), doubling the distance, illumination is reduced 42%. These results refute the common fallacy that doubling the distance of the light fixture from plants always reduces the intensity of illumination by the same amount.

Lights should be hung so that their height can be adjusted to accommodate both the height of the plants being grown and plant growth. We support our light fixtures with lightweight chains.

Keep the fixture close to the growing plants, particularly newly developing ones. Remove 2 of the tubes over young plants to reduce heat and cost. The young plants will have adequate light for healthy and sustained growth. As the plants grow, shorten the chains to keep the fixtures away from the new growth. When growth is well along replace the removed tubes.

For example, when a *Sarracenia flava* rhizome is planted, just the growing tip or the bud is exposed to the light. To provide adequate light, lower the fixture to within a few inches of the growing tip. Since the light source is very close, 2 tubes of a 4-tube fixture can be removed. As the leaves start to grow the light fixture will have to be moved upward to keep it out of the way of the growing leaves. As the light source is elevated, a point will be reached when the tubes must be replaced to provide adequate light. A *S. flava* plant can have pitchers up to 4 ft. (1.2 m) high so with the fixture above the mature leaves, the newly emerging leaves will not have enough light for optimum growth if all the tubes are not present.

Height differences between species are best solved by growing plants of similar height and light requirements under 1 light assembly and another group with different requirements under another. If your space or setup will not permit separate groupings, plant the taller plants in the back of the growing area and progressively plant the shorter ones toward the front. A light assembly can then be positioned in the front and/or sides and angled toward the soil level. (Fig. 7-3)

Normally heat build-up with fluorescent lights is not a serious problem unless the growing area is in an intrinsically warm room. In that case, take steps to lower the temperature.

As fluorescent tubes age, the amount of light they produce decreases. While the aging of the bulbs is quite variable, depending upon the environment, the loss of efficiency after 2000 hours (142 14-hour days) is 5–12%, 8000 hours (571 14-hour days or 1.6 years) 10–38%, 12,000 hours (857 14-hour days or 2.3 years) 10–45%. Therefore, as tubes age, it is necessary to bring the light assembly closer to the plants or replace the tubes.

Use a photographer's light meter to measure the illumination in foot-candles. The light requirement for each genus is indicated in the description of the genera. If you do not have access to a light meter an alternative is to use a camera with a built-in light-meter. Set the film speed to ASA 25 and shutter speed to 1/60. Place a piece of opaque paper next to and in the same plane as the leaves of the plant. The camera-to-paper distance should be no longer than the narrowest dimension of the paper. Adjust the f-stop (lens opening) until the meter indicates the correct exposure. The lens opening will yield the approximate illumination as given in Table 1.

Table 1

f-stop	Foot Candles
f/2	40
f/2.8	75
f/4	150
f/5.6	300
f/8	600
f/11	1,200
f/16	2,400

If neither light meter nor camera is available, continual observation will provide empirical results to guide you. Start with the light source about 2 ft. (61 cm) above the plants. As the plants develop, close observation will tell you if they are healthy and strong. If not, adjust your light distance accordingly. Inadequate light is manifested by weak, spindly, and unusually long growth, whereas excessive light may be indicated by extremely deep red or purple coloration or stunted growth. Always change the lighting to suit your plants, their stage of development and their health. Don't hesitate to make adjustments in the intensity of illumination for a given plant if you find the suggested value is either inadequate or excessive in your cultural environment. There are many environmental factors involved in correct lighting. With experience one will be able to judge the best intensity of illumination for the plants being grown.

Light intensity can be increased in an indoor growing area by using shiny surface coatings on the walls to reflect light back into the container that would normally be lost to the outside. Paint the walls with white or silver paint or line them with a metal foil such as aluminum foil.

The plants' photoperiod is the duration of daylight or artificial light plants are exposed to each day. Plants in their native habitat have adapted to a given photoperiod which is determined by their latitude, that is the distance north or south of the equator. Chart 2 shows how the length of daylight varies with latitude.

Chart 2

Latitude	June 21 Length of daylight	December 21 Length of daylight
90 deg. N	24 hours	0 hours
80	24	0
70	24	0
60	18½	5½
50	16¼	7¾
40	15	9
30	14	10
20	13¼	10¾
10	12½	11½
0	12	12
10 deg. S	11½	12½
20	10¾	13¼
30	10	14
40	9	15
50	7¾	16¼
60	5½	18½
70	0	24
80	0	24
90	0	24

The daylight period for a region at 50 degrees north or south of the equator varies from a minimum of 7¾ hours in the winter to a maximum of 16¼ hours in the summer (June 21). The best guide to a particular plant's photoperiod is the latitude of its native habitat. Some plants such as *Aldrovanda* grow in a wide range of latitudes and can, therefore, survive under various photoperiods. Some plants such as the arctic and subarctic *Pinguicula* are very sensitive to photoperiod. If a wide range of plants from varying latitudes are grown together a compromise in photoperiod will be necessary. A photoperiod of a 14–17 hour day for those plants that do not require a dormant period has been successful.

Some hobbyists are experimenting with a 24-hour photoperiod. Some carnivorous plants have not flowered or if they have, do not set viable seed in cultivation. It could be that the photoperiod is critical to these plants.

The study of photoperiod is almost virgin territory which needs much more investigation.

Water & Humidity

Soils should be kept wet during the growing season; wet does not mean waterlogged. While some species of carnivores will tolerate being waterlogged at times, most will not. During the plant's dormancy period, keep the soil barely damp.

Ideally, the water used for watering carnivorous plants should be free of minerals and noxious impurities. Distilled water and rain water are excellent. It may be inconvenient or too expensive to use mineral-free water. Therefore, well water or water treated by a municipality must be used. The problem with hard water (water with a high mineral content) is that when the water evaporates from the soil and/or from the sides of pots, the minerals are left behind. In time the concentration of minerals can reach levels that are harmful to the plants. This does not mean that the plants will die immediately, but rather that the plants' health will gradually deteriorate. If plants are not as

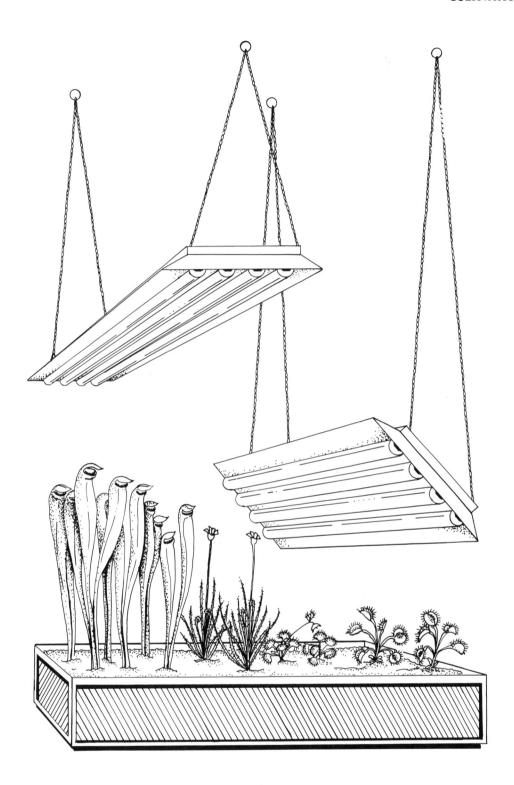

Fig. 7-3 To insure adequate lighting of both tall and short plants in the same planting, lighting fixtures are hung so that their height is adjustable and their light is angled toward the plants.

healthy as they used to be, check the soil for mineral content. An indicator of this problem, often called mineral build-up, is the presence of a variagated crusty material on the soil or pot surface.

While mineral-free water is ideal, this should not be interpreted to imply that hard water cannot be used. Hard water and municipality-treated water can be used to achieve results as good as those obtained with distilled and rain water. Municipality-treated water contains a germicide such as chlorine or fluorine. Allow treated water to stand a day or two in an open container so the chlorine or fluorine will leave the water. This practice is particularly desirable if the plants are grown in a small enclosed container in which the chlorine and fluorine gas can cause problems. We have used city water treated with flourine for over 15 years on all of our plants with no apparent ill-effect. For 10 years preceding this period we used hard well water with the same excellent results.

Frequently growers owning a water softener think that the softened water is low in minerals. This is only partly true. Hard water contains ions such as calcium, magnesium, and iron. When the water is "softened" these ions are removed, but in the process other ions such as sodium replace those removed from the water. Therefore, the water from a water softener still has many minerals or ions. Even though the ones that are troublesome in laundering have been removed, some remain which may cause problems in growing carnivorous plants.

Some growers acidify water used on carnivorous plants that normally grow in acid soil. One of the acidifiers used is aluminum sulfate. A good homemade solution can be prepared by using 1 tablespoon (15 ml) of acidifer per gallon or 4 liters of water. Another type of acidifier contains trace minerals—for example, Miracid. Start with a solution made of 1½ teaspoons (7½ ml) per gallon or 4 liters of water. Either of these solutions are used in place of water.

It is vital that plants be monitored when using these solutions for any possible ill effect. The experience gained with these concentrations is a guide for future dilution rates. To our knowledge these materials have been used on some *Sarracenia, Drosera,* and *Pinguicula* species.

Many of the carnivorous plants grow in bogs, swamps and wetlands. This indicates that many of them need or do best under conditions of high humidity. If the humidity in your growing area is not high enough, you must employ terrariums, greenhouses, aquariums or glass jars. It should be pointed out that many carnivorous plants will grow in a less humid environment than found in their native habitat. See the *Nepenthes* chapter for a *N. anamensis* plant grown in our bedroom to confirm plant adaptability. While this species grew well, do not rely upon it as proving that all the other species will do as well. The humidity levels tolerated by carnivorous plants in culture need more investigation. We suspect that many plants will do well at lower relative humidities than previously thought.

If a higher humidity is needed in a large area, use a humidifier. There are types designed for greenhouse use. We spray the walls and the floor of the greenhouse during very hot weather both to maintain the humidity level and reduce the temperature.

Planting Media

The planting medium serves to anchor the plant as well to provide a reservoir for moisture and nutrients. Most carnivorous plants require an acidic medium (a pH of less than 7), which is permeable and contains a low concentration of nutrients.

Carnivorous plants have been grown successfully in a variety of planting media. Some of the more commonly utilized ingredients are living and/or dead sphagnum moss (long fiber or milled), sphagnum peat moss, sand, horticultural grade perlite, vermiculite and osmundum fibers. Silica sand, which is slightly acidic, is preferred by most carnivorous plants. Limestone sand, which is basic (pH greater than 7), is used for those few species that grow in alkaline soils. Limestone sand can be identified by placing a few drops of a dilute acid, vinegar or orange juice, on the sand which will then effervesce.

The recommended planting media can be used separately or mixed. A few growers have successfully used prepackaged soil mixtures formulated for house plants. The planting medium we use for most of our carnivorous plants is sphagnum peat moss which is readily available and economical.

Living sphagnum moss has some noteworthy advantages which should be mentioned. Its green color provides a pleasing background for the plants. It grows and produces more of itself. It is a sensitive indicator of some toxic materials, so if the moss is in poor health you know your growing conditions are poor. It is acidic, and it helps maintain a high humidity around the plants. The disadvantage of using living sphagnum moss is that it tends to overgrow the shorter carnivores such as some of the smaller *Drosera, Pinguicula,* and *Utricularia* species. To prevent overgrowth cut it back with a pair of scissors or pull it away from around the plants. Both tasks are time-consuming and tedious.

One convenient and suitable planting medium for many carnivores is 1 part sphagnum peat moss to 1 part sand. The ratio is given on a volume basis, that is, the mix consists of 1 volume of sand and 1 volume of sphagnum peat moss. This means that any size container can be used to measure the ingredients. Equal quantities of each material are used. For example, 1 cup or 1 bushel of each ingredient is measured out and mixed together. Mixing media is easier when they are dry or almost dry.

After a planting medium has been made or selected, throughly wet it by soaking for an hour or so before using it. A convenient way to wet the planting medium is to fill planting pots that have drainage holes with medium and place them in a container such that when water is added to the container the water level will be at or very near the top of the medium in the pots. After a short time the water level will drop in the container because it is being absorbed by the planting medium. Fill it again. After the medium has been soaked, remove the pots and allow the excess water to drain before planting. Dry sphagnum peat moss is particularily difficult to wet. It should placed in a pail with some water and kneeded until it is thoroughly wet. The addition of a few drops of wetting agent to the water makes the task easier. A cleaner method of wetting sphagnum peat moss is to put it in a plastic bag, then add water and twist the top of the bag closed. Then the peat moss and water can be kneaded together until thoroughly wet.

POTTING

Pots should be selected of a size such that when the plant is positioned its root system can be spread out and not touch the walls. A pot cannot be too big for a plant; it is best to use one which is too large rather than too small. The only problem in using over-sized pots is that they take up a great deal of space so in a limited growing area the number of plants is limited.

The pot is filled to within 1 in. (2.5 cm) of the top with medium. If the planting medium can leak out of the drain holes, cover them with pebbles, broken pieces of clay pots, or with a thin layer of sphagnum peat moss. Some growers prefer to crock their pots which means to place an inch (2.5 cm) or so of broken pieces of clay pots or pebbles on the bottom of the pot. We have not found this practice to be desirable or necessary.

The terrestrial *Utricularia* and *Genlisea;* and *Polypompholyx* are usually obtained in clumps mixed with the planting medium. A depression is made in the new planting medium such that when the clump is placed in it the surface of the clump will be at the same level as the surrounding soil mix.

For all other species a depression should be made in the soil large enough so that when the plant is positioned the crown of the plant will be at soil level and its roots can be separated and spread out away from the base of the plant. Then the medium should be gently packed around and on top of the roots firmly enough to hold the plant in position.

If *Drosera* and *Pinguicula* spp. are watered from above, it is desirable to place a thin layer of pebbles over the surface of the medium to prevent soil from splashing onto the plants. Once medium is on their leaves it is difficult, if not impossible, to remove all of it. Its presence on the leaves not only detracts from the appearance of plant but also reduces the effective photosynthetic area.

After plants are potted, they should be thoroughly watered, kept out of direct sunlight, and placed in a higher-than-normal level of humidity for a few weeks before exposing them to their permanent growing environment. These precautions are particularly important if repotting is done while plants are actively growing.

REPOTTING

Repotting is required when the plants have grown too large for their containers or too many plants occupy the pot or the planting medium has become unfit.

The latter is indicated by declining plant vigor, meaning that the plants are not as healthy as they used to be. For example, the plant, instead of growing larger each year or at least retaining its size, becomes smaller. Each year the plant produces crops of new leaves which may be the same size the first few years of declining vigor, but later will be smaller. Or new growth is not strong but tends to be weak and "papery." Another indicator is the health of the plant which is difficult to describe, but after one works with them for some time one can tell when a plant is healthy or not.

Conditions that cause declining vigor include mineral build-up, soil deterioration, or infestations of pests.

Mineral build-up is evidenced by grayish-white, mottled deposits on the soil surface and/or sides or edges of the pot and by an increasing pH. As the minerals accumulate the soil becomes more alkaline. Mineral accumulation occurs when water evaporates, leaving the minerals it contains behind in the soil or pot. Ideally, distilled water or rain water (free of minerals) should be used (See section on watering).

Deterioration of the planting medium is another indicator that it should be changed. Media such as sphagnum moss and sphagnum peat moss are spongy when new or unused. If a handful is squeezed it will spring back somewhat when the hand is opened. When these media break down they do not spring back but rather become sticky and mushy.

Sometimes the planting media may become seriously infested with aphids, mites or other pests. Usually it is easier to change the soil than to try to treat the plant and the soil with a pesticide. If earthworms get into the soil they may create problems by tunneling through the soil and leaving castings on the surface. They can be particularily destructive in pots of very young seedlings.

Usually the best time to repot is when the plants are dormant, just before active growth resumes. If there is a serious problem, however, the medium should be changed as soon as the problem is recognized. Remember though that repotting is riskier if done when the plants are actively growing.

The repotting procedure is straightforward. The plants are removed from their present pots with care so as to not damage the roots. This can be accomplished by immersing the pot with the plant in water so that all or almost all of the medium is below water level. It is best to not wet the leaves of plants such as *Drosera* and *Pinguicula* any more than necessary. Let the pot soak for about ½ hour to loosen the medium so that the plant can be easily removed with minimal damage to the roots. Another technique used to separate the plant from the medium is to remove the plant with its ball of medium from the pot and then gently wash away the medium with a mild stream of water from a hose or faucet.

To repot plants follow the procedures outlined in the potting section of this chapter.

Containers

Any container specifically designed for the growing of plants is suitable for carnivorous plants. In addition, less obvious containers such as plastic pails, child-size swimming pools, bushel baskets, wooden boxes, aquariums, large glass jars, and brandy snifters can be used.

While pots are made of almost every kind of material, the more commonly used are plastic, clay and wood. Generally plastic pots are more economical, lighter and easier to use. A problem associated with a porous container, such as a clay pot, is that when water evaporates from its surface the minerals that were in the water are left behind in the pore spaces and on the surface. In time, the mineral build-up in the walls of clay pots or on the rim of plastic pots will adversely effect plants growing in them. A clue to mineral build-up is deposition of variegated crusty-like material. It is very difficult and time-consuming to remove the minerals from clay pots. Soaking in water for several days will remove some of the minerals, but usually the pots must be treated with acid to remove the balance of the minerals. It is easy to remove mineral deposits from the rim of plastic pots by using steel wool, a metal brush or scraping with a sharp tool.

The pore spaces in clay pots provide ideal homes for pests such as fungi while algae and moss may grow on the damp sides. Plastic pots are less likely to harbor disease organisms. Another advantage of plastic pots is that watering need not be as frequent because there is no evaporation from the walls of the pot. We strongly urge the use of plastic pots with drain holes until you become experienced with growing carnivorous plants.

Plastic pots are made with and without drain holes, both kinds are used succesfully in growing carnivorous plants. There are some advantages in using pots without drain holes, the major one being reduced watering. If this type is used, then provisions must be made for monitoring the depth of water in the medium. This can be done by inserting a piece of perforated plastic tubing near the edge of the pot. If perforated plastic tubing is not available, it can be made by drilling numerous small holes in the lower end of solid tubing. (If the media used has a high sand content, it is best to use tubing without perforations.) The water level in the tube will be the same as in the surrounding media so water level can be accurately gauged. An alternative is to plunge a small plastic pot with drain holes into the media in the larger container. These water level monitors not only assure the maintainance of a given water level, but can also be utilized to water the plants by pouring water into them. As experience using containers without a drain hole is gained and/or a grower is very careful in watering, water monitors can be discarded, but they do make it easy to water the plants, particularily *Drosera* and *Pinguicula* whose leaves should not be wetted too often.

We have used wooden pots occasionally, but find they are not as convenient as plastic or clay, because they tend to become heavy when the wood is soaked and will eventually rot, providing a haven for insects and other pests. Redwood pots will last a considerable time, but become heavy when water-soaked. Wooden pots can be lined with plastic to prevent water from soaking the wood and to delay decay. Wooden pots are sometimes treated with a wood preservative to delay decay, but we have never tried them for fear the chemicals might enter the medium and adversely affect the plants.

Some carnivorous plants like to have their root ends in standing water. To accommodate them, obtain a pot or pail without drain holes and drill a hole in the side a few inches from the bottom. When the pot is filled with soil, planted, and watered, the soil below the level of the hole will be saturated with water while any excess water will flow out the drain hole.

The type of container chosen will, in part, be determined by the environment in which the plants are growing. If the growing environment is humid, plants can be grown successfully in pots. If not sufficiently humid it will be necessary to provide humidity by growing them in a second container such as an aquarium, terrarium, large glass or clear plastic jar or greenhouse.

Providing high humidity within a secondary container is not difficult. Choose a glass or plastic container that allows light to pass through and whose opening can be covered if too much water evaporates. Such a container can be as fancy as a large brandy snifter or as practical as an old aquarium or gallon (4 liter) jar.

When selecting your carnivorous plant terrarium, be sure to consider the size attained by mature plants to insure that the container selected will be tall enough for fully grown plants. Most *Dionaea, Drosera,* and *Utricularia* do not create problems, but plants such as *Darlingtonia, Nepenthes,* and some *Sarracenia* species have leaves and/or stems that can exceed 4 ft. (1.2 m). Young plants of all terrestrial species can be grown in terrarium-like containers for several years.

Care of your carnivorous plant terrarium consists basically of providing water and light. The plants should be watered when peat moss in the high spots becomes lighter brown, indicating that it is starting to dry out. The other built-in signal for watering is the pulling away of peat moss from the sides of the terrarium, again indicating drying out. Over-watering can be remedied by leaving the cover off of the terrarium to let it dry out. The plants will not be damaged by occasional over-watering.

Carnivorous plants thrive in direct sunlight as long as they are adequately watered and are surrounded by a highly humid atmosphere. The danger from direct sunlight is the build-up of lethal temperatures within the terrarium. In such a case simply remove the cover of the terrarium. Air circulation will not only keep the internal temperature down, but will also help prevent the growth of fungi.

Feeding & Fertilizing

We usually don't fertilize or feed our plants and they are healthy and grow vigorously. The plants in our outdoor greenhouse catch a few insects in the summer, while those in the indoor greenhouse and terrariums do not get any insects at all. Some growers fertilize and/or feed their plants and feel that the plants benefit from it. The degree of benefit is obviously a function of the nutrient content of the planting media.

FEEDING

Avoid feeding fatty meat as it will more often then not kill the trap or leaf. Do not feed large portions at one time as this can damage or kill the trap. Insects, lean meat, and powdered milk can be fed to all terrestrial carnivores except *Utricularia.* The food is placed in or on the trap about once every 3–4 weeks during the growing season.

It is easier to feed *Utriculria, Aldrovanda,* and *Genlisea* very small animals, known as protozoans, such as *Daphnia* and microworms which are available from tropical fish stores. These organisms can be propagated at home by making a hay infusion.

To make a hay infusion fill a vessel such as a quart jar with dried chopped grass, hay, straw, cattails, etc. Pour boiling water over the material until the vessel is almost full and place it in a warm spot for 3–4 weeks. Draw some of the liquid off and add it to the aquatic carnivore culture about once every 3 weeks during the growing season. The liquid from the hay infusion will provide microorganisms for the plants and help maintain an acid medium.

FERTILIZING

Fish oil emulsions, seaweed mixtures and any of the rich inorganic fertilizer formulations such as Rapid Gro or Miracid can be used to fertilize carnivorous plants. Organic fertizers such as fish oil emulsion in small growing areas or terrariums can cause devastating fungal infections. We strongly recommend that organic fertilizers not be used in small or confined areas.

Various growers recommend different dilutions for the inorganic fertilizers. The recommendations are confusing because the dilution that works for one grower is detrimental to the plants when tried by another. Frequently the deleterious effects of fertilizing results from the addition of nutrients which the planting medium already has in sufficient quantities. We have tried different fertilizers at various concentrations in a variety of planting media and can recommend diluting the fertilizer about 8 times the label recommendation. To our knowledge growers diluting at this rate have not experienced any untoward effects. For example, if the label calls for 5 teaspoons (25 ml) of fertilizer per gallon or liter of water, ⅛ this rate is ⅔ of a teaspoon (3 ml) per gallon or liter. [One tablespoon (Tbsp.) is equal to 3 teaspoons (tsp) and 1 teaspoon is equal to 5 milliliters (ml).]

Application of fertilizer

The fertilizer solution is applied once every 3–4 weeks to the soil during the growing season. The solution can be sprayed on the leaves of some species, a process called foliar feeding. Some of the fertilizer solution can be placed in the pitchers of *Nepenthes*, *Sarracenia*, *Heliamphora* and *Cephalotus*.

Plants should not be fed and fertilized at the same time. One or the other is done, but not both. If plants are foliarly fed, no fertilizer should be placed in the soil.

The addition of fertilizer to the water of aquatic species usually results in algae growth which can be troublesome. To avoid this problem use microorganisms to feed the plants.

Growing Plants in an Outdoor Bog

Some fortunate people live in areas of the world where the natural environment is suitable for growing some carnivorous plants outside the home or greenhouse for part of or the entire year.

For those not so blessed, an artificial bog is an excellent alternative. The site must have at least 5 hours of direct sunlight, be protected from high winds, and have an adequate supply of water if rainfall is insufficient to maintain the water level. The species of plants grown will determine the hours of direct sunlight required. If your site does not have natural shade to limit the light received by the plants, a lath-house will do the job. A lath-house will also protect plants from falling rain. In nature some of the more delicate plants such as *Drosera* and *Pinguicula* often grow intermingled with taller plants such as grasses, which protect them from the direct rain by breaking the fall of the rain drops.

To make the bog obtain a container of the size of the bog you plan. The depth of the container should be at least 6 in. (15 cm), but preferably about 12 in. (30 cm). The container can be almost anything which will hold water such as a plastic or wooden tub, a child's plastic swimming pool or plain plastic sheeting. A hole is dug large enough so that the edge or rim of the container will be an inch (2.5 cm) or so below the soil level. A drain hole ⅛–¼ in. (0.3–0.6 cm) in diameter is made in the side, midway between the top and the bottom of the container. This will allow excess water to drain out slowly, thereby keeping the water table level at the drain hole height.

If the bog is made with sheet plastic, use a heavy grade of at least 6 mils or a double layer if you cannot obtain a heavy guage sheet. A single layer of a thinner sheet is likely to be punctured by stone or debris. If the soil has many rocks, it is advisable to spread a layer of sphagnum peat moss or other such cushioning material over the surface of the depression in order to protect the plastic. Then spread the plastic sheet over the soil surface so that the plastic extends a foot (30.5 cm) or two (61 cm) beyond the opening. As the planting medium is added the plastic will be forced against the bottom and side surfaces and will be pulled down. A drain hole is made in the side, about midway between the top and bottom as previously indicated. Fill the container with wet medium and allow it to set a few days to insure thorough wetting and settling of the medium as well as to drain excess water. The edge of the plastic is then cut so that it is about 1 in. (2.5 cm) below the surrounding soil level. More medium is added, if needed, to raise the level of the medium in the bog to that of the surrounding soil or a little higher. This will result in a bog which will appear to be part of the natural landscape.

Generally speaking, the tallest plants should be in the back and the shortest in the front of the bog. The front of the bog is the side that faces the sun. It may be wise not to follow this rule absolutely because in nature, the plants are intermingled, tall plants mixed with short plants. Avoid planting in straight rows. Plants should be grouped in clumps of several of the same species to simulate a "natural" appearance. Plants such as *Sarracenia purpurea* ssp. *purpurea* and *Darlingtonia* that grow best under cooler conditions must be planted so that they will be shaded by others. The plants can be planted directly in the bog or they can be planted in porous pots which, in turn, are buried in the planting medium. In the latter case, the plants can be removed from the bog without incurring damage or shock. This is an easy method of handling plants that you want outside during the summer and inside when it's colder. After the bog is planted some living sphagnum moss can be 'planted' in various areas of the bog. There is no need to cover the entire surface with sphagnum moss because it will spread and eventually cover the entire surface if the environment is suitable.

If aquatic *Utricularia,* and *Aldrovanda* are desired in the bog, a container such as a plastic pail, preferably green, can be inserted in the bog so that its rim is a bit below the soil surface. The aquatic plant container must be placed in a protected area, as a sudden downpour can wash out its inhabitants. Cut a drain hole about 3 in. (7.5 cm) from the top of the pail and place an inch or two (2.5 or 5 cm) of medium in the bottom of the pail, then add water and adjust its pH to the correct value (see the appropriate chapter for the plants being grown). When the water clears the plants are added.

It may be necessary to fence the bog to keep out animals and/or people to prevent damage and vandalism. Pests such as slugs, that enjoy moist conditions, will surely be attracted to the bog and must be dealt with.

Bogs in the temperate zone can be winterized by covering them with a foot (30 cm) of hay, straw or moss. If needles of evergreen trees, such as pines and firs, are available use them for mulch as when they decay, acid is produced, keeping the bog acidic.

When to Buy and/or Trade and Care of Plants Upon Arrival _____

The best time to obtain plants is when they are in a dormant stage just before their growing season starts. For plants that have a winter dormancy, early spring is the ideal time to purchase and for those with a summer dormancy, fall is the best time. Seeds of the carnivores can be shipped through the mail at any time except for tropical species which can be killed by freezing temperatures.

Plants are usually shipped bare root with the more delicate species wrapped in spahgnum moss. Upon arrival, remove the contents of the parcel and do not discard any of the packing materials until a thorough accounting has been made of all the plants you were supposed to receive. Some of the plants ordered during the dormant season will arrive as winter buds which tend to be small and some shade of green to grey and, as such, they can be easily overlooked if they are packed in material such as non-living sphagnum moss. Some people will unpack the parcel, plant the items received and days or weeks later check their records and discover that something is missing. It could be a mistake made by the shipper or it could be that the item(s) was inadvertently discarded with the packing material. If there is a shortage after checking the packing material thoroughly, a note should be sent to the shipper immediately. Credibility may be questioned if a few months elapse before you notify the shipper.

When plants are shipped by mail or United Parcel Service (UPS), they sometimes look weathered due to packing and transit. *Drosera* and *Pinguicula* that have been wrapped in sphagnum moss may be soiled or dirty-looking because of the moss fragments, particularly on leaves with tentacles. Do not be alarmed as they will recover given time and proper care.

Plants should be unpacked in a humid, shaded area protected from the wind. After plants have been removed from the plastic bags and packing material, if any, they should be cleaned and the damaged leaves should be cut off with a sharp tool such as a razor blade to prevent decay. Cut surfaces should be sprayed or wet with a fungicide diluted to about ⅓ the recommended label strength. The damaged leaves removed from plants such as *Drosera, Pinguicula,* and *Cephalotus* can be used as leaf cuttings by following the procedure given for leaf cuttings to propagate more plants.

Plants should be separated and planted individually except for *Utricularia, Polypompholyx* and *Genlisea* which are kept as a clump. Often, if you order a *Drosera* plant, there may be some smaller ones attached to the main plant. Casually looking at such a plant it may seem to be only one, but upon careful examination you can determine if it is one plant or a group of plants. If it is a group, they should be separated gently.

8

Pests and Diseases

This may seem to be an incongruous chapter for a book on carnivorous plants but, unfortunately, it is not. There are animals (insects, mites and scale) and fungi (plants without chlorophyll) that attack carnivorous plants and can eventually cause their death.

Fungus diseases can be devastating to a collection of plants, particularly to the succulent types such as *Pinguicula* and *Drosera* and to seedling plants of almost all species.

Prevention of pest infestation is usually the simplest, most economical, and the best path to follow. Some techniques for accomplishing this are:

1. Remove all the dead parts of plants such as old flower stalks and leaves. Fungus infection often starts on the dead parts of plants and later spreads to the rest of the plant. Not only will their removal help prevent infestation, it will enhance the beauty of the plants. Also do not leave plant debris on the soil or in the growing area as it provides a breeding site for pests.

2. When new plants are obtained, examine them carefully to determine if any pests or diseases are present. The plants could have a disease and its manifestations may take several weeks to become apparent. Or, there may be eggs or spores which require more time to develop. If possible, isolate new plants from the rest of your collection. One method is to place a new plant in its pot in a plastic bag of sufficient size, inflate the bag and seal it, thereby creating a small isolation chamber. Never place any plant in an enclosed container in direct sunlight.

3. If a pest appears in a pot or on a plant, remove the plant from the rest of the collection while treating it to prevent further contamination. Isolate the plant during treatment using a transparent plastic bag as an isolation chamber. Spray or dust the plant in the bag and seal it. This procedure not only prevents further spread of the pest but also confines the pesticide within the bag.

4. Provide the proper environment for plants so that they will be healthy and vigorous. Low light levels, high humidity, and poor ventilation provide

excellent conditions for fungus infestation and development. Fungal growth occurs most readily when plants are grown in enclosed containers, particularly small ones and in outdoor greenhouses in the colder parts of the world during the fall and winter when the greenhouse is "buttoned up" for the winter. Ventilation windows are closed and, in many cases, sealed until the following spring. The resulting poor ventilation can be circumvented by using a fan to keep the air in the greenhouse circulating. Experience indicates that healthier plants are better able to ward off pests.

5. Knives or scissors used to remove infected plant parts should be disinfected after use. It is a good policy to not only disinfect all tools after using them, but also all pots. A satisfactory solution for treating tools and pots can be made by mixing 1 part liquid bleach, such as Clorox, in 6 parts of water. For example, mix 1 cup of bleach to 6 cups water. Soak the items in the solution for about 1 hour and then rinse thoroughly in fresh water.

SLIME MOLD

Slime mold grows on the soil. While it does not seem to infect the plants directly, plants growing in a medium covered with slime mold do not seem to thrive as well. Very small seedling plants can be smothered by it. When infestation occurs, remove the plants and discard the medium. Wash off the plants and repot in fresh medium.

FUNGUS

Fungi, such as *Botrytis,* are usually more common when soils are wet, light levels low and ventilation poor. Fungus appears as a fuzzy growth, usually on dead parts of the plants first. Upon closer examination, the growth looks like thousands of short "hairs" which have spherically-shaped structures called spore bodies at the ends of the hairs. The spore bodies contain the spores which are the source of a new generation of fungi. New fungi will grow from the small dust-like spores, which are very easily spread by the gentlest air currents throughout a growing area. The infestation can spread with alarming speed among the more susceptible species.

Fungicides containing benomyl, such as Benlate, are effective and safe on carnivorous plants. Follow label directions for the proper dilution. It is important to spray the plants thoroughly and to saturate the upper layer of soil in order to kill the infecting agents in the soil. Once an area has been infected with a fungus it is extremely difficult to eradicate. It is good insurance to spray the winter buds of terrestrial plants with a fungicide to ward off fungal infection.

After treating our outdoor greenhouse for *Botrytis* during one fall and early winter, it appeared we had eradicated it. The following spring we transplanted some seedlings from starter pots into larger ones. There was no trace of *Botrytis* that we could see, but it showed up in the transplanted seedlings. It proved very difficult to eliminate all the spores even with extensive spraying. The following winter *Botrytis* appeared again in numerous areas in the greenhouse. Now we spray fungicide in a regular program starting in the early fall and into the early winter at 2-week intervals. This, together with our regular practice of treating all transplanted plants with a fungicide, has eliminated loss from this pest.

The last few years we have used Exotherm Termil, a fungicide which is released by burning. It comes in a can. To use, the top is taken off and the material ignited with a match or propane burner. Tremendous clouds of smoke (the fungicide) are produced. It is very effective and has not damaged any of our plants.

APHIDS

Of all the animal pests, aphids are the most troublesome in our greenhouse. Their presence is revealed by malformed leaves and flower stalks, or a smattering of tiny white to green particles on the soil surface and the lower parts of the plants. Often the whitish debris is visible before the infestation is serious enough to cause malformed leaves. Close examination will reveal the presence of aphids.

We formerly used liquid Sevin on all of our plants to control aphids, following the label's suggested dilution and applied at 2-week intervals until the aphids were eliminated. After using Sevin for several years we found it was becoming less effective even at higher concentrations and with more frequent applications. Forced to something else we chose Malathion, which is effective but is tougher on the more sensitive plants such as some *Utricularia, Drosera,* and *Pinguicula.* The leaves may be malformed or die after treatment with Malathion, but new leaves will develop normally. We have followed label directions for dilution and use. We are experimenting with a more dilute solution to control the aphids on the more sensitive species.

It is good practice to periodically change the pesticide you use for a particular pest in order to prevent the development of resistant strains of the pest. Sevin may be used for a few years to control aphids, then switch to another pesticide for a few years, and then switch back to Sevin.

MEALY BUGS AND SCALE

Mealy bugs look like small fluffs of cotton and are easily seen. Scale bugs which have a roundish shell, are difficult to see. But their presence is revealed by the growth of a very dark mildew on the sweet fluid secreted by the scale. Malathion will control both of these pests when label directions are followed.

LARVAE

Various larvae (appearing as small worms or caterpillars) infect *Sarracenia* plants by attacking the leaves and/or rhizomes. When the leaves are affected, simply remove and destroy them. If loss of leaves is objectionable or if all of them are involved, Sevin or Malathion can be used, following label directions.

There is a larvae that attacks the *Sarracenia* rhizome whose presence is revealed by piles of reddish brown debris resembling earthworm castings in the area of the plant crown. By removing the material and probing around the rhizome the hole made by the borer (larvae) can be located. Remove the larvae with a pair of tweezers unless the tunnel is tortuous. In this case, some Malathion, diluted to label directions, is poured into the tunnel. Another technique is to uproot the plant, cut the rhizome length-wise along the tunnel, being careful to cut the rhizome so that there are roots on both halves of it. Once cut, remove the larvae, destroy them and replant the two halves which will develop and grow into healthy plants. Remember to dust the cut surfaces with a fungicide. The pest is eliminated with the bonus of an extra *Sarracenia* plant.

MITES

Mites, which are spider-like animals, are difficult to see unless a magnifying glass is used. Their presence is revealed by malformed or twisted leaves. Kelthane 35% WP, used according to label directions, is effective.

ANTS

In outdoor greenhouses ants can become a pest, particularly during the spring. Control them with a saturated sugar solution. Dissolve as much sugar as possible in a half a cup of hot water, then stir in 3 tablespoons (45 ml) of lead arsenate, a poisonous material used in spraying fruit trees. Pour some of this liquid in a shallow container, such as a salad dressing bottle top, and place it in the area infested by the ants, preferably on the path or "run" that they take from the plants to their home. Once the poison is found the problem is solved because they will carry some of the sugar mixture back to the ant hill to feed the young, resulting in the death of both the old and young ants. The remainder of the sugar arsenate mixture can be saved for future use. Label the bottle to indicate that it contains a poison.

MICE

Outdoor greenhouses, particularly in colder climates, make excellent homes for mice. Every year, with the arrival of cold weather, some mice enter the greenhouse. In our greenhouse the only plants eaten have been *Dionaea*. Each fall we set-up several feeding stations of Warfarin in the greenhouse. The dead mice usually end up floating in the aquatic *Utricularia* tank.

SLUGS AND SNAILS

Slugs are very destructive of carnivorous plants, particularly those with succulent leaves. Use a slugicide such as Pyrethrin or Allethrin, following label directions to control them. They also can be easily removed by hand. They tend to be nocturnal, at which time they come out of hiding. After a few hours of darkness, light the growing area and remove the slugs and snails with a pair of tweezers.

General Guidelines for The Use of Insecticides and Fungicides

If a pesticide is used that you have not previously tried on carnivorous plants, experiment with it on a single plant or on 1–2 leaves of a plant at first to determine its toxicity. In the initial trial dilute the pesticide more than the recommendations call for to prevent the loss of plants. If all goes well then gradually increase the concentration as experience dictates.

Often directions for diluting pesticides are given for large volumes.

Listed are some useful conversions for mixing pesticides.
1.   One pound per 100 gallons is approximately equal to 1 level tablespoon per gallon.
2.   One fluid ounce is equal to 30 ml.
3.   One tablespoon is equal to 15 ml or 3 teaspoons.
4.   One pound is equal to 454 grams.
5.   One quart is almost equal to 1 liter.

The term Captan 50% WP means that 50% or ½ of the material is active in combatting the pest and WP means wettable powder. Many growers prefer wettable powders to liquids because the liquids (solvents) used to carry the chemical often damage plants more than the chemical which acts on the pests. Pesticides will often damage the leaves to varying degrees, but the new leaves will develop normally.

When treating plants for pests do not stop with a single application. Repeat the treatment at 1–2 week intervals several times. We recommend this procedure because the chemicals are usually effective only against the living animal or plant (fungus). Thus the eggs and spores may not be affected by the treatment and so will hatch or germinate after the first treatment. Continue treatments until the pest has been eliminated or controlled. Spray the plants thoroughly to insure that the undersides of the leaves and the soil surface are not missed.

Listed below are some of the pesticides that have been used on carnivorous plants with little or no damage.

Miticides
Kelthane 35% WP—Control mites.
   Follow label directions for dilution.

Fungicides
Benomyl 50% WP—A systemic fungicide to control fungi such as *Botrytis* (gray mold)
   and powdery mildew. Follow label directions for dilution rate. Benlate is a brand
   name fungicide containing benomyl.
Captan 50% WP—Controls mildew, *Botrytis,* and damping-off organisms. Follow label
   directions for dilution.
Truban 30% WP—A fungicide for treating soil to control damping-off and stem-rot
   diseases. Follow label directions for dilution.
Exotherm Termil—A fungicide for the control of fungi such as *Botrytis*. Material comes
   in a can and is ignited whereupon smoke (the fungicide) is produced. This material
   is made for treating large greenhouses. Follow label directions.
Chlorothalonil 75% WP Controls foliar blight, a fungus infection on *Dionaea* leaves. Mix
   1 teaspoon (5 ml) per quart or liter of water.

Insecticides
Malathion 25% WP—Controls pests such as aphids, mealy bugs, scale, *Sarracenia* borer
   and larvae. Follow label directions for dilution. It has been reported that this
   chemical will kill *Drosera adelae* and *D. burmanii.*
Sevin 50% WP or the liquid preparation—Controls aphids, *Sarracenia* larvae and borer.
   Follow label directions for dilution.
Plantfume—A gaseous insecticide. It is packed in cans and must be ignited to release
   clouds of smoke which is the killing agent. This material is designed for larger
   greenhouses to control aphids, mites, scales, and mealy bugs. Follow label directions.

Slugicide
Pyrethrin or Allethrin—Controls slugs, snails and larvae. Follow label directions.

Solid Insecticides
Materials such as Shell No-Pest strip and Black Flag solid insecticide. These vaporize
   slowly, producing a vapor which kills pests such as aphids, mealy bugs, and white
   flies. Hang the material in the growing area.

9

Propagation &

Hybridization

Most carnivorous plants can be propagated both by·sexual and asexual means. Sexual propagation involves the production of seeds with their inherent genetic variability. Asexual, or vegetative reproduction, usually results in progeny which are genetically identical to the parent.

Sexual Reproduction

Sexual reproduction requires the union of a sperm with an egg, a process which usually leads to the formation of seeds. Fertilization, union of sperm and egg, is preceded by pollination in which pollen from the anther of the stamen is deposited on the stigma of the pistil.

In most carnivorous species the male reproductive organ, the stamen, and the female reproductive organ, the pistil, occur within the same flower, classifying the flower as bisexual, containing both sexes. The genus *Nepenthes* is an exception, as the flowers of individual plants contain only male or female reproductive organs. Male flowers contain stamens but no pistils, and female flowers contain pistils but no stamens. The flowers are unisexual and the plants that bear them are called dioecious because the male flowers and female flowers develop on separate plants.

There are several ways in which pollination is effected in carnivorous plants. Self-pollination occurs in the flowers of some bisexual species; that is, the pollen from the stamen is transferred to the pistil of the same flower. Other species, even though the flowers are bisexual, must be cross-pollinated; that is, the pistil of one flower must be pollinated by pollen from a flower on a different plant in order for fertilization and seed production to occur. *Sarracenia*, some *Drosera, Darlingtonia, Dionaea, Pinguicula, Heliamphora, Utricularia, Drosophyllum, Cephalotus* and *Byblis* will produce seed either via cross-pollination or self-pollination.

Some *Drosera* species actuate self-pollination when the petals close up on the other floral structures after blooming. But most species need some help from breezes, insects, vibrations or other sources to transfer pollen. Information on pollination specific to each species is found in the chapter devoted to each genus.

Generally, seeds that mature in late spring or early summer will germinate immediately, while seeds that mature late in the summer and in the fall will not germinate without some special treatment such as stratification. The specific requirements for seed germination of each species is given in the chapter devoted to their genus.

Stratification is a cold treatment needed by some seeds before they are capable of germinating. In nature the stratification process takes place during the winter when the seeds are lying on damp or wet and cold or frozen soil. One way to satisfy this environmental requirement is to place the seeds, on the surface of 2–3 in. (5–7.5 cm) of moist medium in a plastic bag. Dust the seed with a fungicide by shaking the seed with a small amount of the fungicide in a small capped bottle before stratifying. The seed is then sprinkled on the medium surface in the bag. Seed should be evenly and, more importantly, thinly spread over the medium surface to minimize chances of fungal infection and to allow a full season's growth after germination before the plantlets are transplanted. It may be easier to sprinkle the seed on the medium first and then sprinkle some fungicide on top of the seeds and medium. Insert a glass or plastic rod in the medium in the center of the bag, inflate the bag and twist the top shut. Secure the bag to the rod with a rubber band or a piece of string. (Fig. 9-1) The rod will support the plastic bag and prevent it from collapsing. Place the prepared seed in the plastic bag in a cool area, 33–40° F (0.6–4.5° C) for 3–6 months.

An alternative method of stratification is basically the same as the one just described, except the medium is placed in pots and the pots containing the treated seed are put in plastic bags with about ½ in. (1.3 cm) of water in the bottom of the bag. The advantage of this method is that, following stratification, the pots can be removed from the plastic bag and placed in a suitable growing area or the pots can be left in the bag which provides a high humidity which is beneficial to germination. After the seeds have germinated and grown for a few weeks the pots can be removed from the plastic bags. This method is preferable because there are fewer problems with fungal disease when seedlings are grown in an area with good air circulation.

A third method for stratifying seeds, which is easier and more efficient for treating large quantities of seed, involves using cloth as the stratifying bed. Select a piece of cloth large enough for the quantity of seed to be stratified. If the seed is small, such as some of the *Drosera* species, the cloth should have a very fine weave. Moisten the cloth and spread it out flat. Sprinkle first the seed, then a fungicide on the cloth. Roll the cloth into a tight roll and secure it with rubber bands or string. Since there is fungicide on the cloth, it is best to wear plastic or rubber gloves when handling the cloth rolls. Moisten the cloth roll again so that it is thoroughly wet and then place one or more cloth rolls in a plastic bag or in a glass container sealed with plastic to preventing drying out. To insure high humidity we place 1 in. (2.5 cm) of water in the plastic bag or glass jar. We also place a small plastic object, such as a short, upside-down pot, in the container to keep the rolls with their seed out of direct contact with the water. (Fig. 9-2) The completed packages are placed in a space cooled to the appropriate temperature for the proper length of time. After the stratification period is over, remove the cloth rolls and unroll them. Allow the cloth to almost dry out, then shake it over a piece of paper to remove the stratified seeds. If the cloth is still moist it will be difficult to shake all the seed off.

If you have only a small quantity of seed to stratify use a petri dish. Filter paper, paper towelling or cloth cut to the size of the petri dish acts as the seed bed. Wet the paper or cloth and put it on the bottom of the petri dish, sprinkle seed sparsely on the bed and then sprinkle fungicide on the seed. Cover the petri dish and seal it to prevent drying. Handle these containers in the same manner as outlined previously.

Seeds of some species must be scarified before they will germinate; for example, *Drosophyllum* seeds. To overcome this barrier to germination, the seed coat must be scratched or cut. Specific details for so doing are provided in Chapter 4 dealing with *Drosophyllum*.

Another barrier to germination is found in seed of *Byblis gigantica*. The seed needs heat treatment which can be provided by wetting them with scalding water. Alternatively the hormone Gibberellin can be used to break dormancy and allow germination.

If seeds are to be stored they should be dried for about 1 week at room temperature and then placed in sealed vials or bottles and kept under refrigeration at 35–40° F (1.7–4° C) until used. The longer the seeds are stored, the lower their germination rate will be.

Better growth and larger plants will be obtained if the stratified or scarified seed is spread very thinly when it is planted so that the seedlings have plenty of space to grow undisturbed; that is, without being transplanted during their first growing season. Overcrowding not only slows seedling growth considerably but creates an environment conducive to fungus attack as well. If the young plants are too close they can be transplanted when they have 2–4 true leaves.

Asexual Reproduction

Asexual reproduction does not involve the combining of genetic information from two different plants of the same species. The genetic characteristics of the one parent are passed on to the progeny.

Some carnivorous plants propagate asexually in nature. This occurs when new plants develop on various portions of established plants. The new plants, or plantlets as they are called, develop from roots, stems, and/or leaves. Not all carnivorous plants are capable of reproducing asexually from the same plant organ. The following paragraphs summarize the natural types of asexual reproduction and list some of the species reproducing in this manner.

ASEXUAL REPRODUCTION—NATURALLY OCCURRING

Budding
The production of new plantlets on established plant organs such as roots, leaves, stems, rhizomes, and runners.

Roots: Plantlets are produced on the roots. Species reproducing in this way include:
Drosera adelae
Drosera binata var. *binata*
Drosera binata var. *dichotoma*
Drosera hamiltonii
Drosera schizandra

Leaves: Plantlets are produced on the leaves. The leaves producing new plants are usually those closest to the soil where the humidity is higher. Leaf budding typically occurs near the end of the growing season. Genera reproducing in this fashion include:
Dionaea
Drosera
Pinguicula

Fig. 9-1 Seeds to be stratified are sprinkled on the surface of growing medium, either directly contained in a plastic bag or in pots that are placed in a plastic bag. The glass rod is inserted into the growing medium. The plastic bag is inflated and secured to the glass rod. After stratification the seeds are germinated in the same containers.

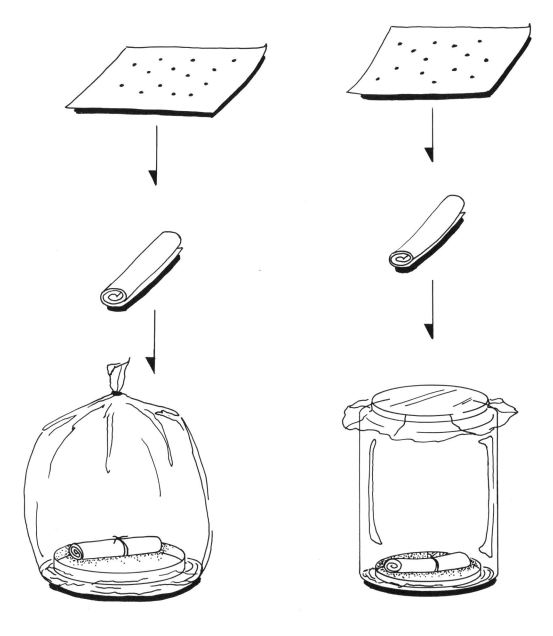

Fig. 9-2 Stratification of large quantities of seed can be accomplished by sprinkling the seeds on a wet cloth, rolling the cloth into a tight roll and securing it. The cloth rolls are put into a plastic bag or jar. To insure high humidity in the container, put water in the bottom of the container, keeping the cloth rolls out of the water. Cover container with plastic wrap.

Stems: Above-ground vertical stems that do not elongate are called crowns. Plantlets develop from the crown. Genera that reproduce in this fashion include:

Drosera
Pinguicula

Rhizomes: Plantlets are produced on the horizontal underground stem that may or may not branch. Genera reproducing in this fashion include:

Cephalotus
Darlingtonia
Heliamphora
Sarracenia

Runners: Aboveground horizontal stems that in some species produce flowers and plantlets and in others produce plantlets only. Genera reproducing in this fashion include:

Drosera
Pinguicula

Vegetative Apomixis

Some flower parts may develop into plantlets without union of gametes. To our knowledge, this characteristic is exhibited by the following species:

Dionaea muscipula
Drosera binata var. *binata*
Drosera binata var. *dichotoma*
Drosera intermedia
Drosera filiformis var. *filiformis*
Drosera filiformis var. *tracyi*

ASEXUAL REPRODUCTION—VEGETATIVE REPRODUCTION

Man has capitalized on the natural tendency of plants to reproduce asexually in order to propagate them vegetatively. We outline here only the general techniques for the commonly used vegetative reproduction procedures to avoid needless repetition. Specific requirements, such as ideal temperatures, have been described in the chapter devoted to each genus.

Asexual or vegetative propagation in carnivorous plants can be organized according to the organ of the plant utilized.

Stem

Rhizome break-up: Large rhizomes are cut into sections about ½ in. (1.3 cm) long. If roots are present, care should be taken to not damage them. Dust the rhizome ends with a fungicide, then place the rhizome sections in damp growing medium in a horizontal position so that the top of each section is about ¼ in. (0.6 cm.) below the soil surface. Keep them damp in a high humidity and well-lighted environment, but not in direct sunlight, until new growth develops.

We have found that living sphagnum moss gives the best results and is a deterrent to decay. The rhizome sections can be placed in the growing medium in a plastic bag which when sealed results in a self-contained unit that usually will not require any additional care until the plants are ready to be transplanted. Genera that can be propagated by rhizome break-up are *Sarracenia* and *Cephalotus*.

Rhizome proliferation: Remove all the leaves from a rhizome. Cut off about ¾ in. (2 cm) from the growing tip of the rhizome. Place the remaining portion of the rhizome horizontally in the damp medium so that about ½ of it is above the medium, after dusting the cut surface with fungicide. (Photo 9-1) Dust the cut end of the removed terminal piece with a fungicide and plant it, cut end in the medium, up to about ½ of its length. In several weeks the planted terminal tip cutting will develop into a plant and several buds should start to develop into plants on the half buried rhizome.

After the new plantlets have developed roots they can be cut apart into separate plants. If the rhizome is small, rather than trying to take a tip cutting, simply cut off the growing tip with a knife or your fingernail. Once the undeveloped bud (growing tip) is removed you should have reached the rhizome which is whitish in color and somewhat woody. The debudded rhizome should be planted as outlined above. The rhizomes of species such as *Sarracenia purpurea* and *S. psittacina* tend to grow in a vertical direction and are usually very short. Since the rhizomes are so short, it is difficult to take a tip cutting. In this case remove the terminal bud as outlined previously for small rhizomes. Then plant the rhizome vertically so that about ¾ of it is above the soil level. *Sarracenia* plants can be propagated by rhizome proliferation.

Stem Cuttings

Since the procedure for taking stem cuttings is different for each of the 3 groups of plants that reproduce easily by stem cuttings, each group will be dealt with separately.

Nepenthes

Cuttings consisting of 1–4 nodes, regions of the stem where leaves are attached, are removed from the plant. We have found that cuttings taken any time of the year will root successfully. About ½–⅔ of each leaf on the cutting is removed and discarded. (Fig. 3-13) The lower end of the cutting is dusted with a hormone such as Rootone, which usually contains a fungicide, to promote rooting. All cut surfaces of a cutting should be treated with a fungicide or powered sulfur to inhibit or delay decay.

The cutting is inserted in a pot containing the medium. Living or dead sphagnum moss seems to give the best and the most consistent results. By placing the cutting in a pot it will not have to be transplanted for at least a year or two, at which time the cutting should have a well developed root system. The cutting is inserted into the medium so that 1–2 nodes are above the growing medium. If a 1-node cutting, the node should be just slightly below the soil level with the leaves extending above the soil.

The pot containing the cutting is placed in a plastic bag which is sealed to maintain high humidity around the cutting. The entire set-up is kept in a well-lighted area but out of direct sunlight. Optimum temperatures are between 70–85° F (21–29° C).

The cuttings should be kept moist at all times, but not waterlogged. It is better to have them a bit on the dry side rather than too wet, as excessive moisture promotes decay. Cuttings will root in a few months, but usually take 8–12 months to become well established plants with vigorous growth of new leaves and traps.

The remaining portion of the plant from which the cuttings were taken, often called the mother plant, will develop new growth from the undeveloped buds in the remaining leaf axils. The buds are normally prevented from growing by hormones produced in the terminal end of the stem which, when removed, eliminates the source of the hormone. As each lateral bud grows it will provide you with more stem tissue for more cuttings. Detailed information on propagating *Nepenthes* is found in the chapter on this genus.

Drosera

To propagate Sundews from stem cuttings, remove the top 2–3 in. (5–8 cm.) of the plant, including the leaves. Dust the cut surfaces with fungicide. Insert the cutting in a pot of sphagnum moss (living or dead) or sphagnum peat moss so that about ¾ of it is below soil level. Place the cutting in bright but not direct light and high humidity. Roots should form in 3–8 weeks.

We have found that this works with all the *Drosera* spp. having elongated stems.

Some *Drosera* spp. can be propagated asexually by decapitation. This means the plant is cut off at or just below soil level. The base of the cut off top is then placed firmly on the planting medium surface if it is a rosette type. (Fig. 9-3) If an elongated stem type, about ½ of the stem should be inserted into the medium. The cutting should be handled just like other *Drosera* cuttings. In a few weeks they will root and continue to grow.

In addition, the roots which are left in the soil will now produce another plant. This technique can be repeated when another plant has grown from the roots. We have one batch of roots which had been decapitated continuously for 12 years. Species which we have propagated this way are *Drosera binata* var. *binata*, *D. binata* var. *dichotoma*, *D. capensis*, *D. hamiltonii*, *D. adelae*, and *D. schizandra*.

Aldrovanda and Aquatic *Utricularia*

Stem cuttings of *Aldrovanda* and aquatic *Utricularia* are taken by cutting the plant into sections about 3 in. (8 cm) long. The sections are then returned to the water. Each plant section will develop into a new plant in a few weeks.

Leaves

Leaf cuttings are prepared from leaves which are removed from plants and then are layed flat on or inserted in the medium and in some cases floated on water. After removing the leaves from the plants, treat them with a fungicide, particularly at the point where they were attached to the mother plant. Best results are usually obtained with mature, older leaves which contain more stored food. The medium must be kept damp and the humidity high. Placing the leaves in sealed plastic bags simplifies care.

Buds appear on the leaves in 2–8 weeks depending on the species and environmental conditions. Leaves of some species of *Pinguicula* and *Drosera*, *Sarracenia*, *Cephalotus*, and *Darlingtonia* can be used.

Roots

Roots of species such as *Drosera binata* var. *binata*, *D. binata* var. *dichotoma*, *D. adelae*, *D. hamiltonii*, *D. capensis*, *D. schizandra*, *D. spathulata*, and *Byblis gigantea* can be induced to produce new plants. The thicker roots give better results. Fifty percent or less of the roots can be removed. Cut the roots into 2 in. (5 cm) lengths or they can be left whole. The pieces are placed on damp medium preferably sphagnum moss, and placed in a humid, bright area, but not in direct sunlight. If they are placed in a sealed plastic bag, maintenance will be minimal. New plants should be visible in 2–10 weeks.

Hybridization

Hybrids result from the crossing of two species and occur regularly in nature. The pollen from one species is transferred to the pistil of another species by insects, wind, birds, etc. The resulting hybrids may or may not survive in nature. If not, they will not be perpetuated.

Hybridization is used in culture to produce plants which differ from the species in respect to vigor, disease resistance, size, growth habits and form.

When we cross-pollinate species artificially the potential for survival increases. We carefully collect, plant and grow the hybrid seed under optimum conditions for maximum survival.

Hybridization is both fascinating and challenging. To date, the hybrids produced are those within a genus, that is *Drosera* crossed with *Drosera* or *Sarracenia* crossed with *Sarracenia* and not, for example, *Drosera* crossed with *Dionaea*.

Successful hybridization is enhanced by crossing species having the same number of chromosomes. While all the *Sarracenia* species have equal numbers of chromosomes, not all of the *Drosera* do. To ascertain the chromosome number of the species, the literature must be consulted. An ideal reference is the *Kew Index to Taxonomic Literature*. Also Katsuhiko Kondo has done much work on chromosome studies, and published his results in *The Journal of Japanese Botany*.

Hybridization by man involves not only the transfer of pollen from anther to stigma,

Fig. 9-3 Propagation of *Drosera* by decapication. The plant is cut from the roots near soil level. The removed portion is firmly replanted. Both the removed portion and the roots will regenerate their missing part.

but also protection of the ovary from unwanted pollen and careful recording of the cross as well as marking the ovary for identification of the seed when mature.

To increase the probability of subsequent fertilization and seed development, it is necessary to use mature pollen. Mature pollen is visible to the naked eye or with the aid of a 10 $\times$ magnifying lens. It usually appears as dense masses of pale to deep yellow spherically-shaped bodies when the anther splits open.

Mature pollen can be transferred using flat toothpicks, small camel's hair brushes or the stamen itself. Toothpicks have the advantage of being inexpensive and disposable. We usually use small camel's hair brushes for our *Sarracenia* hybridizing. To keep track of which brush was used to transfer what pollen, we insert the brush, handle first, in the soil next to the plant supplying the pollen. After each transfer we shake out as much pollen from the brush as possible. Before the brush is utilized to transfer the pollen of another species, it is washed thoroughly in warm, soapy water and allowed to dry. If water or nectar drops are mixed with the pollen, and adhere to the brush, as sometimes happens with *Sarracenia*, the brush should be washed before being used again.

If the stamen is used to transfer the pollen, remove it gently from the donor flower with tweezers. Rub the anther with its pollen on the stigma of the other flower. This operation should be done quickly as the stamen dries rapidly. The anther cannot be used as a pollen source another day unless it is wrapped in wax paper or plastic and refrigerated.

Once you have made the pollen transfer, you should check to make sure the job has been done. There should be pollen on the stigma. If it is not visible to the naked eye, use a magnifying glass to make sure. Whenever possible, transfer pollen each day for several days or until the flower closes.

To insure that the cross you have made is maintained and not contaminated with undesirable pollen, the flower that is expected to produce the seed should be protected from insects that may transfer pollen during their quest for nectar, by covering the flower. Plastic bags, gauze, fine cheese cloth, muslin or paper bags are used to cover the flowers or the whole plant to prevent contamination. If plastic bags are utilized, tiny holes should be punched in them and the plant kept out of direct sunlight while covered.

Unwanted pollen also comes from the anthers of the flower that will produce the hybrid seed. The easiest way to prevent pollen in the same flower from pollinating the stigma is to remove the anthers from the flower before they mature. We usually remove the anthers from *Sarracenia* flowers that are to be crossed unless the pollen is needed to effect another cross. In some *Drosera* species, the flowers open during the day, usually before noon, and close the same day in the afternoon. Upon closure, the petals press the pollen to touch the flower's stigma, thereby causing self-pollination. In order to prevent self-pollination, the anthers must be removed. If possible, it is safest to remove the anthers from the flowers before the pollen is mature to reduce the incidence of accidental self-pollination.

In order to hybridize two species, either they must flower at the same time or the pollen from the anther of one species must be available when the pistil of the other species is receptive. There are two ways to deal with this problem. One is to delay the flowering of the earlier flowering plant so that it will flower at about the same time as the late flowering species. The other method which is the simplest, once a procedure is developed, is to store the pollen until it is needed.

We will use the genus *Sarracenia* to illustrate our technique for delaying flowering of the early flowering species. Experience with *Sarracenia* kept in our greenhouse the year around reveals the following sequence of blooming, which fall in 2 distinct flowering groups, early and late. *S. flava* flowers first, followed by *S. alata, S. oreophila*, then *S. purpurea* and *S. leucophylla*. A few weeks later *S. minor, S. rubra, S. alabamensis* and *S. psittacina* come into bloom.

We have been very successful in producing hybrids between the 2 groups using the following procedure. About 5 dormant plants or rhizomes of each species to be crossed are stored under refrigeration. In the spring, we plant the late flowering plants one at a time, at 2-week intervals. What date in the spring depends upon your location. In Florida it is late February or early March, whereas in New York State, where we grow, it is mid-to late-April in order to avoid the expense of heating the greenhouse when the plants are flowering. When one of the early planted plants produces a visible flower bud, commence planting the early flowering plants or rhizomes one at a time at 1-week intervals. Using this procedure we have made 26 different successful crosses between species.

This timing procedure can be accomplished without refrigeration. The flowering time of the early blooming species is delayed by keeping the plants cooler, by placing them on the ground beneath greenhouse benches, on the side of the greenhouse that is not exposed to direct sunlight or is shaded.

If you are working with species whose blooming sequence you don't know, this sequence can be ascertained as follows. Plant one or two of each species that are involved. The first species to bloom will be classified as the early flowering type. Now follow the procedure described for *Sarracenia*. While plants used in the above illustration are kept dormant by low temperatures other plants such as the tuberous *Drosera* are kept dormant by a dry, warm environment.

A much simpler procedure for making crosses is to collect the desired pollen when it is mature and store it until it is needed. *Sarracenia* pollen can be collected, wrapped in wax paper and stored in a refrigerator (not freezer) for up to 2 months and still retain its viability. Storage of viable pollen for this length of time will enable you to execute any of the crosses in the *Sarracenia* genus by collecting and storing pollen of the early blooming species. Perhaps pollen storage will work for some other carnivorous plant genera.

Freezing pollen until needed has been done with other groups of plants, but as far as we know it has not been tried with any carnivorous species. The procedure, developed by C. D. Clayberg of the Connecticut Agricultural Experiment Station with *Gloxinias*, follows so that if any reader wants to try it with carnivorous plants they will have some guidance.

Gather the fresh pollen, place it in a small open bottle or open vial. This container is, in turn, placed inside a slightly larger bottle (the dessicator) in which about ½ teaspoon or 2.5 milliliters of silica gel has been placed. Then the larger bottle is tightly capped. The purpose of the dessicator is to remove moisture from the pollen for better storage.

The pollen should be left in the dessicator for 3–4 hours at room temperature, after which the pollen, in its dessicator, is placed in a yet larger storage jar containing a layer of silica gel. The storage jar is tightly capped. If you are storing pollen from more than 1 plant or species, each should be placed in its own small dessicator but several can be placed in the storage jar. (Fig. 9-4) Place the large storage jar in a freezer (not refrigerator) at temperatures below 32°F (0°C) until needed. When the pollen is needed, remove it from the freezer and allow it to stand at room temperature for about 10–15 minutes before opening the smaller dessicator. If there is more than one kind of pollen in the larger dessicator, remove only the vial you want to use and immediately return the rest to the freezer. Viability of frozen pollen depends upon the genus and species of the plants and can last from a few weeks to over a year.

It is difficult to know when ordinary silica gel has absorbed all the water it can, whereas Tel-Tale, a brand product, is an indicating gel. It has been treated so that when it is dry its color is blue and when it is translucent pink it has absorbed all the moisture it can. To regenerate the gel, spread a thin layer in a shallow pan such as a baking dish and bake at 250°F (121°C) until it changes back to a blue color. It is then ready to be reused. While still warm the silica gel should be placed in sealed containers for storage until needed.

Record-keeping is a very important part of hybridizing plants. Your records should be accurate and thorough. Minimally they should include: date, plant species receiving, and plant species supplying the pollen. The usual procedure is to indicate the name of the female plant first followed by an "X" and then the male plant, the pollen supplier. For example, if pollen from *Drosera spathulata* is placed on the pistil of *D. capensis*, the cross would be written: *D. capensis* $\times$ *D. spathulata*. Failure to record the cross when it is executed is an all too common mistake. Procrastination in record-keeping can be disasterous, especially if several crosses are made at the same time. A cardinal rule should be to record the cross at the time it is made.

Hybrids resulting from crosses should be identified so that when seed is produced you will know its parentage. Plastic plant markers with the crosses written on them serve this purpose, but care should be taken to make sure they are not removed and replaced in the wrong pot. Visitors in your growing area can, however, make a shambles of markers. So it is wise to tie the plastic tag to the plant. Hybrids growing in beds must be identified in the same way. We use plastic tape dispensed after being printed or numbered by a labeling gun. A hole is punched in one end of the tape, then the tape imprinted with a code is tied to the flower stalk with nylon string or a rubber band.

Do not label hybrids with any label material or marking ink which will fade when in a humid environment, or from water and sunlight. It is very disheartening to have successfully produced seed from a cross and then not know the parentage. Sometimes the hybrid seed yields progeny whose parentage is obvious, but when dealing with complex parentage it is difficult or impossible to determine the parentage by looking at the offspring. So label the crosses that you make.

When dealing with plants which have several flowers on a single flower stalk such as most *Drosera*, we use short pieces of colored thread to identify the cross. For example, we use green thread to represent pollen from *Drosera capensis*. Every time *D. capensis* pollen is used we tie a piece of green thread around the pedicle or base of the flower. Thus, the green thread identifies all the flowers which have been pollinated with *D. capensis* pollen. When we make more crosses than colors of thread available, 2–3 colors are combined to represent pollen from a particular species.

We have found that the basic colors red, blue, green, black, white and yellow are the safest to use. Under greenhouse conditions the thread color may fade and become lighter in color, therefore, shades of the basic color should not be used with the basic color. For example, red thread may fade during the summer so it could look like or be confused with pink or rose.

If a code is utilized, such as colored thread or numbers on plastic tape, be sure to record the code and its meaning in a permanent record book at the time you make the cross. Record keeping is a tedious but necessary undertaking.

Anyone attempting hybridization of small-flowered plants should consider purchasing a magnifier worn on the head such as the Magni-Focuser Mark II. The advantage of such a device is that both hands are free for making the cross.

When working with very small flowers a fine pair of tweezers is necessary to maneuver the floral parts.

Since a slight undesirable movement can result in damage to the pistil or unwanted pollen dispersal, it is safer to sit while you are working rather than stand.

We have noticed that when anthers were removed from some *Drosera* species such as *D. rotundifolia*, the petals closed over the pistil in a relatively short period of time. Whether petal closure was caused by stamen removal or by some unseen injury to the flower due to the procedure, we do not know. There are 2 ways to handle the problem. One is to gently open the de-antherized flower by pulling the petals apart with fine tweezers when the pollen for the cross is ready. The pollen is then deposited on the exposed stigma. The alternative solution is to wait until the desired pollen is ready, remove the anthers from the flower whose stigma will be utilized and immediately

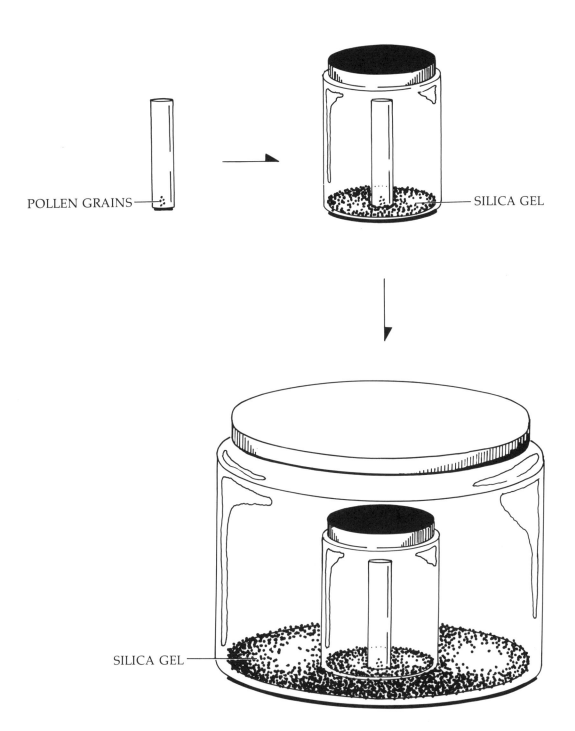

POLLEN GRAINS

SILICA GEL

SILICA GEL

Fig. 9-4 Freezing of pollen necessitates removal of excess moisture. Pollen is placed in a small vial which is placed in a jar containing silica gel which is then tightly capped. After 3–4 hours are room temperature the jar with the vial is placed in a larger jar containing silica gel which is tightly capped. The 3 jar container set-up is placed in a freezer.

effect the cross. Extreme care should be taken so that self-pollination does not occur accidentally.

Tissue Culture

Plant tissue culture is a process by which plants can be rapidly propagated. The new plants contain the same genetic information as the original plant. Tissue culture is a type of vegetative propagation in which many new plants can be propagated in a short period of time.

Commercially, tissue culture is now utilized to produce Boston ferns, *Rhododendrons*, orchids, Staghorn ferns, *Chrysanthemums*, grapes, strawberries, raspberries, and many other plants. Although tissue culture of carnivorous plants is not done on a large scale yet, it is a potential means of satisfying a large portion of the demand for these plants which will reduce natural collection and hopefully in the future it will be a way to provide all the carnivores and eliminate field collection.

Today some *Sarracenia*, *Cephalotus*, *Pinguicula*, and *Drosera* are available in this form. In the future, hopefully all the genera will be propagated by this technique.

When you buy tissue-cultured carnivorous plants they will arrive in a test tube or vial with the plants growing in a special medium. The plants usually can remain in the test tube or vial for a few months, but it's best to remove them from their containers because the media will eventually dry out and/or become depleted of growth substances or the plants will outgrow the container. To transfer tissue-cultured plants from their very humid and disease-free environment to a natural one, your growing area, use the following procedure:

1. Remove the cap from the tube or vial.
2. After 4 or 5 days gently remove the plants and wash the agar, a jelly-like material, from the roots, using lukewarm water. During this step and the following steps it is very important that the plants are not allowed to dry out.
3. If plants are well developed with roots, then individual plants may be separated. If not, simply separate clusters of plants, or wait till roots develop to transfer.
4. Plant the plants or clusters of plants in pots filled with your soil mix. Make sure that all the roots, if any, are below soil levels.
5. Spray with a fungicide such as Benomyl to help prevent fungus infection.
6. Water the plants with a weak fertilizer solution made as follows:
   a. ¼ teaspoon (1.25 ml) of Miracid or RapidGro or other similar fertilizers per quart or liter of water.
   b. 18 drops of Schultz-Instant liquid plant food per liter or quart of water.
7. Cover the plants with a transparent cover such as a plastic cup, clear plastic, or better yet, place the potted plant in a plastic bag, add a little water to the bottom of the bag, insert a stake or glass rod in the soil to prevent the collapse of the plastic and then twist it shut and secure with a rubber band or piece of string.
8. Place the plants in bright light or under fluorescent lights, but never in direct sunlight, for at least one week.
9. If the plants were well developed with roots, the bag may be untwisted and slightly opened. Over a period of a week, gradually open the bag more and lower it until the plants are exposed to the conditions of the growing area. If they were covered with a plastic or glass container, then prop the container up a little for 3 days after which you prop it as high as you can for 3 more days, followed by its removal. If the pot was covered with a transparent flat material, slowly remove it over a period of a week.

After acclimation to your growing area, the tissue-cultured plants should be treated and grown just as similar carnivores are.

APPENDICES

Appendix A
Carnivorous Plant Sources

Asia

Borneo Exotics
262 B/5 Millagahawatta
Hokandara Road
Thalawathugoda
Sri Lanka
www.borneoexotics.com
(*Nepenthes* only)

Malesiana Tropicals
First Floor, Lot 4909, Sect. 64 KTLD
Upland Shop House, Jln. Upland
93300 Kuching, Sarawak, Malaysia
www.malesiana.tropicals.com.my
(*Nepenthes* only)

Australia

Allen Lowrie
6 Glenn Place
Duncraig 6023
Western Australia

Carnivorous & Unusual Seeds
3 Normandy Ave
Para Hills 5096
South Australia

Collectors Corner/Gardenworld
810 Springvale Road
Keysborough 3173
Victoria
www.collectorscorner.com.au

Exotica Plants
Geoff and Andrea Mansell
CMB Cordalba
via Childers 4660
Queensland
www.uq.net.au/intaac/ExoticaPlants/
    index.htm

Southern Carnivores
Phill Mann
P.O. Box 193
Harvey 6220
Western Australia
www.scarnivores.com

Triffid Park
257 Perry Road
Keysborough 3173
Victoria
www.triffidpark.com.au

Germany

The Nepenthes Nursery
Wistuba - Exotische Pflanzen
Mudauer Ring 227
68259 Mannheim
Germany
www.wistuba.com

Great Britain

Cambrian Carnivores
17 Wimmerfield Crescent
Killay
Swansea
SA2 7BU

Hampshire Carnivorous Plants
Ya-Mayla
Allington Lane
West End
Southampton
Hampshire
SQ30 3HQ

Hewitt-Cooper Carnivorous Plants
76 Courtney Crescent
Carshalton on the Hill
Surrey
SM5 4NB

South West Carnivorous Plants
2 Rose Cottages
Culmstock
Cullompton
Devon
EX15 3JJ

Tropic House
Langford Nursery
Carty Port
Newton Stewart
Wigtownshire
Scotland
DG8 6AY

United States

Botanique
387 Pitcher Plant Lane
Stanardsville, VA 22973
www.pitcherplant.com

California Carnivores
7020 Trenton
Healdsburg Road
Forestville, CA 95436
www.californiacarnivores.com

Cascade Carnivorous Plants
P.O. Box 20
Tenino, WA 98589
www.cascadecarnivorous.plant.org

CP Jungle
506 Country Way
Cordova TN 38016
www.cpjungle.com

Dragon Agro Products
P.O. Box 33
Kendall Park, NJ 08824-0033
www.dragonagro.com

Hyde's Stove-House
844 37th Ave S
St. Petersburg, FL 33705
www.stovehouseplants.com

Lee's Botanical Gardens
P.O. Box 669
LaBelle, FL 33975
www.esiwest.com/lees/about.htm

Peter Pauls Nurseries
4665 Chapin Road
Canandaigua, NY 14424-8713
www.peterpauls.com

Plant Delights Nursery, Inc.
9241 Sauls Road
Raleigh, NC 27603
www.plantdelights.com

Tristan's Carnivorous Plants
HCR 2 Box 9568
Keaau, HI 96749
www.tristanscps.com

Appendix B
Carnivorous Plant Societies

The International Carnivorous Plant Society
PMB 330
3310 East Yorba Linda Blvd.
Fullerton, CA 92831-1709
USA
www.carnivorousplants.org

The Carnivorous Plant Society
Derek Petrie
100 Lambley Lane
Burton Joyce
Nottingham NG14 5BL
England
Email: UKCPS@aol.com

Insectivorous Plant Society
Department of Biology
Nippon Dental College
Fujimi, Chiyoda-ku
Tokyo 102
Japan

The New Zealand Carnivorous Plant Society
P.O. Box 10226
Dominion Road
Auckland
New Zealand
www.math.auckland.ac.nz/~waldron/NZCPS

Association Dionée
2 avenue du Bayonnais
40500 Seignosse
France
www.multimania.com/dioneae

Australian Carnivorous Plant Society
P.O. Box 391
St. Agnes, South Australia 5097
Australia
www.acps.org.au

Gesellschaft für Fleischfressende Pflanzen
Frank Gallep
Zweibrückenstr. 31
D-40625 Düsseldorf
Germany
www.carnivoren.org

Appendix C
Bibliography and References

Affolter, J. M., and R. F. Olivo. 1975. Action potentials in Venus' Flytrap. *American Midland Naturalist* 93:443–445.

Bell, Clyde R. 1949. A Cytotaxonomic study of Sarraceniaceae of North America. *Journal of the Elisha Mitchell Scientific Society* 65:137–166.

————. 1952. Natural hybrids in the genus *Sarracenia*. *Journal of the Elisha Mitchell Scientific Society* 68:55–80.

Bell, Clyde R., and Frederick W. Case. 1956. Natural hybrids in the genus *Sarracenia*. Current notes on distribution. *Journal of the Elisha Mitchell Scientific Society* 72:142–152.

Benolken, R. M., and S. L. Jacobson. 1982. Response properties of a sensory hair excised from Venus' Flytrap. *Journal of General Physiology* 56:64–82.

Carnivorous Plant Newsletter, volumes 1–12.

Case, Frederick W., Jr. 1956. Some Michigan records for *Sarracenia purpurea* forma *heterophylla*. *Rhodora* 58:203–207.

Casper, S. J. 1962. On *Pinguicula macroceras* Link in North America. *Rhodora* 64:212–221.

Coker, W. C. 1928. The distribution of Venus Fly Trap. *Journal of the Elisha Mitchell Scientific Society* 43:221–228.

Darwin, C. 1875. *Insectivorous plants*. New York: D. Appleton & Co.

Dean, B. 1890. *Report on the supposed fish-eating plants*. Commissioners of Fisheries of the State of New York, Report 18:183–197.

Erickson, E. 1968. *Plants of prey*. Osborne Park, Western Australia: Lamb Publications Pty. Ltd.

Fassett, Norman C. 1957. *Manual of aquatic plants*. University of Wisconsin Press.

Godfrey, R. K., and L. H. Stripling. 1961. A Synopsis of *Pinguicula* (Lentibulariaceae) in the Southeastern United States. *American Midland Naturalist* 66:395–409.

Green, Sally, T. L. Green, and Yolande Heslop-Harrison. 1979. Seasonal heterophylly and leaf gland features in *Triphyophyllum* (Dioncophyllaceae), a new carnivorous plant genus. *Botanical Journal of the Linnean Society* 78:99–116

Heslop-Harrison, Yolande. 1978. Carnivorous plants. *Scientific American* 238:104–115.

Hooker, J. D. 1874. Address to the department of botany and zoology. B. A. A. S., *Report of the forty-fourth meeting* 102–116.

Hulten, E. 1948. *Flora of Alaska and Yukon,* C. W. K. Gleerup, Hakan Ohlsons Boktryckeri, Vol. VIII, Lund, p. 1422–1429.

Jacobson, S. L. 1965. Receptor response in Venus' Flytrap. *Journal of General Physiology* 49:117–29.

Jones, F. M. 1904. Pitcher-plant insects. *Entomological News* 15:14–17.

———. 1907. Pitcher-plant insects-II. *Entomological News* 18:412–420.

———. 1908. Pitcher-plant insects-III. *Entomological News* 19:150–156.

———. 1920. Another Pitcher-plant insect. *Entomological News* 31:90–94.

———. 1921. Pitcher-plants and their moths. *Natural History* 21:296–316.

Katsuhiko, K., and Richard M. Adams. August/September 1979. Forbidding beauty orchid-flowered butterworts. *American Horticulturist* 29–33.

Kurata, Shigeo. 1976. *Nepenthes of Mount Kinabalu,* Sabah National Parks Publications No. 2, Sabah, Malaysia.

Lloyd, F. E. 1942. *Carnivorous plants.* Waltham, Massachusetts: Chronica Botanica, New York: Dover Publications Inc.

Mandossian, A. J. 1965. *Some aspects of the ecological life history of Sarracenia purpurea.* Ph.D. thesis, Michigan State University.

McDaniel, S. 1971. The genus *Sarracenia* (Sarraceniaceae). *Bulletin of the Tall Timber Research Station,* (Tallahassee, Florida) Number 9.

Muenscher, W. C. 1944. *Aquatic plants of the United States.* Comstock Publishing Co. (Cornell University Press), New York.

Pietropaolo, J., and P. A. Pietropaolo. 1974. *The world of carnivorous plants.* Shortsville, New York: R. J. Stoneridge.

Poole, L., and C. Poole. 1963. *Insect eating plants.* New York: Crowell. (For Juveniles)

Reinert, G. W., and R. K. Godfrey. 1962. Reappraisal of *Utricularia inflata* and *Utricularia radiata* (Lentibulariaceae). *American Journal of Botany* 49:213–220.

Roberts, Patricia R., and H. J. Oosting. 1958. Responses of Venus Fly Trap, (*Dionaea muscipula*) to factors involved in its endemism. *Ecological Monograms* 28:193–218.

Rossbach, G. B. 1939. Aquatic *Utricularias.* A key based upon leaf-characters for the aquatic *Utricularias* of central and northeastern United States and eastern Canada. *Rhodora* 41:114–128.

Rowland, J. T. 1975. Carnivorous seed plants: sources and references. *HortScience* 10:112–114.

Scala, J. et al. 1969. Digestive secretion of *Dionaea muscipula* (Venus Flytrap). *Plant Physiology* 44:367–371.

Schnell, D. E. 1976. *Carnivorous plants of the United States and Canada.* Winston-Salem, North Carolina: Blair.

Shinners, Lloyd E. 1962. *Drosera* (Droseraceae) in the southeastern United States: an interim report. *Sida* 1:53–59.

Simms, G. E. 1884–85. Piscivorous plants. *Bulletin of the United States Fish Commission* No. 4.

Slack, A. 1979. *Carnivorous plants.* Cambridge, Massachusetts: M. I. T. Press.

Smith, Cornelia M. 1931. Development of *Dionaea muscipula,* flower and seed. *Botanical Gazette* 91:377–394.

Stuhlman, O. 1948. A physical analysis of the opening and closing movements of the lobes of Venus Fly-Trap. *Bulletin Torrey Botanical Club* 75:22–44.

———. 1950. The fundamental action potentials developed in the lobes of Venus Fly-Trap (*Dionaea muscipula*) due to a stimulus. *Journal of the Elisha Mitchell Scientific Society* 66:112–114.

Stuhlman, O., and E. B. Darden. 1950. The action potentials obtained from Venus Fly Trap (*Dionaea muscipula*). *Science* 111:491–492.

Swartz, R. 1974. *Carnivorous plants,* New York: Praeger.

Swenson, A. W. 1977. *Cultivating carnivorous plants,* New York: Doubleday.

Taylor, P. 1964. The genus *Utricularia* L. (Lentibulariaceae) in Africa (South of the Sahara) and Madagascar. *Kew Bulletin* 18:1–245.

Walcott, Mary V. 1935. *Illustrations of North American pitcher plants with descriptions and notes on distribution by Edgar T. Wherry, and notes on insect associates by Frank M. Jones.* Smithsonian Institute, Washington, D.C.

Wexler, J. 1981. *Secrets of the Venus's Fly Trap.* New York: Dodd, Mead Co. (For Juveniles).

Wood, Carroll E., Jr. 1960. The genera of Sarraceniaceae and Droseraceae in the southeastern United States. *Journal of the Arnold Arboretum* 41:152–163.

———. 1955. Evidence for the hybrid origin of *Drosera anglica. Rhodora* 57:105–130.

Wood, Carroll E., Jr., and R. K. Godfrey. 1957. *Pinguicula* (Lentibulariaceae) in the southeastern United States. *Rhodora* 59:217–230.

Wood, Carroll E., Jr. 1966. On the identity of *Drosera brevifolia. Journal of the Arnold Arboretum* 47:89–99.

Wynne, Francis E. 1944. *Drosera* in eastern North America. *Bulletin of the Torrey Botanical Club* 71:166–174.

Appendix D
Dealing with Mail-order Firms and Trading

Many carnivorous plants are available only by mail-order from commercial dealers or by trading with individuals. Therefore, a few comments are in order as how to deal with them.

1. Read the ordering instructions and information carefully. Follow instructions explicitly.
2. Read the guarantee and make sure you understand it. Guarantees run the gamut from live delivery to complete satisfaction with material upon arrival. Some of the problem areas in this context are:
   A. Some buyers insist upon having their plants shipped out of season. If you insist, expect to receive plants not at their prime.
   B. Some people who live where there is no freezing weather fail to understand that nurseries located in areas which have freezing weather cannot ship at certain times of the year.
   C. Some guarantees state that plants will be replaced or money refunded if, upon arrival, you are not completely satisfied and the plants are returned immediately. Since the seller has no control over the cultural environment you provide, he cannot guarantee growth. If you keep them, then, the seller's responsibility ceases.

      It behooves the buyer to make sure he is satisfied with them and, if there is the slightest indication that the plants are not healthy, to return them immediately packed in the same manner as they were shipped. They should be snugly arranged in the box so that they will not tumble in transit and thereby be damaged.
3. Follow catalog advice as to the best time to order plants and seeds. The best time is usually just before the plants begin active growth.
4. If you order plants which have a dormant period, do not expect to get actively growing plants if ordered during the dormant season. You will receive a winter bud, rhizome or tuber.
5. If you want to receive plants in their prime they should be ordered for shipment during the peak of the growing season.

6. Plants are usually packed in sphagnum moss for shipment. Plants such as the *Drosera* and *Pinguicula* will seem a little shopworn; that is, the leaves may be bruised when they are unpacked, and their leaves may be covered with small particles of moss. This does not harm them and in a few weeks they will resume active growth.

7. If you buy from sources outside the United States you will need an import permit which is available from the United States Department of Agriculture, Animal and Plant Health Inspection Service, Plant Protection and Quarantine Programs, Federal Center Building, Room 638, Hayattsville, MD 20782.

    If you are a resident of another country you should check with your Department of Agriculture or other appropriate agency to insure that you comply with the laws of your country so that when the plants arrive they will not be returned to the sender or destroyed.

8. Keep a copy of your order.

9. In most cases orders will be shipped faster if payment is made by money order, certified check, credit card (if the firm accepts them), or cash. It is safer to avoid sending cash.

10. If your order doesn't arrive in a reasonable length of time, write to the firm. Don't wait several months before writing.

11. Don't write to a nursery about a problem in a hostile tone. More often than not, if you write in a civil manner, they will bend the rules in your favor.

12. Last, but not least, you should be thoroughly familiar with the cultural requirements of carnivorous plants before they are purchased and have a suitable growing area ready before they arrive.

Trading or Exchanging Plants

1. Pack the plants in damp sphagnum moss in sealed plastic bags. Pack the bags in a strong corrugated cardboard box. Send by special handling via the post office or by United Parcel Service (UPS). Airmail is preferable, particularly when sending plants overseas, because it can take up to 3 months or more for a parcel to reach some countries by surface mail.

2. When plants are sent to other states in the U.S.A. a state certificate should be obtained from a state plant inspector and enclosed with the shipment.

3. If plants are to be sent to other countries, you should ascertain what documents, if any, are needed. Usually a phytosanitary certificate is required and is obtainable from a federal plant inspector (in some states the state plant inspector can issue it). If you can't locate a state or federal plant inspector, contact your county agricultural agent for assistance.

4   If plants are being sent to you from another country you will need an import permit. The permit is available from the address given in item 7 previously.

5. Seeds crossing most borders require no documentation.

6. Be honest. Send what you have promised to those individuals who send material to you.

Glossary

Abaxial The side away from the axis, such as the underside of a leaf.

Abscission The natural falling off of plant parts such as leaves and flowers induced by biochemical processes in the plant.

Adaxial The side toward the axis such as the upper side of a leaf.

Angiosperms Flowering plants that bear seeds and that develop in an ovary.

Annual A plant that grows from seed, germinates, produces more seed and dies in one growing season, which is usually one year.

Anther The part of the stamen which produces the pollen.

Apical bud The bud at the tip or apex of a stem.

Areolae See Fenestration.

Ascidiform Pitcher-shaped, or with hollow tubular leaves.

Axil The upper angle formed by a leaf and the stem from which it is growing.

Bilabiate A corolla and/or calyx having two lips.

Bladder The trapping structure of *Utricularia*.

Bract A leaf-like structure subtending a flower or flower stalk.

Bristles Hairs along the outer edge of the lobes of the trap of *Dionaea* and *Aldrovanda*.

Bud A mass of tissue that will develop into a stem, branch or flower.

Budding The development of a plant from a proliferation of cells.

Bulb An underground bud surrounded by scales or leaf bases which enclose it. The so-called *Dionaea* bulb is not a true bulb, but rather the growing point (apical bud) surrounded by the remaining basal portions of the leaves which have been cut off. See Tuber, Rhizome.

Calyx A term used to include all of a flower's sepals.

Cambium The living tissue just beneath the bark that gives rise to secondary xylem and phloem cells.

Carpel In flowering plants the ovule-bearing structure.

Carpellate Having or consisting of carpels.

Chasmogamous Flowers which are pollinated when open.

Cilia Sometimes used to refer to the bristles of the *Dionaea* trap.

Cleistogamous Flowers that do not open and therefore, are self-pollinated.

Clone   A group of plants reproduced asexually from one plant and, therefore, genetically identical.

Corolla   Includes all of a flower's petals.

Corolla tube   A hollow 'cylinder' resulting from the fusion or joining of the petals.

Cotyledon leaves   The leaves present in the seeds and the first to appear following germination. These leaves seldom resemble the mature leaves of the plant.

Cross-pollination   The transfer of pollen from the anther of a flower on one plant to the stigma of a pistil of a flower on another plant.

Decumbent   Growing flat along the soil surface with the terminal ends erect or ascending.

Dichotomous   Dividing into parts or branches.

Digestive juices   Secretions which act to break down prey so that the organism, plant or animal, can use it for nourishment.

Dioecious   A plant that has either male or female flowers, but not both.

Dropper   A shoot that usually grows from a plant down into the ground terminating in a tuber.

Ecosystem   An interacting community of organisms and their physical environment that is self-sustaining.

Ensiform   Leaves that are sword-shaped and are not hollow.

Epiphyte   Plants that grow on other plants using them for support.

Exserted   Protruding beyond an enclosing structure. In some flowers the palate extends beyond the petals.

Fenestration   Transparent or translucent areas in the hood of *Sarracenia* and *Darlingtonia* plants. Areolae is a term that is also used for this feature.

Fibrous root system   When all the roots arise from the same area and are about the same thickness and length.

Filament   Thread-like; stalk of a stamen.

Filiform   Leaves whose shape is thread-like.

Flexuous   Curves alternately in opposite directions, zig-zags.

Fresh water   Water with very few dissolved minerals.

Fry   Baby fish.

Fungi   Simple plants lacking chlorophyll and, therefore, unable to make their own food. They must live on the nutrients manufactured by other plants and animals.

Fungicide   A chemical used to kill fungi.

Gamete   A sex cell, contains half of the chromosome number of the organism. Two gametes combine to form a diploid cell.

Gametophyte   The portion of the life cycle of a plant in which gametes are produced.

Gemmae   Reproductive structures which are vegetatively produced by plants and which will grow into new plants.

Genus   A group of related species. Some genera consist of one species.

Gibbous   Swollen or distended on one side.

Habitat   The native environment in which an organism naturally lives.

Heterophyllous   Plants that have different shaped and/or sized leaves at different times.

Hibernaculum   Winter bud produced by a plant to survive the winter.

Hybrid   The off-spring resulting from a cross between two species or previously established hybrids.

Hypogynous   Flowers that have superior ovaries—the petals, sepals, and stamens are attached below the ovary.

Inflorescence   The flower cluster or flowering area of a plant.

Juvenile leaves   The leaves that form after the cotyledons appear. Juvenile leaves do not usually closely resemble the mature leaves.

Lamina   The flat, widened portion of a leaf or petal.

Larvae   Immature insects in the 'worm' stage.

Midrib   The central vein of a leaf. In the *Dionaea* trap both lobes are attached to the midrib.

Mucilage   A thick, sticky fluid, a gelatinous substance.

Mutation   A change in the genetic or hereditary material in a plant or animal.

Nectar   A sweet, sugary liquid produced by plants.

Niche   The place an organism occupies in an ecosystem.

Ovary   The lower portion of the pistil which forms the fruit or seed pod and in which the seeds develop.

Ovule   A part of the ovary that will develop into a seed after fertilization.

Palate   A projection or platform-like structure on the lower lip of a sympetalous corolla.

Panicle   The axis of an inflorescence from which secondary branches arise that bear flowers.

Pedicel   A stem supporting a single flower and arising from the peduncle.

Peduncle   The major flower stalk which bears a cluster of flowers, or a flower stalk which bears a single flower.

Peltate   Shield or umbrella shape supported by a stalk attached near the center of the lower surface.

Perennial   A plant that lives for more than two growing seasons.

Perianth   The calyx and corolla of a flower or tepals.

Peristome   Teeth-like structures.

Personate   A two-lipped corolla with an arched upper lip and the protrusion of the lower lip into the throat area that almost closes the throat.

Petal   The leaf-like structure inside the sepals that is often colored.

Petiole   The slender stem that supports a blade of foliage, the leaf stalk.

Photoperiod   The length of the daylight period.

Phyllodia   Broad petioles without leaf blades. Often used to refer to the winter or ensiform leaves.

Pistil   The female reproductive structure of a flower, consisting of the stigma, style, and ovary.

Pitchers   Leaves of *Sarracenia, Darlingtonia, Cephalotus, Nepenthes* and *Heliamphora*. Typical leaves are ascidiform; that is, tubular or hollow. Ensiform leaves tend to be sword-shaped and are not ascidifrom.

Pollen grains   The male gametophytes that give rise to sex cells. They are produced in the anther of a flower.

Prostrate   Lying flat on the ground.

Pubescent   Covered with hairs.

Pupa   The resting stage of the larvae from which it will emerge as an adult.

Raceme   An unbranched inflorescence with pedicelled flowers along its axis.

Rhizome   Horizontal underground stem.

Rootstock   An inaccurate term used in the past for rhizome.

Rosette   A circular cluster of leaves.

Saccate   Forming or having the shape of a sac or pouch.

Scale leaves   Small leaves resembling scales.

Scape   The stem or stalk which bears flowers, has no leaves but may bear bracts.

Self-pollination   The transfer of pollen from the anther of a flower to the stigma of the same flower or other flowers on the same plant or clone.

Sepal   An outer leaf-like structure of a flower.

Sessile   Without a stalk.

Species   A group of organisms that interbreed and are reproductively isolated from others. It is designated by a binomial consisting of the genus and species name.

Stamen   The pollen-producing structure of a flower. It consists of an anther and a filament.

Stigma   The upper part of the pistil where the pollen is deposited.

Stipule   Usually pairs of small structures at the base of the petiole. They are quite variable and can appear as scales, glands, spines or be leaf-like.

Stolon   A runner; an aerial stem that grows on the surface of the soil often producing roots.

Style   The slender part of the pistil that connects the stigma with the ovary.

Suberect   Almost erect.

Sympetalous   Flowers having petals which are partly to completely fused.

Tentacles   Stalked glands which produce mucilage and other secretions, and which help trap prey.

Tepals   Segments of the perianth that have not differentiated into distinct sepals or petals.

Trigger hairs   Spike-like structures which must be stimulated in order to induce the trapping action in *Aldrovanda, Dionaea, Polypompholyx* and *Utricularia*.

Tuber   A fleshy, usually subterranean stem that serves to store food and water and propagate the plant.

Turions   The winter buds produced by tight, overlapping, undeveloped leaves.

Variant   A plant or group of plants which is different from typical species.

Ventricose   Unequal swelling.

Zygomorphic   Bilateral symmetry.

INDEX